Introduction to C#
Joes 2 Pros

Hands-On Guide to C# 2010 for Beginners, Volume 1

(C# Exam Prep Series 70-536)

By: Peter Bako

ISBN10:   1451581718
ISBN13:   978-1451581713

D1504909

Acknowledgments

I went into this project thinking I would just type out a few pages, have somebody look over the spelling and call it good! Little did I realize just how much help it takes to get a book to look right, make sense and hopefully to be of use to the readers. Looking back over this process, there are so many people to thank, but a small handful of contributors whose efforts simply must be acknowledged in these pages:

- Rick A. Morelan – for staring the Joes to Pros series, encouraging me to author my own book, and once started to make sure I actually finish it. His expertise and insights were wide and varied and I cannot thank him enough for it!
- Suzanne Bako – my wife, who is not a programmer, did a most amazing job in reading the book over and giving me tons of advice on proper formatting, terminology, layout and other elements of the writing process. (I guess a degree in English Lit is useful after all!)
- Ward Henneberry – I could not have asked for a better reviewer, proof reader and fountain of knowledge about writing! Ward probably read through every line of text and code more times than probably even I did, and each time found another chunk of code or turn of phrase that did not make sense! Without questions this book would not have happened without all of Ward's invaluable help!
- Joel Heidal – for finding all of the missing commas, and grammatical errors that I should have caught! Your suggestions and keen eye brought this book from just good to great!
- Sweep/Sooty/Ginger/Barkley – Otherwise known as the Bako cats and dog. Having a cat jump into your lap when you are in the middle of writing a critical paragraph, or when you groping desperately for the right words, is both a blessing and a curse – usually at the same time!

Table of Contents

Chapter 1 – Introduction

Everything has to start somewhere and it is usually best to start at the beginning. In Chapter 1 I explain the benefits of C# compared to other programming languages, get our programming environment installed and configured, write our first program and even do a bit of debugging – otherwise known as troubleshooting.

Who is this Book for?

It's easy for those of us who have been using computers for many years, to assume that everyone has at least some level of basic computer skills. But, as with everything else in life, this varies from person to person. I've known people who have used a computer at work for years, decades in one particular case, and within the context of their daily computer usage they are experts. Yet outside of that narrow range they really have little to no computer skills.

One person, who comes to mind, had been working with a highly customized accounting program for about 11 years when I met her and without doubt, was almost as knowledgeable as the system administrator on that particular product. She considered herself to be of average computer skills, yet when faced with a new operating system and a new set of programs, she did not have even the most basic skills. This is hardly something to be embarrassed about – after all, in our highly modern society, we are all specialists to a certain extent with few general skills outside of our areas of interest.

In writing this book, I took the assumption that the person reading it has at least a basic set of general computer skills, possibly even more, but little to no actual programming experience. If that's you, then you are reading the right book! We will start at the beginning and work our way steadily up to where you can create complex windows based applications!

How to Use this Book

We all have our unique ways of learning, and trying to cover all of the possible learning styles in a single book would lead to a giant volume! Instead, I will try to present the material in a way that allows for easy adaptation to the different learning styles. For example, some people are able to simply read the text and visualize the results in their mind, while others need to actually try it out before they fully understand the topic. For most of us, a nice mix of these two styles works the best. Therefore, this book is written using a textual explanation as well as instructions on how to create the sample projects yourself. While you are welcome to just read straight through, I would strongly recommend working through the code samples on your own system. As you enter the code and replicate the results, you are also encouraged to spend time making changes to the code to see how it behaves.

Each chapter will end with four common elements:

1) *Points to Ponder*
So what is a Point to Ponder? Think of these as the highlights of the chapter just completed, a type of review. However unlike a regular review, Points to Ponder also show you some new possibilities and variations on your learning. In other words, they are a quick and easy way to boil down all of that description into just a few short points. Now if you were to read these points on their own before reading the chapter, they are likely to not really make any sense. However, once you have read through and understood the information presented in the chapter, these little points will serve as a memory reminder of what you read.

I find the Points to Ponder especially useful when going back to review material that I covered a while ago. As each item is reviewed, this unlocks all the knowledge in my memory without having to spend the time re-reading the entire chapter!

2) *Challenges*
Remember getting homework in school? Homework was designed to build on the knowledge you acquired in class with the hope that by using those skills at a later time it will cement that information into your head. The same idea applies here! By taking the material just presented, as well as subjects from previous chapters, the challenges allow you to expand your skills and experiment with the material presented.

Each challenge problem will have the final solution to it available for download at the *Joes 2 Pros* website (http://www.joes2pros.com/). Compare your solution to the answer presented!

3) *Review Quiz w/Answer Key*
   Each chapter will also contain a quiz based on the materials presented up to that point. (Yes, that does mean both the current chapter and all previous chapters!). Use this quiz to check your understanding of the material! You can confirm your answers by looking for the Answer Key in the Appendix at the end of the book.

4) *Your Notes*
   Instead of having to scribble notes into the margins, at the end of each chapter you will find a couple of blank pages into which you can organize your notes, ideas and other information.

Speaking of the *Joes 2 Pros* website… this site contains not only the solutions to the Chapter Challenges, but you will also find each of the chapter projects available for download. While to gain the maximum benefit from this book you should follow the chapters and type in each program as presented, if you just do not want to type in that much code, you can download the final versions (quite often the programs start out as a simple example but are built upon as the chapter proceeds.) Also at the site, you will find links and download materials for the rest of the books in the *Joes 2 Pros* series.

A Walk down Memory Lane

Back in the dawn of the modern computer age (oh, somewhere around the 1940's – makes you feel quite old, doesn't it?), all computer users were to some extent, programmers. Back in those heady days we did not have mice, graphical menus, or in most cases, even color displays. Turn a computer on and you were simply presented with a black (or green or amber) screen, and a blinking prompt. If you were lucky, you might get a nice friendly "ready" prompt, but even that wasn't guaranteed!

So what was one to make of or do with such an austere display? Just like today, one could load up a program to complete a variety of tasks, such as edit a document, copy a file, or play a game. Of course we didn't double-click on a nice icon, but rather, would type something as complex and esoteric as:

```
load "*", 8,1
```

If memory serves me right, this was the command for the old Commodore-based systems that told the computer to start loading the first program it found on the tape drive attached to port 8. Now, even after this finished, your program would still not run, all that would happen is that your happy little `ready` prompt would display. To actually start the program, you would have to issue the `run` command.

What if instead of running the program you wanted to see what it looked like, or how it did what it was supposed to do? Easy! Instead of a `run` command you could always type `list` and the computer would happily show you the code (Figure 1)! Heck, you could even modify any part of it! Many early computer <geeks/hackers/enthusiasts>[1] got started like this.

Figure 1: Typing LIST on an old Apple ‖ computer.

---

[1] Personally I've always considered myself a geek and took no offense at it, but others may not feel the same, so choose your favorite term and go with it!

Unfortunately, today we are not so lucky. Instead, we get a nice pretty icon to launch our program(s), but there is actually no way to see what it does or how it does it. More importantly there is no way for anyone to pull the code apart and learn how to make a dialog box display, or draw a line across the screen and then use that skill in a program of their own. Instead, we have to be a bit more organized and learn our skills from other sources, such as this book!

What is C# and why Should I Care?

In those old days, a programmer pretty much only had two choices in programming a computer, either using the old BASIC language or directly programming using a machine language. BASIC is what is known as a high level programming language, which is just a fancy way of saying that an average Joe can read it, whereas to read machine language (basically a long series of numbers) you needed to be superhuman!

Today, there are a number of high-level computer languages, such as C, C++, C#, Java, Perl, Pascal, Visual Basic, and so on. Different languages have different strengths and uses, but over the years the C family of languages has come to dominate most professional programming circles. Within this family, the original C language (first developed back in 1972) is the granddaddy of them all, and it is still used by many. However, as time went on new concepts were introduced and the language modified to include them. C++[2] came along in the late 1970's and introduced into the language the concept of objects and object oriented programming. Both of these languages were developed by Bell Labs.

C#[3] came to us from Microsoft and was first introduced to the world in 2001. As its name suggests, it is based on the C language style, and for those who have any kind of a background in either C or C++ much of its syntax will be quite familiar. One common question regarding C# has to do with the name itself. There are a lot of theories as to the source of the name, but none has been officially "blessed" as the real source. There are two common theories: The first comes from the world of music where the # sign is called a sharp and indicates a half step above the note which it graces. You could read into that that the programming language C# is (at least) half a step better than its predecessor, C. The second theory is purely visual, and it has to do with the ++ notation that all the C based languages

---

[2] Pronounced as C plus plus.
[3] Pronounced as C sharp.

use. If you take two sets of ++ signs and visually slide them over each other, they sort of form a # sign. Take your pick…

So what makes C# unique? Unlike either C or C++, both of which need to be compiled for a specific processor type before they can be used, C# is compiled to the .Net environment and not to any processor type.

Let's try to make that a bit clearer. In the past (or still, if using an older programming language), when your code was completed you would go through a process called compiling which turns your human readable code into something that your computer, or more precisely your processor, could understand. As an analogy think of your processor as speaking English, while another one speaks British or Australian English. There are some words and concepts which do not exist in one or the other, but in general they can understand each other.

That's great for you and anyone else running a similar class of processors, but what about somebody else running a totally different kind of a system? Think of this processor as speaking French or German. They would not be able to run your compiled code, so they would either be out of luck or would have to take your original source code and compile it for their type of processor. This poses a number of problems. What if you did not want them to see your source code, or perhaps this person does not have a compiler for their system, or maybe even they do not have the skills to use a compiler? The problem of having to take the same programming code and compile it in many ways needs to be addressed.

This is the problem that .Net solves – using our analogy from above, think of .Net as a translator. This translator speaks two languages, one is specific to your processor (English, Spanish, German, etc.) and the other is a universal language such as Esperanto[4]. Now in computer terms we do not refer to .Net as a translator, but rather as a "layer" between the top level (your compiled program) and a bottom layer (the computer itself). The .Net layer lives between these two other layers and as data moves through it, it gets translated (Figure 2). In other words, you compile your code to the "translator" already installed in each machine.

---

[4] Yep, this is a real language that was invented in the late 1800's with the idea that without any country or culture being able to lay claim to it, it could serve as a universal common language that all could adopt – needless to say it never came into fashion, though it did have resurgence in the 1970's.

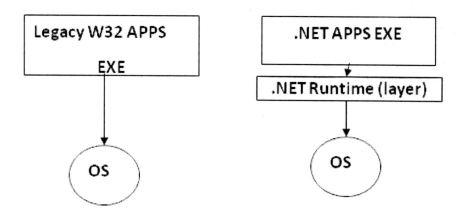

Figure 2: Path of code on a Legacy system vs. one using .Net

When we take our C# code and run it through its compiler, this generates a universal language which your .Net layer can then translate to your specific processor. As long as there is a .Net layer for any given type of processor, you can just hand off your compiled C# program to another person and they can run it, without even having to be aware of or worrying about what processor it was designed for!

Now we all know that computer folks have their own terminology for things, and things here are no different.

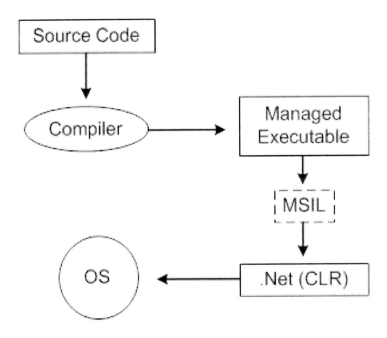

Figure 3: The flow of a C# program from source code to executable on your Operating System.

So the flow of a C# program looks like this (Figure 3). The first two steps (the source code and the compiler) are the same for any language, but the output is not. For a traditional language such as C the process would stop there and the output would be a fully functional executable (a fancy word for a program). However, in the C# world this executable is not able to run on its own since its execution is managed by .Net, so it is referred to as Managed code or as a Managed Executable. The "Managed" in this term refers to the fact that another process is required to handle it before it can do anything useful.

The Managed Executable actually contains our source code (or just code) in a format called the "Microsoft Intermediate Language" or MSIL. The .Net layer (or as it is correctly known for this step, the Common Language Runtime, aka CLR), speaks this language on one side but then translates it into something that the processor can actually understand. If you could actually capture what comes out of the .Net layer, it would be very much the same as a traditional compiler would create. However the C# compiler does something called Just-In-Time compiling, meaning that the result is compiled to the processor specific language as needed and not all at once as a traditional compiler would.

Let me explain that a little bit further. For a traditional language the compiler goes through the entire source code and turns it into an executable program in one single step. For example, imagine if you had an accounting program that calculates tax rates all over the world, but you only need to run a calculation on a single purchase in Seattle. You would have to load the whole program, and all its parts, just to do this one task. Depending on the size of your code, this process can take anywhere from a few seconds, to hours, or even days. In the case of .Net, the process it broken up into two parts – first the source code is turned into a Managed Executable (MSIL), but this does not result in a program that can run on its own. The second part, done by the CLR, finishes the compile process turning the Managed Executable into a format which your processor can understand. However, if you remember, I said that a traditional compile can take hours or even days to finish since the entire code has to be compiled. The .Net CLR does not compile the entire Managed Code in one single effort, but rather compiles the parts as it is used, in other words it gets compiled "Just-in-Time".

Besides being platform independent, C# has a number of other benefits that make it a great programming environment. Here are just a few:

- Large groups of developers are using it, so there is plenty of help
- Supported, maintained and used by the largest software development company in the world
- Huge .Net libraries provide tons of functionality, which have been tested and proven by many other developers
- Development time is faster as compared to C or C++
- Automatic garbage collection (automatic memory allocation - this will be explained later in the text) saves the developer tons of time

Even with all of these benefits there are a few negatives that need to be kept in mind:

- Currently C# is primarily a Windows based development option. There is an open source .Net CLR developed for the Unix platform (Project Mono), but its support is not guaranteed
- C# is not a good choice for embedded systems, or other small memory based devices, due to the .Net layer requirement
- Fully compiled programs, such as those generated by C or C++, tend to run faster and are better suited for real-time applications or for embedded systems

Now that you understand what makes C# and the .Net layer so special we are almost ready to start coding! But before we can do that, we need to get ourselves set up with the C# compiler and development environment.

The Programming Environment

There is actually no specific way, method or program you have to use to program in C# - or pretty much in any other language. Source code is stored in the simplest of all computer file structures, namely that of a simple text file. If you so desire you can use Notepad to create your code, feed that into your compiler and create your executables.

While this is certainly a viable way of doing things, I think we can find something a bit more elegant and useful. In fact we don't even have to look very far, since Microsoft provides a wonderful programming environment for C#, namely Visual Studio. Of course it is rare that one tool can adequately serve the purposes of all users, so Visual Studio was made to be very modular allowing developers with a whole range of needs to use the same basic tool. For example the needs of a developer creating a web-based program are quite different from those of one working on a database or of somebody writing in C#. Yet each of these developers with their unique needs can all use Visual Studio, simply by adding one or more specialized packages to their copy of Visual Studio. Some of these combinations have become so popular (like Visual Studio Professional or Visual Studio Team Suite) that they were turned into packaged products and released as complete kits, all under the same Visual Studio name.

Of course all versions of Visual Studio have one thing in common – they all cost money. If you are a company or a professional developer, then spending a bit of money on a great tool is a no-brainer, but what about people like us just getting started? To help us out, Microsoft has released Express editions of some of their popular programs, including Visual Studio. These Express editions are free to download and use by all, but lack some of the advanced features which the for-pay versions support. Regardless of which version you use, the program looks and behaves the same, so as you get better and decide to get that high paying job as a professional developer, the fancy version of Visual Studio at your new company will look and behave the same way.

With that said here is the list of what you need to actually do the coding samples and examples further on in this book:

1. A computer running some flavor of the Windows Operating System
2. Microsoft .Net Framework
3. Microsoft Visual C# Express or greater
4. An open mind and the desire to create something wonderful

Let's examine all of these requirements in greater detail...

1) A computer running some flavor of the Windows Operating System.
   Basically that is any computer capable of running Windows XP with SP2 or higher. Other valid Operating systems are Windows 7, Windows Vista, Windows Server 2003 with SP2 or Windows Server 2008.

   The actual minimum hardware specs as recommended by Microsoft are[5]:

   - Pentium 4 at 1.6Ghz
   - 192M of RAM
   - 1024x768 display
   - 1.3 GB of free hard drive space

   Now these are truly very minimal. In reality, the faster the processor the better and since memory is not very expensive, at least 1G of RAM. For a display use whatever is comfortable for your eyes but keep it at least at 1024x768, otherwise some of the dialog boxes are going to be cut off. For storage space, considering that hard drive nowadays are pushing a terabyte, I'm pretty sure you can find at least 1.3G of free space...

2) Microsoft .Net Framework
   At the time of writing, the current version of the Visual Express tools are the 2010 series and, within that, the C# 2010 platform requires the .Net 4.0 framework. Odds are you probably already have this installed on your computer (If you are not sure, check the *Programs and Features* icon in your *Control Panel* and scroll down until you see if *Microsoft .NET Framework 3* is listed.) If you do not have this, you can either install it using the Windows Update function of your OS, or the installer for Visual C# Express will take care of it for you.

3) Microsoft Visual C# Express or greater

---

[5] You can always find out what kind of a processor, speed of processor and amount of RAM you have in your computer, by right-clicking on the "My Computer" icon and selecting "Properties".

As many developers are likely to agree, one of the greatest environments for developing code in is the Microsoft Visual Studio family of programs. However the entry level version of this software starts around $300, which is great if you can afford it. For the rest of us, Microsoft has released an Express edition of many of their programming languages for free! While these free editions do not have the entire feature set of the full Visual Studio products, they have more than enough not only to learn on but even to develop rather complex applications, and are true members of the Visual Studio family!

At the time of writing, the URL to download the Visual C# Express Edition is http://www.microsoft.com/express/vcsharp/. This might change, but if it does, just go to the main Microsoft web site, and search for *"Visual C# Express"*. While it is free to download, install and use, Microsoft does want you to register your new software and they enforce this with a pretty simple method – if you do not enter the registration code, after 30 days the program stops working! So take a few minutes after installation and follow their registration process.

You can use any member of the Visual Studio family to execute all of the code in this book. However all of the screenshots were taken using Visual C# Express Edition, which has different looking dialog boxes from the rest of the Visual Studio family. If you are using a version other than the Express Edition, some of the screenshots will not fully match what you will see!

Before we go any further I need to point out a bit of a naming issue. The Visual C# Express Edition is a member of the Visual Studio family, but is officially known as "Visual C# Express Edition" or just as "Visual C#". However most people, me included, will refer to the Visual C# product as Visual Studio – after all Visual C# is part of the family!

4) An open mind and the desire to create something wonderful.
I can only hope that your reading of this book is proof of your desire to learn and with that comes an open mind just waiting for new knowledge!

Now that you have Visual Studio installed you might be wondering what the heck is it and why did I need it if Notepad can do the same thing?! Think of it like this – in a pinch you can always use a rusty pipe to pound a nail into a board somewhere, but it is hardly the most efficient tool for the job. Personally I'd rather use a nice hammer and not get rust all over my hands, but hey it's up to you!

While it is true that you can code with pretty much any text editor, Visual Studio is much more. It is what is known as an IDE or Integrated Development Environment. Think of an IDE as a one stop shop for all things having to do with development. From this one environment you can not only type in code (with plenty of context sensitive help as you will see), but at a click of a button you can compile your code, or step it through a debugger to see where things are going wrong. Let's fire this puppy up and get to it by writing our first C# program!

Welcome Developer!

Go ahead and find your new program and launch it. You should see a screen much like the picture below (Figure 4).

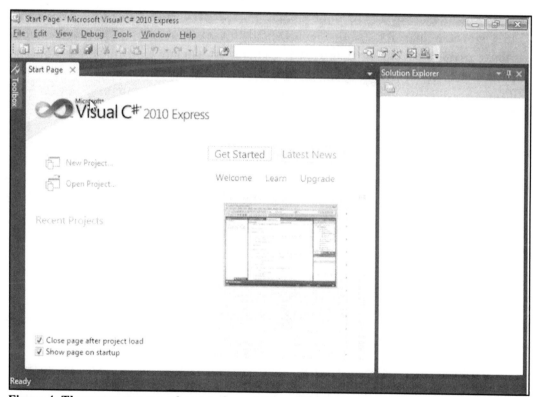

Figure 4: The screen you see when you launch Visual Studio Express

It may look like there is a lot going on here, but if you break it down piece by piece, you will quickly see that it's not so bad! Of course, as with all windows programs, you have a menu bar at the very top with a toolbar below that.

Underneath those, filling up the rest of the screen, are the *Toolbox* (currently minimized to the left edge of your screen), the primary work area currently showing the start page, and the *Solution Explorer* area on the far right. We are going to be dealing with each of these areas as we learn about C#, so I am not going to go into any detail on their purposes here, but rest assured we will! After all, right now we are here to write our first program, so let's get to it!

Before we can do any kind of actual programming we need to create a new project into which our code can be put. Obviously our first program is going to be quite small, just a few lines, but even so it has to go into a project. Think of a project as a kind of a briefcase were all the parts of a single large document are. Individually these pages of your document do not work, but as a whole they can be as powerful as a legal brief, project proposal, or perhaps a book.

Ok, so we need a project. If you examine your screen carefully you will note a section near the top left of your screen labeled as *Recent Projects*. Above this area are two links for *"New Project"* and *"Open Project"*. If you hover your mouse over these labels, note that it changes to a hand icon, meaning you can click there! (Alternatively you can go to the File menu and select "New Project...".) This is how we are going to create not only our first project, but many others to come!

As soon as you click on the New Project link the New Project dialog (Figure 5) comes up. There are a few important decisions that need to be made here, so let's take the time to examine this carefully.

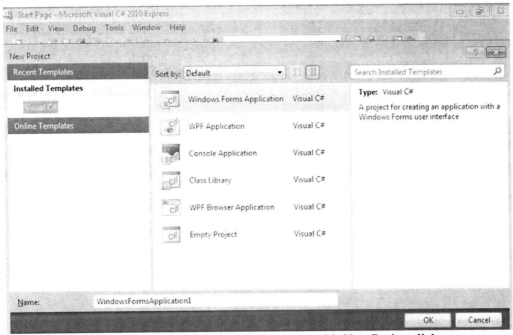

Figure 5: After you click the "New Project" link, you get this New Project dialog

In the middle of this dialog are a series of icons, with the first icon already highlighted. These icons represent the types of projects that you can create right out of the box. The highlighted icon, *Windows Forms Application*, is what you would use to create a standard windows program, one with windows, dialogs, buttons, etc. The fourth icon from the top is called *Console Application*, which is what you would use to create command line-based applications.

If the very term "Command Line" strikes terror into your heart, fear not – it is not as bad as it sounds. In fact these will be the type of programs we are going to be writing as we learn the basics of the C# language. Once we understand the language we can create the much more complex, and much more useful, Windows applications. Finally at the bottom is a text box labeled as *Name*, where we need to type in the name of our new project.

To create our first masterpiece, please click once on the "Console Application" icon and type "Hello World" (without the quotes!) into the *Name* box. When you are ready to proceed click the OK button. Your computer will spin its drive for a few seconds as it creates the project you asked for and, when it is ready, you will see the beginnings of your new program (Figure 6).

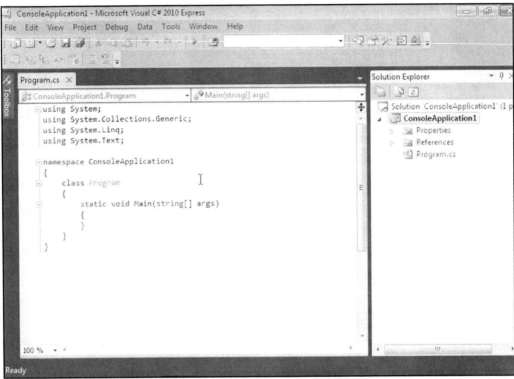

Figure 6: Your new program is opened in Visual Studio and the initial C# file is called "Program.cs"

The same basic parts presented on first launch of Visual C# are still there, but there is also data in the parts that were empty before! The Toolbox is still there and is still shrunk down on the left edge of your screen, but the main work area now has a new tab on it labeled as "Program.cs" (more on this later), and on the right side of the screen the Solution Explorer area has changed in a significant way – there is stuff in there!

Actually, if you take a look at the "stuff" in this window you will note that your project name shows up on the first line – "Solution 'Hello World' (1 project)", as well as on the line below that. Take a look at it. Notice that your project name on it is in bold letters and it has a little C# project icon to the left. That means that this is the current project (yep, you can have multiple projects in one solution), and this project is written in C#.

By now you might be asking yourself what the difference between a Project and a Solution is – after all it seems like we are using these two words interchangeably. Simply put, a Solution is made up of multiple components, including Project(s). In the case of small programs, such as the ones we are going to be creating all through this book, each Solution is going to contain a single Project and therefore can be thought of as the same thing. However in the case of a very large program, the Solution is going to be made up of multiple Projects that together form the final application.

You might think that marking your project that it is written in C# is sort of redundant – after all this program we are using is the Visual C# programming environment, what else could it be? Well it could be quite a few things. We may be using the Visual C# environment, but this is actually a scaled down version of the full Visual Studio, and that can support a number of other languages. Even this express edition is able to import in non C# code such as C, C++, J#, Visual Basic, etc. While normally a single project is written in a single language, the complete solution may be made up of multiple projects and they could be written in any number of other languages. Having a quick visual indicator of the language used is actually quite useful.

So what else can we learn from the rest of the lines in the Solution Explorer window? Notice how your project name (Hello World), has a small black triangle next to it, with three additional lines below it. Those three lines are indented, meaning they are part of the entry above, but are visible because we have expanded that area. If you click on that black triangle those three lines will fold up and disappear – but we want to examine them, so let's not hide them (click the now hollow triangle to expand them again). The next two entries, "Properties" and "References" we are not going to deal with for now, so go ahead and ignore them for the moment.

However the last line, "Program.cs", is one we should talk about. If that name sounds familiar, it should – it is the same label that we see in that new tab in the main work area that showed up when we created this project. Remember our briefcase example from earlier on? Think of the *Solution Explorer* area as the file folder holding each individual page. Each page has a title, which of course is listed as part of our project in the Solution Explorer, and can be examined. When you "examine" a page, it opens up in the main work area as a new tab and that tab gets labeled with the name of the page (or file) that you are looking at.

As our programs get more complicated and we start to split them into multiple files, the Solution Explorer is going to become quite important. However until then it is taking up a valuable chunk of our screen real estate. Personally I am not fond of having to scroll left and right just to see a particularly long line of code, so unless I need it, I like to either shrink the Solution Explorer out of the way or simply close it all together.

To shrink the Solution Explorer down (as the Toolbox is shrunk down on the left edge of your window), you can click the small pushpin icon just to the right of the Solution Explorer label. If you ever want it back you can simply hover over the small tab on the right and it will pop back out, but will shrink away as soon as you move your mouse out of its area. To make it stay permanently, just click the pushpin icon again. Now if, instead of the pushpin icon, you clicked the small X to the right and closed the Solution Explorer totally, don't worry you can still bring it back! Click on the "View" menu, select "Other Windows", and choose "Solution Explorer".

Why did Visual C# call this new file "Program.cs"? The "program" part is just a default name and can be changed as soon as you save this file and make it real – at the moment it only exists in memory! The "cs" part is an extension that stands for C#, and just marks this file as a C# source code file.

Basic C# Coding

Enough description, time to code! Take a look at the main work area at the open Program.cs file. Find the line that says "`static void Main(string[] args)`" and notice the open curly brace under it. Put your cursor after the curly brace, press enter once and type in this line of code. Upper and lower case does make a difference, and all punctuation is required, so type this in exactly as you see it!

```
Console.WriteLine("Hello World!");
```

If you did it correctly, your work area should look like Figure 7.

```
Program.cs* ✕

Hello_World.Program                                        ▼  Mai

  using System;
  using System.Collections.Generic;
  using System.Linq;
  using System.Text;

  namespace Hello_World
  {
      class Program
      {
          static void Main(string[] args)
          {
              Console.WriteLine("Hello World!");
          }
      }
  }
```

Figure 7: The first line of code has been added to the Main method

As you were typing in that line, did you notice how a small drop down list kept coming up? That is called IntelliSense and it is one of the really cool benefits of using the Visual Studio IDE instead of a plain text editor, such as Notepad. Basically, the way it works is that as you type the editor keeps track of your keystrokes, and based on what has already been entered makes a best guess as to what you are trying to type. If it has guessed correctly and the word you want is the very top entry in that small dropdown, you can press the key that would normally follow the word and IntelliSense will finish that word for you.

So what do I mean by "the key that would normally follow the word"? For example in our line above we know that after the word "Console" the next character is a period. So as I start to type in "console", as soon as I get to that second "o", it becomes unique enough and the word Console gets highlighted. At that time I can press the period button, which is the next character I want after Console, and the word "Console" gets automatically completed, and even correctly capitalized! (Besides pressing the period button, you can also use the Tab key to get the auto-complete!)

Try it with the next word, which is WriteLine. Notice as soon as you enter the first two letters, it highlights "Write" and under that is what we want, which is "WriteLine". Instead of typing in the rest of the word, press down arrow to select `WriteLine` and type in the character we want after it, which is the "(" character. Again the IntelliSense finishes our word for us (with proper capitalization). Besides using the next character we want, you can also always use the tab or enter key to complete the word that IntelliSense is suggesting. Once you get used to this, your typing speed will dramatically increase and your coding accuracy will go up with it! It minimizes the need to find problems caused by typos.

Up to now we have written only a single line of code, yet there are 15 lines of text on this page! What are the other 14 lines for? Let's break our code down and see what each part is for.

```
using System;
using System.Collections.Generic;
using System.Linq;
using System.Text;
```

These four lines tell the compiler to load in additional namespaces so we can use code from them below. What the heck is a namespace? All C# code lives in containers, which can contain either additional containers or actual code. A namespace is the primary container for all parts of a C# based project. Using our briefcase example from before, think of a namespace as the file folder that the individual pages for a section belong to. Of course, a C# project can be made up of multiple namespaces, just as a large document in our briefcase can be made up of multiple file folders, each with its own set of pages.

```
namespace Hello_World
{
```

While the `using` lines above loaded in additional namespaces for us to use, our own code also has to live in a namespace, and therefore the first line of code internal to the project is to declare a namespace using the `namespace` keyword, followed by a name for this specific namespace. By default the name of the namespace is that of our project, but since you cannot have a space within the name, the Visual C# program used an underscore with which to replace the space.

Also notice the open curly brace. C# uses the curly braces (as do C and C++) to encompass a block of code. Therefore right after the namespace we use an open curly brace to indicate that code will follow, and at the end of that code we will use a close curly brace to let the compiler know where the code ends.

```
class Program
{
```

Within the namespace you will find one or more classes. Just as when we defined the namespace by using a keyword followed by a name, so we do for a class. Again we use an open curly brace to indicate that code will start.

```
static void Main(string[] args)
{
```

Finally, within a class we have one or more members, and the most common member is a method. If you have done any kind of programming before, you might be more familiar with the term Function. In C# functions are called methods. Programmers who have been around for a while and have worked with other languages tend to use the term "method" and "function" interchangeably.

The name of this method is *Main*. The keywords `static` and `void` are special indicators that mark the Main method with additional specifiers which we will cover later. The part inside the parentheses `(string[] args)` are the parameters that the Main method takes. We are going to be spending quite a bit of time talking about methods and their parameters later on, so we are going to skip them for now. Once again an open curly brace is used to indicate that the guts of this method are to follow.

```
Console.WriteLine("Hello World!");
```

Ah, our actual bit of code that we had to provide! There are quite a few elements in this line, but for now the important part is that the `Console.WriteLine` method call is used to display something onto the screen. The parameter within the parentheses is what this method will display, and since it is a string (i.e. text to display as we typed it), it gets put into quotes. Finally note the semicolon at the end. All lines of code in C# (or for any of the other C family of languages) use the semicolon to indicate the end of the line. But you might ask yourself, how come there aren't any semicolons after the lines that defined the namespace or the class? Those lines are not actual code but rather lines that structure the code – therefore they are not terminated with a semicolon.

```
        }
    }
}
```

Finally we have a whole sequence of closing curly braces. If you were keeping score, you noticed that we had three opening curly braces, one each for the Main function (or method), the Class and the Namespace. These three are their respective matching closing pairs!

All that work for just one line of code! I don't know about you, but I'm ready to actually see this thing do something useful! If you remember, before we can run this code it needs to be compiled. True, but that is the advantage of using an IDE, it does all that for us. To save, compile and run this code we just need to click a single button!

On the main toolbar look for a small green arrow icon pointing to the right (should be the 11th icon from the left – Figure 8). If you hover over it with the mouse, it will display "Start debugging (F5)". The F5 means I can just press the F5 key on my keyboard instead of clicking this button. Great, but what does "Start debugging" mean? Shouldn't it be compiling and running my program? Actually it will do exactly that, but how this does it is through the debugger. We are going to be spending quite a lot of time working with the debugger, but for you now don't worry about how it works – just click that button!

Figure 8: The "Start Debugging" button

Wow, that was underwhelming! All that happened is a small green bar showed up to the left of the line I typed and a black window popped up and then went away before it could even be read! What the heck was that!?

Ah computers, so very literal in what they do. So what did happen? The green bar to the left of your code means Visual C# saved your program file and the only line(s) that have changed since the last save are marked in green. Useful to know, but does not help us with that disappearing black screen. For that we have to think a little bit like a computer and try to follow what we told it to do.

Looking over our code, the compiler loaded in four namespaces (System, System.Collections.Generic, System.Linq, and System.Text), created a new namespace called Hello_World, within that created a class called Program, and within that, created a class method called Main. The method has a single command to display a bit of text to the screen, for which that black window was opened up and the text "Hello World" printed.

After it completed that command there is nothing else to do, so the program just ended. When that happened it closed the black window. Speaking of that black window, what the heck is that thing? If you have ever used the Command Prompt window on your computer, then you have probably recognized the black window as a command window, or what we in .Net circles refer to as a console. Remember when we created our project we specified that it be a console application? That means that all of our output will show up in a console window (or Command Prompt if you prefer).

Hmmm, ok very smart of the computer, but personally I cannot read that fast! As a slow human, I would prefer to actually get a chance to see the results of my coding and not have it go away until I am good and ready.

This is easy to fix, but will require one more line of code. Modify your Program.cs file to look like Figure 9.

```csharp
using System;
using System.Collections.Generic;
using System.Linq;
using System.Text;

namespace Hello_World
{
    class Program
    {
        static void Main(string[] args)
        {
            Console.WriteLine("Hello World!");
            Console.ReadLine();
        }
    }
}
```

Figure 9: Adding the `ReadLine()` method to the end of the program will pause the program before terminating

Notice how the new line typed is marked with a yellow tag on the left edge of the screen? Just as the green mark told us that this change had been saved, the yellow tells us that a change has been made but not yet saved!

Once again let's run this. Either click the little green arrow or press F5.

This time the window popped up, our text got displayed, and the cursor is blinking below waiting for something. Press the Enter key when you are ready, so our program can end, and the window can close. Let's take a look at our two lines of code to truly understand what is going on.

```
Console.WriteLine("Hello World!");
Console.ReadLine();
```

The Console is an object that refers to the black screen. WriteLine is a command to write a given bit of text out to somewhere. By putting the WriteLine after Console, we are telling the WriteLine method to send its parameter to the Console. More precisely put, the Console class has a method called WriteLine which takes as its input a string.

The next line is quite similar, again the Console class has a method that we are calling, but this time the name of that method is ReadLine. Notice that there are opening and closing parentheses after the name of the ReadLine method. This method contains no arguments (the official term for parameters when speaking about methods). As a method it could, so you need to provide the framework into which those parameters could go, even if there is nothing to be provided.

Whereas the WriteLine method sends text to the screen, the ReadLine method reads a line from the keyboard. If you had pressed any other key besides the enter key, nothing would have happened, except those characters would have shown up on the screen. When you pressed Enter, the line was completed, sent back to our program and, with the last line executed, the program terminates. Go ahead and try it! Run your program again, but press a bunch of other keys before hitting enter.

Saving C# Projects

Before we can call our program truly done, we need to save it. Just as with any other program, until you save it to the hard drive, it just lives in memory and if the power goes out, poof – there goes the masterpiece! But wait, didn't you just say that when you run your program the IDE saves it automatically before compiling it? True, I did but there is Save and there is Save!

In order for the compiler to compile something, there must first be a file – therefore it will have to save it first! But where? Normally this would be saved as part of your project, but you have not saved your project yet, so the IDE has no idea where to save it. All of the saves so far were into temporary files that the compiler could work with, but are of little use to you. To actually save things for real from the File menu choose Save All (Figure 10).

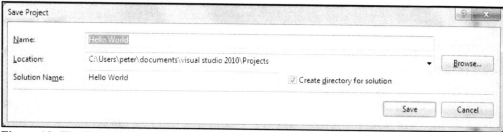

Figure 10: The Save Project dialog box

Click the Save button to save the project and its files to the default location. Note that location; we are going to need it in just a little bit. Since our project is now complete, go ahead and shut Visual C# down as well.

Next, using your Windows Explorer, navigate out to the location that your project was saved to. (If you do not remember, just refer to Figure 10, but instead of "peter" your path will include the name of the user you are logged in as.)

You will find a folder with your project name "Hello World" within which is a number of files and subfolders. These files store the linkages to the various .cs files which make up your project so you can open them up again in the future and continue to work on your program. But there is something else interesting in there! Inside this folder there is another one also called "Hello World", and in there you can find the Program.cs that you created (and yes, you can use Notepad to open it up and look at it).

Also in here is a folder called bin. Go ahead and open up this folder. Note the two sub-folders: Debug and Release. Remember when you hovered over the Run button it actually said Start Debugging? When the compiler did its job, it created a compiled, but debug version of your program, and saved that in the Debug folder you see here. At the same time it also made a non-debug version, which is in the Release folder. If you look in there you will find a number of files, but the most interesting one is called "Hello World.exe" (Figure 11). You can double-click on this program and run your new application outside of the Visual C# IDE! Go ahead, try it!

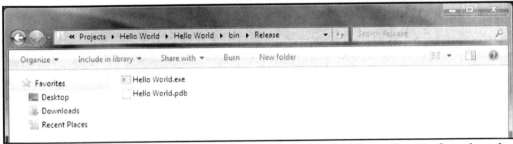

Figure 11: The Release folder shows the Hello World.exe, which can be run from here by double clicking

Pretty cool, eh? You can copy this new program file to any other computer, and as long as the .Net 4.0 Framework is installed, it will run just great!

So we created a new project, put some code into, saved it, compiled it, and when done, shut the development environment down. What if you want to go back and do more work on this project? Just as with any other Windows application you can launch the editor again, reopen the project and continue to work as needed.

However the important part to remember is to open up the project file and not the Program.cs file – the latter only holds the code of that particular C# file, whereas the project contains all of the files. A given project could have quite a few C# files. By opening up the project file, Visual C# will automatically open up all of the C# files within the project. If you just browse out and open up a .CS file, it will come up in the editor, but project itself has not been opened – if you take a look in the Solution Explorer window it will remain empty. (This is not what we want to do, but just in case you ever see an empty Solution Explorer you know to close Visual Studio and reopen the project – not just the .cs file!) Let's try to open up our Hello World project up again to see how it is done.

First, launch the Visual C# application again. Notice when the program starts, there is one change immediately visible in the left hand area, labeled as "Recent

Projects" – the last few project(s) you have worked on are listed. Of course we have only worked on one project so far, so it only shows "Hello Word" (Figure 12).

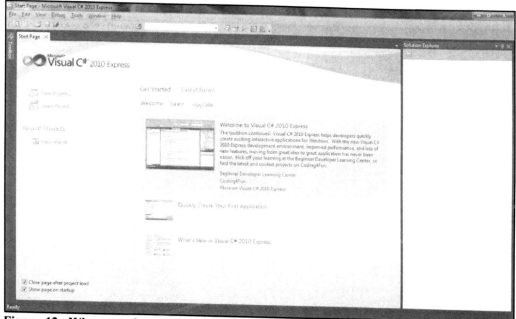

Figure 12: When you launch Visual C# again, you see Hello World listed under Recent Projects

With our recent project listed, we can simply click on the name of it and Visual C# will open up the project for us. But what if the project we would like to open is not listed in the Recent Projects box? In that case we have to manually browse to the project file and open it up ourselves. To do that we can either click on the "Open Project..." link above the the Recent Projects area or from the File menu choose "Open Project". Both methods will present you with an Open Project dialog. Navigate into your Hello World folder and you should see the Hello World project file, "Hello World.sln" listed (Figure 13). In case you are wondering what the extension ".sln" stands for, it is an abbreviation for "solution".

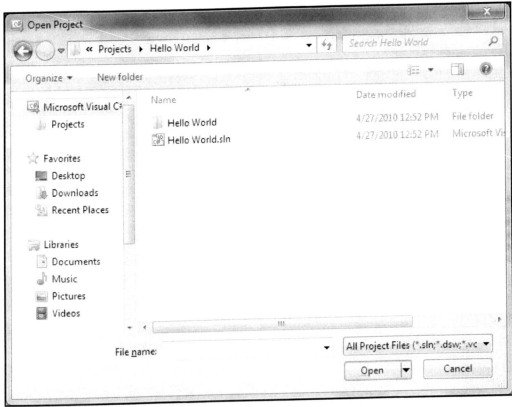

Figure 13: The Open Project dialog

Select this file and click Open. Once you do, Visual C# opens up and shows you your source code ready to edit again. If you are using an older version of the Visual C# environment or have a project with multiple C# files in it, things might not go quite as smoothly. Since our project has only a single C# file, the Visual C# program can deduce which file you want to edit and opens it up without any problems.

In cases with multiple files it cannot make that guess, so it will not open up any C# file automatically, leaving you to think that nothing actually happened. (Interestingly enough, older versions of Visual C# tend to have this behavior even with a single file project.) If that happens, the solution is easy! Just expand the Solution Explorer window, find the file you wish to edit and double-click on it!

Points to Ponder

- C# is a programming language created by Microsoft
- C# talks to the .Net layer. The .Net layer than then talks to the hardware underneath
- While you can write C# code with any text editor, the recommended development environment is the Visual Studio family of products
- Visual Studio is an intelligent environment with many abilities, such as IntelliSense, designed to help developers
- All C# code lives within a structure called a Class, which itself usually resides within the structure called a Namespace
- Once a program has been compiled, it can be run from outside of the Visual Studio environment, simply by finding the .EXE file that was created

Challenge

1. Customize your Hello World program to make the program display the following two lines. Put your name in the <your name> section.
   "Hello Computer."
   "My name is <your name>"

Review Quiz

1.) You have a C# project with 10 classes. Which statements are true? (Choose all that apply)
- ☐ a. These 10 classes can be stored in 1 CS file.
- ☐ b. These 10 classes must be stored in 10 CS files.
- ☐ c. These 10 classes can be stored in multiple CS files.
- ☐ d. These 10 classes must be stored in at least one CS file.
- ☐ e. These 10 classes must be stored in multiple CS files.

2.) What is the starting point for a C# application? (Choose only 1)
- O a. The `Main` class.
- O b. The `Main` method.
- O c. The `main` class
- O d. The `main` method.

3.) What do you call a set of related classes?
- O a. importing
- O b. namespace
- O c. using
- O d. system

4.) What will turn your HelloWorld.cs source code file into a HelloWorld.exe executable file?
- O a. A Translator
- O b. A Layer
- O c. A Project file
- O d. A Compiler

5.) You go to work on your HelloWorld project and notice that there is nothing listed in the Solution Explorer. What caused this to happen?
- O a. You opened the HelloWorld C# file but should have opened up the HelloWorld Project.
- O b. You opened the HelloWorld project but should have opened up the HelloWorld C# file.

Notes

Chapter 2 – Variables

It's time to really learn the C# language and the place to start is with variables. Without doubt, variables are the most basic building block when writing code and therefore the most important to truly understand. We are going to explain what they are, why they are used, the different types of them and their limitations.

When I was much younger I saw the Mel Brooks comedy *Blazing Saddles*. There were tons of really funny scenes in the movie, but there was one that especially stuck with me. In this scene the main bad guy is hiring a bunch of bandits and wants them all to take a pledge. He stands up and says to the group "Repeat after me". He then goes on, "I, your name …", expecting everyone to say their own name instead of "your name". In other words, with this one sentence he was able to cover everyone regardless of their actual names. Of course the crowd did not get this and they all dutifully yelled back "I, your name …". Truly a funny scene, but it does illustrate what a variable is and how it can be used.

Remembering High School Algebra

How many times did you ask yourself while sitting through another class of High School algebra, when and where am I going to actually use these skills in the real world? Well I can't help you with figuring out the real world application of proofs, calculating the angles of a triangle or trying to find out where two trains running at different speeds are going to collide, but you will finally get a real use for variables!

Just in case you slept through that day, here is a quick refresher…

```
5x = 10
```

Yep, looks like a math problem. As my math teacher used to make us say it aloud, here is how you read this: "Five times X is equal to 10". I'm not going to go through the official way to actually calculate this, but I'm pretty sure by now we have all guessed that X is equal to 2. Wow, that wasn't too bad! Let's make this a bit more complicated. If I change this problem like so, what does X become now?

```
5x = 15
```

Again, a bit of basic math tells us that for this equation to remain true X is now equal to 3. In these two simple examples X is the variable since its value is initially unknown. The entire central concept to variables, both in math and in programming, is that they are a temporary placeholder for something which we do not know the value of in advance.

A simple example from the world of computers would be a program that asks you for your name and then prints out a simple greeting using your name. Obviously the guy programming this bit of code could not guess the name of every person who will use his code, so instead he uses a variable to store the name the user enters and then uses the variable again (this time filled in with a name) to print out his greeting.

Now here comes a critical bit of difference between how variables are used in math versus those used in computers. In math, a variable can hold any type of a number, whole numbers, fractions, even entire formulas – however computers are a bit pickier. With computers, you have to define a variable before using it and include in that definition what kind of a variable it is going to be. So if I make a variable to hold an integer (a fancy way of saying a whole number), I cannot then use that same variable to store any other kind of data, such as a name or even a different kind of a number, such as a fraction.

There is another difference in computer types of variables and that is of size. Size is actually kind of tricky here since there are two ways of looking at the size of a variable. The first way is with regard to how big of a number the variable can hold, and the second is how much space it takes up in memory. These two "sizes" are actually linked, so as the ability of a variable to hold a bigger number is increased so does its size in memory (more on memory later). For example a variable of type Byte can hold a value between 0 and 255, while one of type Integer can go from 0 to 4,294,967,295. (For those of you with a bit of knowledge here from other systems, yes I am leaving out the concept of negative numbers here, but just for a little bit!)

Now if you looked at that very large number at the upper end of Integer you might be asking yourself, with such a large range why would we even need other types, why not just use that for all number type variables? Actually that is a very good question and the answer has to do with memory. Basically the bigger value a variable can hold the more memory it needs to operate. Since as programmers we try to make our programs as small, tight and efficient as possible, why would we waste a bunch of space on something that is never going to be used?

Let me give you a real world example. Imagine a program that asks for the age of its user. The answer is going to be a number, so we declare ourselves a numeric type variable and put the answer in there. Now personally I don't know of many people older than about 120 (the verified age of the oldest human on record!), so while I could use an Integer variable it would seem rather wasteful, since it tops out above 4 billion! However a variable type of Byte has a maximum upper limit of 255, which means it is way more than I will ever need, but in memory usage it is just 1/4th the size of an Integer.

So a Byte is smaller than an Integer, but why do I care? As we all know in the real world everything has a cost and we have to make tradeoffs between the financial value of an item and the usefulness of that item in our lives. For example, a Ferrari will certainly get me to work, but so will a Honda, but the price of that Ferrari is so much higher than the Honda that not many of us can afford the Ferrari.

The same concept applies in programming. When we declare a variable it takes up a bit of memory, a very finite resource indeed. Using our example above, the Integer can be thought of as the Ferrari (large, fancy and can do a lot more than we need), but the Byte, or the Honda as it were, will do all we need but at just 1/4th the cost of memory space. So how do I know what the "costs" of the different variables are? Later on in this Chapter there will be a chart with all of the numeric type of variables, their valid ranges and how much memory they take.

Naming Conventions

Many people laugh and joke how the boxer George Foreman has 7 kids all named George. Conventional wisdom says it is probably a good idea to give your kids unique names, which takes into account their uniqueness and gender. While in the real world you can name all of your kids the same, in computers you must have all unique names for your variables.

As with most things in life, we have rules we need to follow. For variables the rules are fairly minimal but are important to know about.

1) A variable name must start with either a letter or the underscore character
2) Characters after the first can be letters, numbers, or underscores
3) The maximum length of a name can be up to 255 characters, but generally shorter is better

4) You cannot use reserved keywords[6]. Reserved keywords are used by the C# language itself, so for example using "integer" as a variable name would be very confusing to both the compiler as well as to anyone else reading your code.

5) Names are case sensitive, so "foo", "Foo", "FOO", and "fOo" are all considered different names

That last point is quite important as some other languages do not have that rule and invariable somebody will get the case wrong and wonder why the compiler does not recognize their variable names.

With C# there is a semi-formal convention for naming of variables and other objects. While it is not enforced by the compiler or any other standards body, it is one used by the vast majority of C# programmers, so it is both a good idea to know and use it. Besides it will make reading your code easier.

While keeping your variable names short is a golden rule, it also needs to be something that makes sense. In other words while you can name your variable "x", you probably should not, since "x" does not really mean anything and the odds are even you are likely to forget after sometime what that variable is used for. The solution is to use a name that describes the purpose of the variable.

For example, if you have a variable used for counting you could call it myCounter. Notice how this name is made up of two words, but the first word "my" is all lower case while the second word "Counter" is capitalized. This convention is called camelCase and is the recommended way to name all of your variables. For other objects, such as classes, namespaces or methods (all of which we will discuss later), the convention is to use something called PascalCase. In this convention you capitalize all words of the name, for example MyMethod.

Time to program

Enough talk, time to use our new skills! If you are not already running your Visual C# program then please go ahead and launch it, otherwise close down any open projects you might have so we can start fresh.

---

[6] See the Appendix for a list of the C# Keywords.

Just as we did in our earlier example, we are going to start a new project and once again it will be a Console Application program. Feel free to check back in the previous chapter if you need a reminder on how to create a new project.

For the name of this project go ahead and use "CH2a", for Chapter 2, project A. I know that it's a boring name, but it will make it easy to keep track of our various projects as we go forward. If you did everything correctly you should end up with a screen like Figure 14.

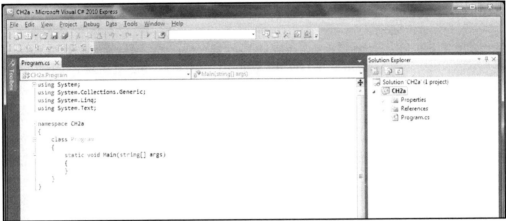

Figure 14: In the CH2a .cs file, we put our cursor between the braces of the Main method

As before, the Visual C# program gives us the framework for a new application with a new Namespace and Class and our empty Main method. If you recall, our code goes between the open and close curly braces of the Main method.

Before we go any further, let me show you a cool trick. Right now the Main method is very small, in fact it is empty, so you can easily see and find both the opening and the closing curly braces. That's great, but what if your code gets larger, how can you figure out which opening curly brace matches a closing one? Once again the Visual Studio environment comes to your rescue! Simply click on any curly brace, opening or closing, and it gets highlighted. The matching pair is also highlighted!

Go ahead and type in the following code:

```
byte myNum;

myNum = 7;

Console.WriteLine("Your lucky number is {0}!",
myNum);

Console.ReadLine();
```

Before we run this, let's examine each line to make sure we understand what everything is doing.

The first line creates a variable of type byte called myNum. In C# as in all C type languages, you must declare your variables before using them. The syntax for doing so is to first specify the data type that it is to be followed by the name. As usual the line is terminated by a semicolon.

The second line uses our new variable and assigns a value to it, in our code that happens to be 7. This initial assignment of a value to a brand new variable is called "initializing" the variable. Until a value is actually assigned, the variable is considered declared, but not yet initialized.

The third line uses the same `WriteLine` command from our first example but adds a number of new elements. As before, we have information in a string format that we want to display and as always that string is surrounded by quotes. However there is something rather strange in there, specifically a number surrounded by curly braces {0}. This is a variable of sorts as well, not one that we defined but one that the `WriteLine` method uses as a placeholder. What it does is provides a space to be filled in with something that is not part of the static string we supplied, but rather some other value, not known in advance. As the computer prints out our string, when it gets to this placeholder it then looks outside of the string to find what it should put in there. Notice in our code that after the closing quote of the string, there is a comma followed by our variable. This is the value that the `WriteLine` method will place into the string instead of the {0} when it actually gets printed to the screen.

One more thing about this {0} placeholder – notice how the first one is labeled as 0 not as 1? Unlike humans who start counting at 1, computers generally start at 0. As you use multiple space holders, as we will do later, you always start at 0 and work up from there.

Finally, the fourth line is our command to make the computer wait until we press Enter so we can see our results before closing the window. `ReadLine` tells the computer to stop executing the program and wait until the user enters something from the keyboard and presses Enter.

Go ahead and run your program by clicking on the green run icon on the toolbar, or pressing F5. If you typed in the code correctly, you should end up with a screen like that in Figure 15.

Figure 15: Hitting F5 runs your program and the `WriteLine` shows the variable value of 7

Well so far using a variable hardly seems useful, since we could have just typed that entire line directly into the `WriteLine` string and gotten the same result! True, but we are just barely scratching the surface of the capabilities of variables!

Before we go on and make our variable actually do something neat, let's try a few simple changes to our code. The first change we are going to make is to change the value of our variable from 7 to some other number. (But remember this variable is of type Byte, so its maximum range is from 0 to 255, so keep it within that range!) Run your program and verify that the line now uses your new number.

Hmmm, so what would happen if we put in a number bigger than 255? Ok, admit it – you've already tried it! Simple, the compiler knows what the range of this type of variable is and will complain that your value is not correct. In fact, you should get an error message as shown in Figure 16.

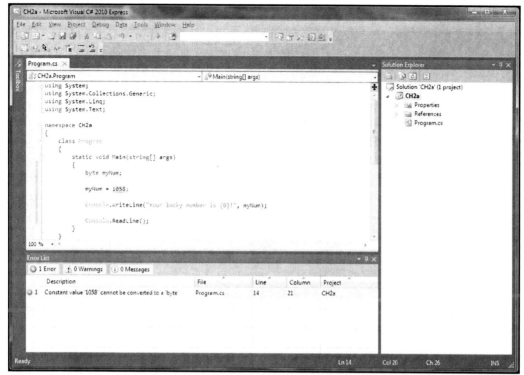

Figure 16: Trying to initialize a variable with a value that it too large, results in an error

So if the problem is that the number I specified, 1058, is bigger than the maximum value of our Byte variable, why is the error message talking about trying to convert it? Because, in effect, that is what the compiler does when you have an assignment line like we do on our second line of code. It tries to take our specified value (or literal as it is known among the programmer crowd) and convert it to the variable type specified on the left hand side of our assignment. Since this value is too large it cannot be converted and you get this error message.

After trying a few different values, let's make a more interesting change and see what it does. First, if your code still has a value above 255, please fix it and verify that it is all correct by successfully running your program.

This time I want you to change the type of your variable from `byte` to `int`. Yep, the type is officially called `int` and not integer. Remember rule 3 in our variable naming convention? Shorter is always better! Even in my code I called my variable "myNum" instead of "myNumber" simply to keep it shorter and easier to type.

Ok, now our variable is of type `int` and not `byte` – what did this get us? Well on initial examination nothing much, everything still runs as before. (Go ahead, try it!) However our variable is much bigger now, so go ahead and change the value of the variable to something else, something larger than 255 and see what it does! Yep, it will happily take our larger values (up to 2,147,483,647) and not a peep of complaint! Wait a minute, didn't you say the upper limit of an `int` is above 4 billion, why is this smaller?

Remember earlier I mentioned negative numbers? There are actually two types of `int` variables, one that will take negative numbers and therefore has the upper limit of 2,147,483,647, and one that does not take negative numbers and can go all the way to 4,294,967,295. When you simply specify an `int` the compiler automatically assumes that you want the ability to use negative numbers. To force it to give you the entire range of positive values, you want to specify your variable type as `uint`, where the u stands for "unsigned".

Try it! Change your variable type to `uint` and give it a number above 2,147,483,647!

Numeric Data Types

As promised, here is a table of the possible numeric data types you can have and their valid ranges. Besides this list, there are also non-numeric data types, which we will cover later.

Alias for	Type	Range	Bits	Bytes
`bool`	System.Boolean	True or false (aka 0 or 1)	1	1[7]
`byte`	System.Byte	0 to 255	8	1
`sbyte`	System.SByte	-128 to 127	8	1
`decimal`	System.Decimal	$\pm 1.0 \times 10^{-28}$ to $\pm 7.9 \times 10^{28}$	128	16
`double`	System.Double	$\pm 5.0 \times 10^{-324}$ to $\pm 1.7 \times 10^{308}$	64	8
`float`	System.Single	$\pm 1.5 \times 10^{-45}$ to $\pm 3.4 \times 10^{38}$	32	4
`int`	System.Int32	-2,147,483,648 to 2,147,483,647	32	4
`uint`	System.UInt32	0 to 4,294,967,295	32	4
`long`	System.Int64	−9,223,372,036,854,775,808 to 9,223,372,036,854,775,807	64	8
`ulong`	System.UInt64	0 to 18,446,744,073,709,551,615	64	8
`short`	System.Int16	-32,768 to 32,767	16	2
`ushort`	System.UInt16	0 to 65,535	16	2

As you can see from this list you certainly have some choices! As a best programming practice, if you can guarantee that the value of a variable will never exceed a certain amount pick the type that is the closest in value range to reduce the amount of memory that will be used.

Also notice the first two columns. The first column is what we have been using as the data type for our variables, but is actually labeled as "Alias for" and the second column is the one actually labeled as "Type". In actuality it is the second column that is the Type that C# uses and understands, but to keep things short (remember rule 3?) and to keep the names familiar to programmers from other languages, the compiler will accept the Alias name in place of the much longer C# name.

Variables and Math

So far, our use of a variable to print out a number seems rather pointless – we could make our program give us the same output without having to use a variable.

---

[7] Hmmm, why are both 1 bit and 8 bits equal to 1 byte? A byte is actually made up of 8 bits, but memory is always assigned in bytes, so anything less than 8 bits will still take up a full byte. We'll cover bits and bytes in greater detail in a later chapter.

That's true, so now we are going to expand our little program and actually make the variables do something productive.

If there is one thing that computers are very good at it is math. We can give them a set of numbers and they can add, multiply, divide and so on faster than humans can. In fact no matter what your program does, somewhere in the code I can guarantee you will have variables getting added, multiplied, and divided. Let's write another program to which we will provide a pair of numbers and the computer will calculate their sum and their product.

As before, we are going to start a new C# project, so if you need to go ahead and launch Visual C#. If you already had it open, then close the current project down before starting a new one. We've done this a few times already, so I am not going to walk you through the steps, just remind you to make it a Console Application. For a name let's use "CH2b".

When your new project comes up, enter the following code between the opening and closing curly braces of the Main method:

```
int num1, num2;
int theSum, theProduct;

num1 = 3;
num2 = 5;

theSum = num1 + num2;
theProduct = num1 * num2;

Console.WriteLine("The sum of {0} and {1} is {2}",
                num1, num2, theSum);
Console.WriteLine("The product of {0} and {1} is {2}",
                num1, num2, theProduct);

Console.ReadLine();
```

When done, your screen should look like Figure 17.

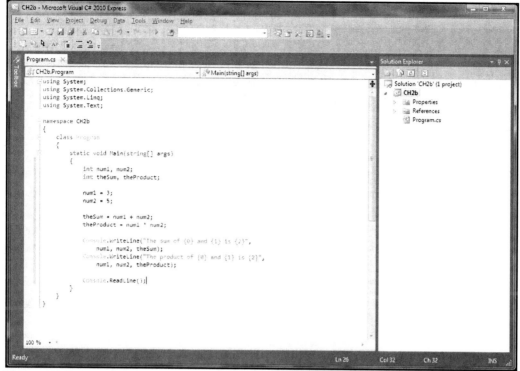

Figure 17: Project CH2b is open and displaying the values of 4 variables to the console

Run the code to verify that you typed it in correctly and to see the result. After you have closed the result window let's take a closer look at the code.

Right off the bat you should notice a couple of things we have not seen before. Examine carefully the first two lines of the code, where we define the variables num1, num2, theSum and theProduct. Notice how I can put multiple variable declarations all on the same line, separated by a comma! I could have even put all four onto the same line and the result would have been the same.

As long as you are defining multiple variables of the same type, you can list as many after a single type declaration as you want – however it is considered good practice to keep ones that have some relationship to each other together. The rest of the variables get their own line(s). In my case num1 and num2 are on the same line since they will be holding our input values, while theSum and theProduct are on a different line since they will hold our calculated values.

The other interesting thing to note is our two Console.WriteLine statements. The first thing to notice is that they span multiple lines. This is allowed and is normally done to break up very long lines so they can be read without having to scroll left/right all the time. You can put a break anywhere, as long as you are not breaking up the individual parts that make up the method call. In our example I could not have put a break within the quotes, since that is a literal string I want to display as is, nor could I have put a break within one of the variable names. Think of it like when writing a sentence in English. You can end the line between words, but you cannot break the words themselves. Yep, in English we can put a hyphen between syllables of a word, but not in programming.

Also note that in the string part of the `WriteLine` command, I have three placeholders: `{0}`, `{1}`, and `{2}`. You can use as many of these as you need and the numbers will correspond to the order of the variables listed after the string. So in our example, `{0}` refers to `num1`, `{1}` to `num2`, and `{2}` to `theSum` or `theProduct`. In fact you don't have to use the values in the order you defined them, meaning I could have written the first line like this:

```
Console.WriteLine("The sum of {1} and {2} is {0}",
                  theSum, num1, num2);
```

Not only is this legal, but it would work in the exact same way! Feel free to try it if you wish!

Now programmers are an interesting bunch. They spend all day long typing code, yet most of them will tell you that they do not necessarily like to type. This, among other reasons, is why most programmers like to keep variables names short, as well as to make other keystroke saving shortcuts. Take a look at the code below. This will work exactly the same way as our sample above, but notice a few shortcuts.

```
int num1 = 3, num2 = 5;

Console.WriteLine("The sum of {0} and {1} is {2}",
                  num1, num2, num1 + num2);
Console.WriteLine("The product of {0} and {1} is
{2}",
                  num1, num2, num1 * num2);

Console.ReadLine();
```

Notice the differences? I got rid of the declarations for the two variables `theSum` and `theProduct`. They are not needed since I am doing the math directly within the `WriteLine` statement. I also got rid of the two lines which set the values of `num1` and `num2`, since they are now assigned as part of the declaration! Both of these shortcuts are quite common and you will see them a lot when reading other people's code.

So is this shorter method better? Technically it is neither better nor worse; rather it is a matter of style and speed. Normally, advanced programmers are more likely to use such tricks simply because it is faster to type. Also for small calculations it is just as easy to put the calculation into the `WriteLine` command. However for larger more complex calculations, it is worth the time and effort to declare a result variable and put the calculation onto a separate line – it will make it easier to read the code or to find and change code elements in case there are coding errors or the requirements for the program change.

Now what about subtraction or division? Of course it works the same way, but there are a few additional things to think about. In the case of subtraction if your result could be a negative value, make sure you use a variable to catch this result which can hold a negative value. For division be careful about dividing by 0.

If you make either of these errors, the compiler will not complain or care, but the program will crash when you actually run it. Now of course there are cases when such an error cannot be prevented, so there are solutions in place to allow you to catch these errors and deal with them, but that is a subject for another chapter.

Can we get some Input?

Our last program is sort of interesting, but not very useful. What if you want to add or multiply numbers other than 3 and 5? Well, we could modify the code, recompile and run it again, but that is hardly convenient. What if, instead of hard coding these values, we could actually make the program ask us for the values each time the program runs? Sounds like it is time for a new project!

Using the same steps as before, startup a new Console Application project and call it "CH2c". Visual C# again gives us a nice blank new project and we can begin to code. As before, type this between the opening and closing curly braces of the Main method:

```
int num1, num2, theSum;
```

```
Console.Write("Enter the 1st number: ");
num1 = Int32.Parse(Console.ReadLine());

Console.Write("Enter the 2nd number: ");
num2 = Int32.Parse(Console.ReadLine());

theSum = num1 + num2;

Console.WriteLine("{0} + {1} = {2}", num1, num2,
                  theSum);

Console.ReadLine();
```

Once typed in, verify that it is all correct by running your program. When the prompt comes up, type in a number and press enter, then do the same thing for the second prompt. It should look like Figure 18:

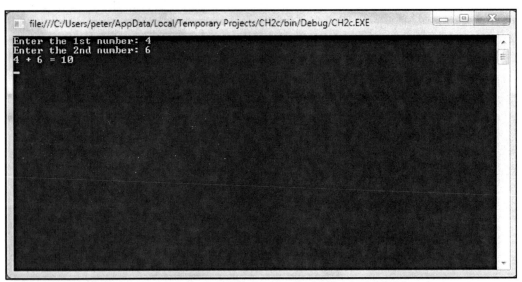

Figure 18: The console output shows it takes the user input for its variable values

Neat! Looking over the code, most of it should be familiar by now, but once again there are a few new things to find and examine. Take a look at the two lines which make up the query for each number:

```
Console.Write("Enter the 1st number: ");
num1 = Int32.Parse(Console.ReadLine());
```

Hmmm, we're using `Console.Write` instead of `Console.WriteLine`? Doesn't that sound the same? Actually they are quite similar in that both commands are used to write a piece of string out to the Console window. The difference is in what they do after they have printed out their respective bit of text. `WriteLine` will put a carriage return after the string, while `Write` does not – that's it! Another way of saying this is that `Write` just writes, but `WriteLine` writes and then moves to the next line.

I could have just as easily used a `WriteLine`, but in that case the cursor would have been on the second line waiting for your input. (Go ahead and try it!) Using the `Write` command instead, kept the cursor after the prompt which made it much easier to figure out what the program was asking

Wow, look at the second line! Quite a bit there, but as we break it down, it becomes quite logical and even easy to understand. Just as with a math problem that uses a number of parentheses to organize itself, we need to read this line not from the left to the right, but rather from the inside out. At the very center of this line is the `Console.ReadLine()` method call that we have used at the end of all of our programs to keep the output window from going away once the program ends.

If you recall Chapter 1 where we first used this line, I told you that you could punch in anything you wanted but nothing would happen until you pressed Enter. That was true then and is still true now, but with a caveat. When you press Enter, anything you typed in is actually collected by the `ReadLine` method and returned to the program. If there is something there to catch it then we can use that as input to our program, which is what we are doing here. So what are we doing with it?

Reading out from our central call to `Console.ReadLine()`, we find the code `Int32.Parse()` surrounding it. In other words the return value of the `ReadLine` method (the stuff we type to the keyboard), is sent as input to the `Parse` methods of the `Int32` object. If you remember from our list of Numeric Data Types, the type we call an `int` is actually a `System.Int32` type. As with everything else in C#, these data types are objects and all objects have methods that they support.

In the case of the `Int32` object[8] (as well as all of the other numeric data types), one of those methods is `Parse`. What the `Parse` method does is quite simple, it takes a string which contains an all numeric set of characters and turns it into an actual number. In other words, it takes the stuff that you typed in and turns it into a number, which then gets placed into our `num1` variable. Whew, that's a lot of explanation for a just a single line of code!

Now if you read that last couple of sentences very carefully, you are probably asking yourself a really good question! What if what I typed in are not all numeric characters? In other words, what if I entered "hello" instead of "5"? Will that work? Nope, it will not and in fact if you try it – go ahead try it, I can wait! – Figure 19, you will get an error.

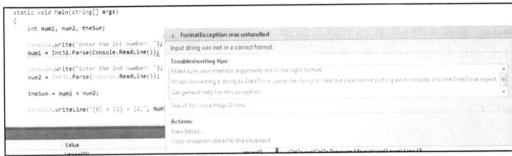

Figure 19: Entering alphabetical characters into the `ReadLine` causes the `Int32.Parse` to fail

As mentioned before, there are ways within C# to capture such errors and deal with them in a nice way (i.e. give the user a nice prompt to remind them that you asked for a number not a word), but that is for another chapter. For now, just be a nice user and only enter numbers! (BTW, while we humans like to put commas to separate out long numbers computers do not, so if you are trying to be really smart and enter something like "1,536" in as a number, it will still generate an error.)

Once the program has collected the two values and placed them into the variables `num1` and `num2`, it calculates the sum of these two values and displays it for us in an easy to read format – pretty much the same as our previous project did!

---

[8] Yes, you could have used just "int" instead of "Int32". I wanted to use the Int32 to demonstrate that these names are interchangeable.

Points to Ponder

- Variables are containers that hold data
- Variables are defined to be of a specific data type and can only hold data of that type
- The bigger value a variable can hold, the more bytes of memory it takes up
- You can name a variable anything you want, but the first character of the name must be either a letter or the underscore character
- Variable names are case sensitive
- To define a variable you first enter the data type it is to be followed by the name
- Variables' values are not fixed, but can be changed at any time
- You can use the `ReadLine` method to get input from the user, but that input must be parsed into the data type of the variable you wish to assign the result to

Challenge

1) Write a program that asks for three numbers and adds them together. Display the three values and the sum
2) Repeat challenge 1, only this time, multiply the three numbers
3) Write a program that asks for 2 numbers and divides the first number by the second. Display both numbers and the result.

Review Quiz

1.) For maximum readability, you must ensure that each string appears on a separate line. Which code segment should you use?

  O a. `Console.WriteLine("StudentUpdate");`
  O b. `Console.Write("StudentUpdate");`
  O c. `Console.Read("StudentUpdate");`
  O d. `Console.ReadLine("StudentUpdate");`

2.) What are 2 methods that are used to display data on the screen?

  ☐ a. `string()`
  ☐ b. `Write()`
  ☐ c. `ReadLine()`
  ☐ d. `WriteLine()`

3.) If you have a variable called `bal` which contains an integer value, how would you make the following output?

    Your balance is 4200

  O a. `System.Console.Write("Your balance is {0}", bal);`
  O b. `System.Console.Write("Your balance is {1}", bal);`

4.) `Write()` and `WriteLine()` are methods of what class?

  O a. System
  O b. Console
  O c. IO

5.) What determines what a variable can store?

  O a. The I/O method
  O b. The Data Identifier
  O c. The Data Scope
  O d. The Data Type

6.) What do you call the name you give to a variable?

  O a. Data type
  O b. Variable type
  O c. Variable Identifier
  O d. Variable length

7.) You want to declare an integer that does not hold negative numbers and will not go beyond 65,535. You decide to declare an unsigned short integer with the ushort keyword. What class is this keyword using?

O a. System.Int16

O b. System.UInt16

O c. System.Int32

O d. System.UInt32

O e. System.String

Notes

Chapter 3 – Decisions

Getting input from the outside world, processing it, and then sending it back out again is nice. However, without the ability to make decisions based on our data, our programs are never going to be very exciting. The ability to decide which bit of code to execute, based on expected values, is known as flow control.

There are three primary decision-making processes used in C#, or most other programming languages for that matter: (1) the `if/then` method, (2) the `switch` method and something called the (3) Ternary operator. For many situations you can use either one of these, but as with many other things in life, generally the simpler solution is usually the better one, in this case, the `if/then` method.

What If?

What if you knew next week's lotto numbers? Would you still play the ones you always play or would you use the ones guaranteed to win? Based on that bit of knowledge you can make a very simple if/then decision and change the course of your life!

The most common way to compare values and change the execution flow of your code is with the usage of the `if/then` statement. This is quite a simple structure which compares one value against another and if the comparison is true it will execute the set of lines that follow. Throw in an `else` statement and you can have a different set of lines execute if the result is false. Notice how I said it will execute a set of lines – ok, but how does the compiler know which set you wanted? Just as we use curly braces to surround a method, we also use curly braces to delimit the set of lines that we want to run if the if condition is true or false.

Let's take a look at a pseudo code version of the common if statement. (Pseudo code means it looks like programming code, but is not real and would not actually make it past a compiler. It is normally used to show the syntax and logic required by a particular method of programming command.)

```
if (<condition>)
{
    <execute for true>
}
else
{
    <execute for false>
}
```

What can we learn about the `if` statement from this bit of pseudo code? We know that the command starts with the keyword `if`, which is then followed by a conditional statement enclosed by parentheses. Below that, are a set of line(s) enclosed by curly braces which will only run if the condition above is true. Should we choose to, we can also have an `else` section to execute if the condition is false – in other words the keyword `else` and the section below it are optional.

Let's talk about what we mean by "conditional" for a bit. Computers have a very simple logic, where everything boils down to either 0 or 1 – which you can think of as either false (0) or true (1). As long as a statement eventually boils down to either true or false, no matter how complicated, we have ourselves a valid condition.

So what kinds of comparisons can we do? Pretty much all comparison functions come down to one of these variations:

==	equal to
>	greater than
>=	greater than or equal to
<	less than
<=	less than or equal to
!=	not equal to

Notice how I typed two equal signs in a row for the "equal" statement? No, that is not a mistake, but rather a very deliberate symbol used by all of the C type languages. The reason is quite simple once you think about it. There are two concepts of "equal" – the first is used to set or assign a value to a variable and the second is to compare or evaluate if two things are equal to each other. For example, if your child does something bad you need to ground him or her. That would be you assigning the status of "grounded" to his freedom, or in the terms of the C type languages you would say: "freedom = grounded".

A single = sign means you are assigning a value on the right hand side of the = sign to a variable on the left hand of the equal sign. If we use the same symbol to now also mean "is equal to", it would be very easy to misread a line like this:

```
if (x = 1) then <do something>
```

as:

"If (set x to be one) then do something".

Wait, does that make sense to you? No – well it would not make much sense to a compiler either. So, instead when comparing values we use the == symbol, which you should always read as "is equal to". That would mean that the following line:

```
if (x == 1) then <do something>
```

Should be read like this:

"if x is equal to 1 then do something".

Ah, much better! Enough talking, let's put our newfound skills to use!

Once again, launch your Visual C# program and start a new project. As usual, it will be a Console Application and this time it should be called "CH3a". As soon as you are ready type in the following code: (Remember to put the code between the curly braces of the Main method!)

```
int secretNum = 5, guessNum;

Console.Write("Guess a number between 0 and 10: ");
guessNum = Int32.Parse(Console.ReadLine());

if (secretNum == guessNum)
{
    Console.WriteLine("Great guess, you win!");
}
else
{
    Console.WriteLine("Sorry, that's not it!");
}
```

```
Console.ReadLine();
```

If you did it right, your screen should look like Figure 20 below.

```
Program.cs ×
CH3a.Program                                              Main(string[] args)
  using System;
  using System.Collections.Generic;
  using System.Linq;
  using System.Text;

  namespace CH3a
  {
      class Program
      {
          static void Main(string[] args)
          {
              int secretNum = 5, guessNum;

              Console.Write("Guess a number between 0 and 10: ");
              guessNum = int.Parse(Console.ReadLine());

              if (secretNum == guessNum)
              {
                  Console.WriteLine("Great guess, you win!");
              }
              else
              {
                  Console.WriteLine("Sorry, that's not it!");
              }

              Console.ReadLine();
          }
      }
  }
```

Figure 20: Using an if/else statement to conditionally run different code

Before you run the code, read through it and try to understand what it will do. When you are ready, try it and see whether you were right.

By now most of the lines in this little program should be quite clear to you. We have used all of these commands in previous programs, with the exception of the if line, but it should not be difficult to guess its purpose. We simply take the value that you entered, store it in guessNum, and compare it to our secretNum variable, which we set during its declaration. If the two match then the program displays a congratulatory message and comes to an end. But if the two values do not match the else statement is run instead, which displays a message telling you that you are wrong.

Now as far as games go, this one lacks a few of the usual refinements, and no I do not mean the fancy graphics! Normally in a guessing type game like this if the user guesses wrong we would expect the program to let the user try again. That is actually quite easy to do, but to do that we would have to use something we are going to cover in the next chapter. So for now, let's just keep our excitement in check until then and try to go on...

In keeping with the "less is more" philosophy of programming, there is a very interesting and commonly used trick that we could have used. Take a look at this version of the program and see if you can notice it:

```
int secretNum = 5, guessNum;

Console.Write("Guess a number between 0 and 10: ");
guessNum = Int32.Parse(Console.ReadLine());

if (secretNum == guessNum)
    Console.WriteLine("Great guess, you win!");
else
    Console.WriteLine("Sorry, that's not it!");

Console.ReadLine();
```

Ok, enough guessing – I'll tell you. Notice how there are no curly braces around lines of code that make up the true or the else sections. This actually would work just fine, and you are welcome to change your code and try it. But why does it work? Doesn't the compiler need to know where the lines that make up the true and else sections of the if statement start and end? Yes, it still does and in actuality no rule has been violated.

The rule is actually that if the condition is true the if command will execute the *next* line of code following the if statement, and that if it is not true then it will execute the *next* line of code after the else statement. Since we only have a single statement for both the true and the else sections, everything still works as normal and the curly braces become optional. As soon as you have more than one line, those curly braces become required; if they are not there the compiler will complain.

Think of it this way. In effect the if statement's true and else sections always only execute a single line of code, because when you surround a block of lines with curly braces, the compiler will treat that block as a single unit of code. Now all this may be good and true, but good programming practice is that you should always use those curly braces, even if you are only going to have a single line of code. It makes things much easier to read and that is a goal you should always stride for!

So far we have only used the equals to (==) in our condition, which is the most common, but there are other ways to compare values. Let's update our guessing program so if you get the answer wrong the computer will give you a clue if you are too low or too high. This will require multiple if statements. Save your project and start a new one, this time calling it "CH3b". When ready, type in the following code.

```csharp
int secretNum = 5, guessNum;

Console.Write("Guess a number between 0 and 10: ");
guessNum = Int32.Parse(Console.ReadLine());

if (secretNum == guessNum)
    Console.WriteLine("Great guess, you win!");
else
{
    if (guessNum > secretNum)
        Console.WriteLine("Sorry, too high!");
    else
        Console.WriteLine("Sorry, too low!");
}

Console.ReadLine();
```

When you are ready, review the code and try to visualize what it will do. If you think you know, run it and play with a couple of values to confirm your understanding of the code.

This is still our guessing program, but with an additional if statement inside the else clause of the original if statement. Notice how I had to put curly braces around the code of the else block since it is made up of more than one line of code. Let's walk through the logic of these two if statements and all of its possible outcomes:

1) The guess is correct. The first if statement compares our guess to the secret number and if they match it prints a congratulatory message. So far no different from our original program.

2) The guess is incorrect and it is higher than the secret number. The condition of the first if statement is false, so we have fallen into the else block. In here we find another if statement where we compare whether the guess is larger than the secret number. If that condition is true then we know the guess is too high and we print a message to that effect.

3) The guess is incorrect and it is lower than the secret number. This condition becomes the else result (or the false result) of both if statements. We know it is not correct, so the first if statement's condition is false. Since it is lower than the secret number, the condition of the second if statement is also false. Therefore the message in the else condition of the second if statement is generated.

Now this is a very simple conditional logic tree with only three possible outcomes, but you could easily imagine one where there could be any number of conditions to check. We could keep on putting if statements into the else blocks of the one above it, but that would get very ugly really quickly.

There is a cleaner solution and that is to put the if command directly after the else command – this is known as the else if statement. The easiest way to demonstrate this is to rewrite our program using this new statement:

```
int secretNum = 5, guessNum;

Console.Write("Guess a number between 0 and 10: ");
guessNum = Int32.Parse(Console.ReadLine());

if (secretNum == guessNum)
    Console.WriteLine("Great guess, you win!");
else if (guessNum > secretNum)
    Console.WriteLine("Sorry, too high!");
else
    Console.WriteLine("Sorry, too low!");

Console.ReadLine();
```

Notice the difference. There is no longer a set of curly braces after the else clause of the initial if statement, since this is not counted as multiple lines. (You are right, based on my comment earlier you really ought to use curly braces even for a single line of code, I'm trying to both prove a point and save some typing.) Rather it goes directly into another if statement, which has its own true and else blocks – each of which is only a single line, therefore curly braces are not needed here either.

This type of logic can be extended quite deeply. The second else statement could become yet another else if statement, and so on. For example, you could have a set of if/else if statements where you would compare the guess to each value between 1 and 10 so you could print a custom message for each number. In actual practice, past a few levels, this becomes much too unwieldy to use and is not common at all. For such complex types of comparisons there is another method more suitable. (Generally speaking if you have more than three nested if statements you might want to rethink your decision logic and try to find a simpler solution.)

Time to Switch

If you guessed from my clever title that the name of this command is switch, then you are right. Whereas the if/else statements are best for a comparison with one or two possible outcomes, the switch statement can have as many alternative results as you can type in. Here is the general structure of a switch statement:

```
switch (<value being tested>)
{
    case <possible value>:
        <code to execute>
        break;
    case <possible value>:
        <code to execute>
        break;
    ...
    default:
        <code to execute>
        break;
}
```

That may look like a lot, but once you get the hang of it you will find it so much easier to use than nesting tons of if statements together! Let's take a look at it by writing a new project, "CH3c" using the following code:

```
Console.WriteLine("Your options are");
Console.WriteLine(" 1) Coffee");
Console.WriteLine(" 2) Tea");
Console.WriteLine(" 3) Hot Chocolate");
Console.Write("Please make a selection: ");
int myChoice = int.Parse(Console.ReadLine());

Console.Write("Thank you, here is your ");

switch (myChoice)
{
    case 1:
        Console.Write("coffee.");
        break;

    case 2:
        Console.Write("tea.");
        break;

    case 3:
        Console.Write("hot chocolate.");
        break;

    default:
        Console.Write("hot drink.");
        break;
}

Console.WriteLine("  Please enjoy!");

Console.ReadLine();
```

That is a lot more code than we have written so far, but none of it should be really problematic to understand by now. But there are a few tricks to watch out for! Notice the usage of Write vs. WriteLine, the declaration of the myChoice variable, and of course, the switch statement itself. Let's walk through this code!

The first five lines are just to display a bit of text to the screen. Of these the first four use the WriteLine command, so each line has a termination at the end (aka a carriage return), moving the cursor down and readying it for the next line. However the fifth line of code just uses a `Write` command, so when it finishes the cursor stays after the string ready for your input.

The next line is our normal line for getting input from the user into a variable, in this case called `myChoice`. However, notice that instead of defining this variable at the top of the program as we have done in the past, this time I put the declaration directly onto the beginning of the line. One of the advantages of C# over the other C languages is its ability to define variables anywhere in the code you would like, instead of just at the top of the code block (yet you will find that many developers still prefer to cluster their variable declarations at the top of a code block).

In the same way that we have declared a variable in the past and directly assigned a value to it, we are doing a similar thing here. The only difference is that the source of the value is not being hard coded by us, but comes from the `ReadLine` method through the `int.Parse` command.

Once we have the user's input, we print out a partial line. Since no matter what they order the first part of our response will always be the same, there is no reason to type that in multiple times. Instead we just display it once, but using a `Write` command so the cursor remains at the end of the line ready for more text. Once that is done we jump into the `switch` statement.

After the keyword `switch` we have, in parentheses, the value we want to test against. Think of this value as what would come on the left hand side of a `==` symbol if this were a normal `if` statement. The next section is enclosed in a pair of curly braces and contains one or more `case` statements followed by a single optional `default` statement.

Each `case` statement is like the right hand side of a `==` symbol in a normal `if` statement, so we end up comparing this fixed value (1 for the first case block) to whatever is inside the `myChoice` variable. If it matches then we execute the next set of line(s) until we come to a `break` command. The `break` command tells the compiler to stop processing the rest of the `case` statements and instead jump to the ending curly brace which contains the guts of the `switch` command.

Now if the value after that first `case` statement does not match the variable specified after the `switch` command, then we just keep on checking the rest of the `case` statements until one of them matches. If none of the `case` statements match, then the compiler looks for a default section and executes what is in there. However the default section is optional, so if none of the case statements match (for example if the user selected number 4) and there is no default section then nothing gets processed (yep, that's valid and does happen).

Finally in our program we finish our partially completed "thank you" line with a final bit and then wait for the user to press the enter key before ending the program.

Go ahead and run your program and experiment with entering different values and see what results you get.

What about a situation where you have two (or more) case statements and you want the same code to be executed for each? Of course you could just type the same lines of code multiple times, but that is never a good idea! Remember, developers do not like to type!

You can actually put multiple case statements together. Let's take our earlier program and add an option for both regular and decaf coffee. For both options we want our output to be the same.

```
Console.WriteLine("Your options are");
Console.WriteLine(" 1) Coffee");
Console.WriteLine(" 2) Decaf Coffee");
Console.WriteLine(" 3) Tea");
Console.WriteLine(" 4) Hot Chocolate");
Console.Write("Please make a selection: ");
int myChoice = int.Parse(Console.ReadLine());

Console.Write("Thank you, here is your ");

switch (myChoice)
{
    case 1:
    case 2:
        Console.Write("coffee.");
        break;

    case 3:
        Console.Write("tea.");
```

```
            break;

        case 4:
            Console.Write("hot chocolate.");
            break;

        default:
            Console.Write("hot drink.");
            break;
    }

    Console.WriteLine("  Please enjoy!");

    Console.ReadLine();
```

Notice how the two `case` statements for options 1 (regular coffee) and 2 (decaf coffee) are listed together. When this runs, if you choose either option 1 or option 2, the same line of code will execute, giving you the same message.

Can you Say Cryptic?

There is one final way to execute a decision sequence, which is called the ternary operator. In essence this is a very (and I do mean very!) shortened style of the basic `if/then/else` process to just one statement. It is rather cryptic and lots of developers are not particularly fond of it, but you do need to know it. Besides it is always fun to stump a developer with something that they may not see (or use) very often.

The basic structure of the ternary operator looks like this:

```
    x = <condition> ? <result if true> : <result if
    false>
```

Unlike the full `if` statement which can contain blocks of code within either the `if` result or `else` result area, the ternary operator simply returns a value depending on the condition. Take a look at this code fragment:

```
    int x = 5, y = 3, answer;
    answer = (x == y) ? 1 : 0;
```

We first define three variables named x, y and answer (yep, bad variable names, but this is just a sample bit of code). We set x to 5 and y to 3, but leave `answer` undefined. When the ternary operator runs, it compares x and y to see if they are equal. If they are equal then `answer` would get set to 1, but since in our example it is not, `answer` gets set to 0.

To help understand, let's rewrite this example using a standard `if` statement – the result will be the same, just using a different command.

```
if (x == y)
    return 1;
else
    return 0;
```

Of course instead of just returning a fixed value such as 0 or 1, we could have put something a bit more complex in there such as x+1. Actually the most common usage of this line is to do something like the example below – try to figure out the purpose before reading the explanation:

```
int x = 5, y = 3, answer;
answer = (x > y) ? x : y;
```

Using our sample values of "5" and "3", what do you think the value of `answer` would be after the ternary operator is executed? The condition tests to see if x is larger than y and if it is then it returns the value of x, which then gets assigned to `answer`. If the test fails and x is not larger then y then y gets returned into `answer`. This is a common usage of this operator to return the larger of two values.

That's it! Not kidding when I said it was cryptic!

Points to Ponder

- There are three ways to make decisions in your code: `if`, `switch` and ternary
- `if` is the most common

- You need to use curly braces around the block of code (if your block of code is more than one statement), you want to execute if the expression is true
- Using the else statement you can instead execute a block if the expression is false
- You can never have the true and the else blocks both execute – it is always one or the other
- You can chain multiple if statements together by the use of the if else statement
- To check for equality (i.e. one item is equal to the other), you use two equal signs (==). A single equal sign is used only to assign a value to a variable
- For a series of values to be compared to a single expression, use the switch statement
- For a switch block, you must have at least one case block. The default block is optional
- The ternary operator does not execute a block of code in either its true or false blocks, but rather returns a value
- The ternary operator is hard to read and is not used very often

Challenge

1. Write a program asking the user to enter a number between 1 and 10. Using if statement(s), check to make sure that they actually entered a number between 1 and 10. If the number is less than 1 display a message that their input is too low and if the number is above 10 remind them of the upper limit.
2. Write a program that asks the user for two numbers. Using the if statement, determine which number is the larger of the two and print that number.
3. Write a program to print the name of the month based on the month number that the user enters. For example, if the user enters 3, then the output should be March.

Review Quiz

1.) What will an `if` statement execute without a {} block if the expression is true?
   O a. Just run the next statement.
   O b. Jump directly to the else statement.
   O c. Skip the next line and continue

2.) How do you cascade many `if` statements to make three or more decisions in your control of flow?
   O a. `if`
   O b. `else if`
   O c. `else`

3.) What keyword is good at handling complex conditions that would normally require nested if statements?
   O a. `break`
   O b. `while`
   O c. `goto`
   O d. `switch`
   O e. `do`

Notes

Chapter 4 – More Math

Oh come on, who doesn't like Math? You in the back – put your hand down - geez, some people!

Like it or not, Math is part of our daily lives – from balancing our checkbook to figuring out how much to tip our wait person at lunch time. While we all need to know and use Math, human beings are geared to think more in terms of words, pictures and colors, than in numbers. Computers, on the other hand, are exactly the opposite. To them everything is just a number, even when they are displaying letters on the screen – in memory it is stored as a series of numbers. Because of this they are very efficient at all kinds of calculations and we as programmers have to get very familiar with how to express ourselves using their mathematical notations.

One plus One

When we got our dog, Barkley, we proudly told our friends and family that we had a new addition to the family. Before there were the two of us plus the three cats, so our FamilyNum == 5. With Barkley we had to increment the FamilyNum counter by one – in other words whatever the size of the family was before, when a new member arrives you increment the family size by one.

Probably the most common Math problem we give our computers is getting them to add one to (or subtract one from) a value or a variable. You wouldn't think it, but I am willing to bet you quite a bit of money that every single program you can think of has somewhere within its source code a line that does nothing but add or subtract a 1 from another value. Let's write a few lines of code to illustrate this:

```
int myNum = 5;
myNum = myNum + 1;
```

Yep, it is just that simple. After that second line is executed, the value stored in myNum is going to be not 5 but 6. Now I remember the very first time I ever saw this expression, back when I was still very new to computers. My first reaction was that this will cause a problem, since we are trying to both use and modify the value of the variable myNum at the same time. While that is true, you have to understand how the compiler would approach this line in order to understand why this is not a problem.

Instead of trying to use the myNum variable on both sides of the equation at once, the compiler breaks this down into two very specific chunks. The first chunk is what is listed to the right of the equal sign, which is to take the value of myNum and add one to it. Once that calculation is done, and the result stored in memory, it then looks to the left of the equals to see what it needs to do with the result of the calculation. That assignment tells it to take this value it now has in memory and put it into the myNum variable, where it overrides the current value of "5" with the new value of "6".

Now this particular line is so very common that programmers have come up with a great shorthand for it (remember, lazy typists). This line here does the exact same thing:

```
myNum++;
```

It does not get shorter than that! What if you want to subtract one from the myNum variable? In that case try this:

```
myNum--;
```

(And they say programming is difficult!) This notation is known as a unary operator. Now programmers are an interesting lot and when they first came up with this notation they all liked it, but some of them just could not resist "making it better" and they made a small tweak to it. Take a look at this bit of code:

```
int num = 1;
Console.WriteLine("{0} {1} {2}", num++, num, ++num);
```

Whoa, you can put the ++ both before and after? Yes, but while in both cases it adds a 1 to the value, when it does that is the trick here. Before you run this line, what do you expect the output to be? If you answered "2 2 3" you would be wrong. The difference between having the ++ before or after the variable, has to do with when the value gets increased in relation to when we see the value.

In our example, the variable num starts off as containing a 1. When it gets to the num++, the compiler notices that the plus signs are after the variable so it first returns the value of the variable (which is currently holding a 1), then increases its value by 1. The second thing it has to print out is just the variable by itself. Since it has been increased, the num variable now holds 2, so that is what gets printed out. Then we get to the third one which is the ++num. The compiler notices that the plus signs are before the variable name, so this time it increments num before sending its value to the WriteLine to print out. So the final output of this program is going to be "1 2 3". Try it!

Ok, trust me on this – go back and read that last paragraph again. This is a really weird concept that takes a while to truly understand. The -- notation works exactly the same way when it is placed before or after a variable, except it subtracts 1 instead of adding 1.

What about adding more than 1 to a value? Well for that you cannot just use more plus signs (i.e. num+++++), that will cause the compiler to get quite confused, since it is not a defined operator. Instead, you have to type the full equation:

```
num = num + 5;
```

Just as adding one to a variable is a very common task, so is adding a larger number to it, so the C# gods have come up with a shortcut for this as well.

```
num += 5;
```

This line is totally identical to the one above: whatever the number was before, it is now higher by 5. However, this method only works as long as you are adding a value to a variable and then assigning that value back to the same variable, such as the examples above. If you want to add 5 to the num variable but store the results in the answer variable, you will have to type out the full statement:

```
answer = num + 5;
```

There is no shortcut for that. What about subtracting, multiplying, dividing and so on? All of the same rules and shortcuts apply, so the following lines are all valid:

This:	Is the same as this:
num -= 5;	num = num - 5;
num *= 5;	num = num * 5;
num /= 5;	num = num / 5;

All of these are standard math operators that we have all known and used since grade school. About the only difference is the symbols used. In school we learned to use the "x" to mean multiply by and the ÷ to mean divide by. For computers the multiplication symbol becomes the * (aka the asterisk[9]) and division is a /. This was originally done to prevent confusion between the letter x and the multiplication symbol and the fact that the division symbol is traditionally not part of the character set that computers can display.

Computer languages, including C#, add one more operator, which is a special version of the divide function, to this basic set. In normal math, if I divide 8 by 5 the answer is 1 with a remainder of 3. Therefore if I write the following line of code:

```
answer = 8 / 5;
```

the value of answer will be 1. So, what happened to the 3? There is a special division operator, called modulo or mod for short, which will do this same calculation but instead of 1, it will return the remainder of 3. The symbol for mod is %. So this line:

```
answer = 8 % 5;
```

will set the value of the answer variable to 3. Just as with the rest of the operators, the mod operator supports the %= syntax as well, when operating on the same variable.

Order of Precedence

If you went to a grocery store and saw a 6 pack of your favorite drink on sale, you might decide to get two. In that case you actually have 12 cans, right? What if there was also a manufacturer special where every 6 pack had a bonus can in it (I guess you could call that a 7 pack). Buying two of these packs would net you a total of 14 cans. Putting that into a math formula would look like this:

```
6 + 1 * 2 = 14
```

---

[9] Weird computer tidbit. In the Unix world the asterisk symbol is commonly known as "splat".

Seems simple to us that a 6 pack with a bonus can would make it into a 7-pack, and two of them would total 14. Just as with English, we read this math problem from the left to the right.

With that in mind, here is a question for you. What is the result of the following math problem?

```
5 + 3 * 2
```

Depending on how you read this, you could answer either 16 or 11. To know which answer is correct you need to know something called Order of Precedence, or which mathematical operator has the highest precedence? Turns out that if you program this formula into C# and run it, the answer will be 11 – Hmmm, why? Simple, because the multiplication function has a higher precedence than the addition function, so the computer evaluates this as 3 * 2 or 6, plus 5. (This concept of precedence is taken from the world of mathematics where the same rules apply.)

Hmmm, sounds like it would be a really good idea to know what order the compiler will evaluate our math problems in so we do not get surprised. Here is the list of the math operators in order of precedence (in other words, which is the most important, meaning it gets evaluated first):

```
++ and -- (as a prefix)
*, / and %
+ and -
=, *=, /=, %=, +=, -=
++ and -- (as suffix)
```

So, multiplication and division come before addition or subtraction. If you have both a multiplication and division operator in the same formula, the multiplication will happen before the division. (Same thing with addition and subtraction, addition comes first.) Notice the ++ and -- functions are treated differently, depending upon whether they come before or after the variable.

Now, there is no question that knowing this order is important, but it turns out that you can also ignore it, or more precisely you can force the various elements of your math problem to come in the order you want, not as dictated by precedence. Remember that problem from the beginning? What if I really wanted the answer to be 16 and not 11? Well, I should have then written it like this:

```
(5 + 3) * 2
```

Basically, this means that whatever is in the parentheses has to be calculated first. Of course, you can use as many parentheses as you need and nest them any way necessary in order to guarantee that things are calculated the way you want them.

My recommendation is no matter how well you know the order of precedence or how simple or complex your math is, always use the parentheses liberally to guarantee that your function is calculated the way you expect and want it, not the way the compiler thinks it should be performed.

Math Theory 101

Before we go on, let's take a bit of time to talk about some basic math theory, otherwise known as "how many fingers do I have"? Way back in our history, there once was a caveman, happily sitting in front of his cave, looking over his special pile of rocks. All was right in his world, until he looked over to the next cave and saw his neighbor examining his own pile of special rocks. As he looked more carefully and compared his rock pile to that of his neighbors, it dawned on him that the other guy might actually have more rocks in his pile than he did! So, he picked up his largest rock and threw it at his neighbor – and that is how war got invented. Oh wait, wrong story...

As he looked at his pile and that of his friend, he finally noticed something. His pile might have been smaller, but his individual rocks were smaller as well. If that is the case then maybe he did have more rocks, just they were smaller so the pile must be smaller then as well. So then, how to impress the cave babes if on first glance the other guys rock pile seems so much larger? Ah, the birth of mathematics is at hand!

Our smart caveman took his pile of rocks and split them into groups of 10. Since he had ten fingers on his hands, each pile was now equal to a handful. When he explained this new way of comparing rocks at the next caveman's meeting and had everyone else do the same, the number of his handfuls were more than those of his neighbors. Wow, he did have more rocks! (Not sure if his caveman buddy was quite as happy with this new system...)

Luckily for us, our caveman ancestors had ten fingers, just as we do, and 10 became the basis of our entire math. Computers don't have fingers; rather they use electricity to do all of their calculations. Electricity is a simple kind of a beast and really only has two states, it is either on or it is off. Put that into number terms and off can be expressed as a 0 and on as a 1. Hmmm, a two state math system, a kind of binary system? I think I've heard of this...

Before we get into Binary math (the fancy name for a two state math), I need to teach you how to count in decimal. Ok, I am going to assume that you didn't sleep through your entire set of math classes from grade school to college. However, unless you were a total math geek, I am going to assume that you have never thought about math like this.

Back in my early school days, I had a math teacher who loved to put a large number on the board, say 16,247, and then break it down like this:

```
1 x 10,000   =  10,000
6 x 1,000    =   6,000
2 x 100      =     200
4 x 10       =      40
7 x 1        =       7
                ---------
                 16,247
```

This was sort of fun once or twice, but frankly after a couple of dozen times I started getting annoyed with it. It wasn't until my high school days (when I had a computer teacher who used to moonlight as a math teacher) that this all actually started to make sense.

Look at that series of numbers on the right side of the multiplication sign – see a pattern? Starting from the bottom, each value above is exactly 10 times as large as the one below it. In other words, 1 x 10 equals 10, 10 x 10 equals 100, 100 x 10 equals 1000, and so on. Hmmm, base 10 math, 10 times as large – there has to be a correlation. Of course there is, it's Math!

Math is even more formal than computer programming, so it turns out that there is another way to show this relationship between these numbers:

$$10,000 = 10^4$$
$$1,000 = 10^3$$
$$100 = 10^2$$
$$10 = 10^1$$
$$1 = 10^0$$

So, for each place in our number, the value is equal to whatever number is in that location multiplied by the value of the base system raised to the positional location of that number. (10^0 is a special case, in fact any number raised to the power of 0 is special in that the answer is always 1.)

Boolean Logic and Binary Math

Before we get started, a quick word on terminology – trust me, we are about to get hip deep in this stuff!

At the lowest level, computers deal in only two states. Those can be thought of as true or false, or if you prefer as on or off. A state of true or on is considered as a 1, while a state of false or off is considered as a 0. This reflects their reliance on the existence, or lack of, an electrical charge.

The physical architecture of a computer is way outside the scope of this book. For the sake of simplicity, let us just say that a computer's ability to store data or make a logical decision is based on a single true/false state. A single spot of memory which can be either on or off is called a "bit". These bits are grouped into larger units, in order to make dealing with them easier. (Figure 21)

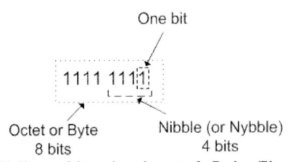

Figure 21: Names of the various elements of a Boolean/Binary value

The smallest element is a "bit", which is a single unit of a Boolean/Binary value and can be either a 0 or a 1. A "nibble" is the term for a collection of four bits, which gives it a value range of 0 to 15 in decimal, or 0 to F in hexadecimal (more on hexadecimal in just a little bit). Finally, a collection of 8 bits, or two nibbles, make up a "byte" which has a range of 0 to 255 in decimal or 0 to FF in hexadecimal. The term "octet", which is another word for a byte, comes from the telecommunications world where an IP address is made up of four octets, each of which has to be in the range of 0 to 255 (decimal). Who said computer folks don't have a sense of humor?

In case you don't know yet how to count in base 2 math (or Binary math as it is officially known), trust me, by the end of this chapter you will! It only uses two characters. As such, it tends to be rather large with relatively small numbers. Let me give you a few examples:

Base 10	Base 2	Base 10	Base 2
1	1	10	1010
2	01	15	1111
3	11	100	1100100
4	100	200	11001000
5	101	255	11111111

I think that's enough for now. As you can guess, really large numbers (say 1,452,824) would be a lot of zeroes and ones to print out. So what is the point and why do I need to know this? Not only do computers internally express all things as numbers and not just any numbers but as Binary numbers, they also use Boolean logic and Binary math to compare things. Of course we are not computers and, frankly, it becomes hard to read Boolean/Binary stuff. Unfortunately, our computers like them so we have to find a way to deal with them as well.

It turns out that you can build math on any base value, not just 10 or 2, so to make things a bit easier for us humans, we came up with alternative number systems to make dealing with all this stuff a little bit easier. For quite a while, octal math, aka base 8 math, was quite the rage and occasionally you can still find references to it nowadays. Turns out that base 16 math, or hexadecimal, has a unique relationship to Binary. Also, since it uses 16 digits instead of 2 or 10, it is even more compact than our normal decimal system. But I'm getting ahead of myself – this chapter is about Binary not hexadecimal math.

You mean besides this Boolean/Binary stuff, we have to learn even more base systems? No, you don't actually have to learn all of these different math systems – it turns out they are all based on the same logic, so if you know one you pretty much know them all! Since we are all familiar with decimal math, let's use that to explain this whole math theory bit.

Let's run the same process we did for decimal, but using base 2, and then look at those sample Binary numbers I gave earlier. To make things a bit easier to understand, I'm going to table this horizontally:

	2^7	2^6	2^5	2^4	2^3	2^2	2^1	2^0
	128	64	32	16	8	4	2	1
255	1	1	1	1	1	1	1	1
200	1	1	0	0	1	0	0	0
100	0	1	1	0	0	1	0	0
15	0	0	0	0	1	1	1	1
10	0	0	0	0	1	0	1	0
5	0	0	0	0	0	1	0	1
4	0	0	0	0	0	1	0	0
3	0	0	0	0	0	0	1	1

Did you notice the pattern? Each increasing digit is twice the value of its neighbor to the right. This makes it very easy to remember the bit values of a Binary number.

Take a look at the line that has 200 as its value. In Binary, 200 is written as 11001000. For each location where there is a 1, we take the decimal value of that column and add them up. For 200, those columns are 128 + 64 + 8. To be more precise, for each location where there is a value other than a zero, we multiply the value of the field by the bit value of that field. In Binary, each field can either be a 0 or a 1, so all of these multiplications would be by 1 – I think we can skip that step.

So, why is this useful? Remember when we were talking about the condition part of the `if` statements? I said that all expressions have to either boil down to a true or a false. With a simple expression like 2 == 3, there is only a single expression and we can, at a glance, know if it is true or false. But what about a more complex one, such as comparing multiple sets of values? For example:

```
if ((num1 == num2) && (num3 >= num4))
{
    <do something>
}
```

Each set of parentheses encloses a single condition, each of which can be either true or false, depending on the values in those four variables. But what does that && symbol in the middle mean? This is known as a logical "and" operator and simply says that both expressions have to be true for the entire expression to be true. What if one expression (say num1 == num2) is true but (num3 >= num4) is not – would that still make the entire expression true? Simple logic with English tells us that when using the word AND, both sides have to be true for the entire thing to be true. Thus, if the first statement is true and the second is false, the whole statement is considered to be false.

Of course, we can always try to look at this in terms a bit less mathematical and more apt to our day-to-day lives. For example, you could have two individual choices to make in order to decide what to have for lunch: If I have more than 10 dollars and my cholesterol is not too high, then I can have a burger. Two individual decisions exist, but to decide if I can have that burger or not I have to evaluate them together.

But Boolean logic has other conditionals besides AND, such as OR and XOR. Which conditions make them true? A list of this nature is known as a truth table, and it looks like this:

num1	num2	AND
0	0	0
0	1	0
1	0	0
1	1	1

num1	num2	OR
0	0	0
0	1	1
1	0	1
1	1	1

num1	num2	XOR
0	0	0
0	1	1
1	0	1
1	1	0

How do you read this? Each table has four possible combinations of either true (1), or false (0). In the case of the AND table, you would read the four lines as:

    0 and 0 equals 0
    0 and 1 equals 0
    1 and 0 equals 0
    1 and 1 equals 1

Put that into something a bit more English like and you get:

False and False equals False, False and True equals False, and so on. Basically, with the AND function both sides have to be true for the entire thing to be true.

The OR function is much easier, as long as one side is true the entire thing is true. Finally we have XOR (or eXclusive OR), where only when one side differs from the other is the entire thing true. Another way to state this is "one or the other but not both". We can more expressively write these out like this:

0 or 0 equals 0	0 exclusive or 0 equals 0
0 or 1 equals 1	0 exclusive or 1 equals 1
1 or 0 equals 1	1 exclusive or 0 equals 1
1 or 1 equals 1	1 exclusive or 1 equals 0

Within decision statements such as if and switch, you will see AND (&&) and OR (||) used quite a bit, but XOR in that context does not make sense, and in fact there is no XOR comparison operator. But you are not out of the woods yet with XOR. Since computers store everything internally as Boolean values, turns out that you can manipulate the individual bits that make up a value, using the AND, OR and XOR logic.

Now, if you are really into this stuff, or just happen to enjoy mental pain, it is actually possible to add, subtract, multiply and divide using pure Binary math. I've done some basic addition and subtraction with Binary and trust me it wasn't particularly fun, so we are not going to really go into it here. (But if you are really interested, search Google or Wikipedia and you can learn all about it.)

First Binary now Hexadecimal

Since trying to read or manipulate Binary is rather an unpleasant task, an easier solution had to be found. One solution early on, and still used by some people, is to just convert all Binary values back into decimal, run whatever processes you need and then convert them back. While that works just fine, the conversion process between base 2 and base 10 is not exactly straightforward. Enter base 16, otherwise known as hexadecimal. Turns out that since 16 is a power of 2 (aka 2^4), the conversion is very simple. Before we go into that let us examine how base 16 math works.

We already know, from our earlier discussion, that you can use any number as a base and simply raise it to the positional value to get its actual value. While that is quite true, whenever you deal with a numbering system that has more than 10 digits (i.e. 0 through 9), you need to come up with a way to represent those additional digits. For hexadecimal, the solution was to simply use the first 6 letters of the alphabet. In other words, the order would be: 0, 1, 2, 3, 4, 5, 6, 7, 8, 9, A, B, C, D, E, and F. In hexadecimal notation the number F is the highest single digit value.

So, the digits 0 to 9 still represent their normal value, but then we get A for 10, B for 11 all the way up to F for 15. Traditionally, these letters are always written in uppercase letters. To try and use this, we will create the same grid we did for Binary.

	16^4	16^3	16^2	16^1	16^0
	65535	4096	256	16	1
1048575	F	F	F	F	F
65535		F	F	F	F
402			1	9	2
255				F	F
200				C	8
100				6	4
16				1	0
15					F
10					A
2					2
1					1

As you can see, this is a very space efficient way to write down some very large numbers. However, an interesting problem develops that you did not have with Binary notation. Take the following number: 192. We know it cannot be a base 2 number, since it uses digits above 1. It could be a base 10 number, since it only uses normal number characters, but it also could be a base 16 number, in which case its actual value is 402 in decimal.

How do you mark a number to indicate which base it belongs to? There are actually a number of solutions to this problem but the two most common come from the world of mathematics and the world of the C programmers (which includes the languages of C, C++ and C#). In math, the normal way to indicate the base is to put a subscript (value of the base) after the number, so that 192 in base 16 would be written as 192_{16}, and the same number if base 10 would be 192_{10}. In the C programming world, we do not mark decimal values in any special method but for hexadecimal values we prefix the number with the characters 0x. So, our base 16 number 192 would look like this: 0x192. Other common methods are (all using 192 as the number):

XML/HTML	#192
Unicode	U+192
Assembly	0192h
Visual Basic	&H192

There are a number of other methods that are more specialized to their environments, but these are the most common ones that I have seen.

So, how do we convert from Binary to hex? Let's take a number, say 171 (notice there is no subscript, so this is in base 10) and get its forms in the other bases. (BTW, the Windows calculator, when in scientific mode, is able to convert between decimal, octal, hexadecimal and binary.)

$$171_{10} = 10101011_2 = AB_{16}$$

To start off, first write out your Binary number, but break it in half, or into two nibbles. For the purpose of this conversion, we are going to treat this not as a single number but rather as two smaller numbers. That gives us:

1010   1011

As you recall from our discussion at the beginning of the Binary section, I made a comment that the value pattern for each Binary bit is easy to remember since it is always the double of the number to the right. So, from the right to left, those values are 1, 2, 4, and 8. If you can remember that, just lay that down on a piece of paper (or after a while you can do this in your mind) and put the Binary bit numbers below that. Notice that we treat each nibble as an individual number, so the Binary bit values start from 1 for each nibble.

Then simply add up the bit values whenever there is a Binary bit with a 1 in it – like this:

Boolean bit values:	<u>8421</u>	<u>8421</u>
Boolean digits:	1010	1011
Totals (decimal):	10	11
Totals (hex):	A	B

And there you are! The only thing you have to memorize are the first four Binary bit values and the first 16 hexadecimal numbers, which are just 0-9 and then A-F with A being 10 and F being 15. That's it!

To convert backwards, from Hex to Binary, you can do the same thing. Take each digit of your hexadecimal number, convert each to its 4 bit Boolean value and stick them all in a row, done!

Are we done with the Math and Logic Yet?

Ok, enough of the Math lesson, let's get back to the coding. So far, we have covered the five basic math operators that C# knows about, specifically +, -, *, /, and %, otherwise known as addition, subtraction, multiplication, division and modulo. So far, all of our operators took two numbers and crunched them into a new number (for example 5 + 3 becomes 8). Sometimes you just want to crunch a single number, like the Las Vegas term "Double Down", which will double the value of the bet already placed. Here you take a single number, apply an operator to it and get a valid result out.

For our logic operators there are actually 6 more, collectively known as bitwise operators. Since these all work at the bit level of a number, you now understand why we had to have that whole discussion on Boolean/Binary. With that, here is the list:

~	complement
&	and
|	or
^	xor
<<	shift left
>>	shift right

That's it, my work here is done, time for the next subject. Oh, wait you want an explanation of all these? Yeah.....

All kidding aside, they aren't that difficult, but you do have to start thinking in Boolean to truly understand them. First the easiest of the lot, the complement function. This one really is quite simple – it simply flips all bits to their opposite state, or put another way all 1's become 0's and all 0's become 1's. For example:

```
byte myNum = 5;
Console.WriteLine("{0} -> {1}", myNum,
(byte)~myNum);
```

What do you suppose this will print out? The first part is easy, the {0} spot will print out a 5, since that is the value of the myNum variable. But what the heck will ~myNum be? (For now ignore the (byte) part in front of the ~myNum. That is called casting and we are going to cover that in detail later on.) Let's write our myNum value out in Boolean first:

00000101

Notice I padded it out to eight bits, since a byte (the type of our variable) is eight bits in length. Remember the ~ command complements all of the bits, or flips them to their opposite value, turning our 5 into this (in Boolean):

11111010

Hmmm, now what would that be in decimal? Use your Windows calculator or just lookup the bit value for each spot with a one and add them up. Both ways the answer becomes 250 and that is exactly what shows up.

Well that was easy – maybe not really practical in our day to day life, but trust me there are times when working at the bit level where this might be of use, but that's for another day. Let's move onto our next three operators, the &, | and ^, otherwise known as the AND, OR and XOR operators. I am going to cover these three together since they work the same way, the only difference is which logic table you apply to the bits. Let's start with a code fragment again:

```
byte myNum1 = 10, myNum2 = 9;
Console.WriteLine("AND: {0}, OR: {1}, XOR: {2}",
    myNum1 & myNum2, myNum1 | myNum2, myNum1 ^
myNum2);
```

As with all bitwise operators, we have to examine this problem at the Boolean level and to start with that we have to convert our two numbers first:

		AND	OR	XOR
10_{10}	=	00001010_2	00001010_2	00001010_2
9_{10}	=	00001001_2	00001001_2	00001001_2
Equals	=	00001000_2	00001011_2	00000011_2
Aka		8_{10}	11_{10}	3_{10}

What the AND, OR and XOR operators do is compare each bit in our variable to the corresponding bit in the other variable and apply the appropriate type of logic to it. (Figure 22) If you recall our logic tables from earlier on, the AND function only returns a 1 (or true) when both of its inputs are also a 1, the OR if either input is a 1 and the XOR as long as only one of the inputs is a 1. Depending on the operator, either a 0 or a 1 gets returned. When it is done with all 8 bits, the result is interpreted as a number. So, our sample code fragment from above should return 8, 11, and 3 as shown in our calculation. Easy, no?

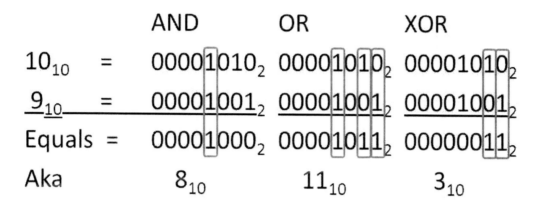

Figure 22: Highlighting the bits affected by the different operators

That leaves us with just two more bitwise operators; the shift left, and the shift right. If you liked the complement operator, then you are just going to love these two! Quite simply, each operator takes the set of bits that make up a number and moves each bit one position to either the left or to the right, depending on which operator you use. That's it!

If you were selling your house and someone came to you with a ridiculously low offer, you might say something like, "You need to put one more zero on that before I can consider it!" For example, if the offer was \$50,000 then by putting a zero onto it, the number would become \$500,000. This is the basic idea of the shift left operator. Of course, with Binary we only use 0 and 1's, so a number like 101 would become 1010 if shifted once to the left.

Now, this may seem quite silly but turns out that these two have a very unique property, due to the nature of Binary math. Remember how each bit value in Binary is double of the one to its right? Guess what, if you take a number, for each shift of its bits one to the left you effectively multiplied that number by 2 and correspondingly, if you shift all the bits to the right you just divided it by 2! Turns out that computers are so fast at dealing with bit manipulation that if you just want to multiply a number by 2 or divide by 2, using the shift method is faster than using the multiply or divide methods. Take a look at this code fragment:

```
byte myNum1 = 10;

Console.WriteLine("Left: {0}, Right: {1}",
    myNum1 << 1, myNum1 >> 1);
```

Notice the 1 after the << and >> operators. You can shift by more than 1 bit at a time, so the 1 here means to just shift by one bit. If we start with a base value of 10, what will be the result of a single bit shift to the left or the right? Again, convert your number to Binary first, then make the changes and convert back:

$$10_{10} = 00001010_2$$
$$<< \quad 00010100_2 = 20_{10}$$
$$>> \quad 00000101_2 = 5_{10}$$

That's it, we are done, no more operators of any kind!!!!!!

Points to Ponder

- You can use the shortcut ++ or -- when you need to add or subtract 1 from a value
- Putting the ++ or -- before or after the variable has different results. Placed before a variable, the value is incremented (or decremented) before returning its value, but when placed after a variable the value is returned and then modified
- All operators have a shortcut when modifying the same variable. For example num += 5 is the same thing as num = num + 5
- Use parentheses to control which parts of a math problem get executed first. Otherwise the Order of Precedence will determine in which order a problem is evaluated
- Binary math only uses two digits, 0 or 1
- Hexadecimal uses 16 digits, 0 to 9 and A-F
- Converting between Binary and Hex is quite easy, just break the Binary into chunks of four bits. Each chunk corresponds to a single Hex digit.
- Shifting one bit to the left doubles the value, while shifting by one bit to the right divides the value in half

Challenge

1) Write a program that takes a number from the user and outputs the number in hexadecimal. Try the numbers 4, 15, 20 and 100 as inputs.
2) Complete the following grid:

Decimal	Binary	Hexadecimal
25		
	1001 1111	
	1111 1001	
		25
		D5
1024		
		FACE
	0010 1000 0110	

Review Quiz

1.) Computer Memory is addressed in?
  O a. Bits
  O b. Bytes
  O c. Pages
  O d. Segments

2.) What are 3 ways you can increment the Amt variable by 1?
  ☐ a. Amt++;
  ☐ b. Amt$;
  ☐ c. Amt += 1;
  ☐ d. Amt + 1 = Amt;
  ☐ e. Amt = Amt +1;

3.) What are 3 ways you can triple a number?
  ☐ a. Amt***;
  ☐ b. Amt *= 3;
  ☐ c. Amt = Amt * 3;
  ☐ d. Amt * 3 = Amt;
  ☐ e. Amt = Amt + Amt + Amt;
  ☐ f. Amt = (3)Amt;

4.) What shorthand will let you know that 20 % 9 leaves a remainder of 2? *Assume that f = 20.*
  O a. f / 9;
  O b. f /= 9;
  O c. f %= 9;

5.) What is ttl equal to?
  O a. 1
  O b. 5
  O c. 10
  O d. 15
  O e. 60

```
ttl = 5 + 1 * 10;
```

Notes

Chapter 5 – Loops

It always surprises me how many things in life need to be done multiple times in order to actually get something useful out of them. In school various lessons were always repeated multiple times so the idea would get properly stuck in our heads, and at work most of us tend to do the same set of tasks over and over. Even in something common as brushing your teeth, you go up and down (or back and forth depending on your personal brushing style) more than once.

This is also true with computers and programming, where you will find some functions need some or all of their parts run a number of times before you get to the end. One really simple example, and probably one that most of us would never think about, is division. After all, a division problem is really nothing more than subtracting one value from another as many times as possible and along the way counting how many times the subtraction worked. Or, how about filling out an electronic form where you enter your name once but then it gets copied onto all of the subsequent pages? All of these are examples of a single task being repeated multiple times.

In programming there is actually more than one way to cause a set of lines of code to be repeated multiple times. While you could probably use one method for most circumstances, each different looping method has advantages for certain types of tasks.

Let's Make a Loop

Before we talk about the logic of a loop, think about how an athlete in the 100 meter dash thinks during a race. They know where the starting line is (0 meters), and they know that they have to step one foot in front of the other repeatedly until they get to 100 meters. So at all distances between 0 and 99, they take another step. But as soon as they get to 100 meters, they can stop. This applies quite well to the concept of a loop. Think of the starting line as the initialization, the goal of 100 meters is the condition, and each step is an iteration.

The most common way to loop a bit of code over and over again is using the keyword for, otherwise known as a for loop[10]. This kind of a loop is best when you know in advance how many iterations of the loop you want. The structure of a for loop looks like this:

```
for (<initialize>; <condition>; <iteration>)
{
    <code to repeat>
}
```

As you can see this structure has four parts that you need to fill out: (1) the initialization where you create or provide a counter, (2) the condition by which the loop ends, (3) an iteration which is how you increment or decrement the counter, and (4) one more lines of code that get executed with each iteration of the loop. By far the easiest way to explain this further is to actually put it to use, see what it does and then walk through the code. To do that we need to start a new project, calling it CH5a, and using the following code:

```
Console.WriteLine("Before the loop!");

for (int i = 1; i <= 10; i++)
{
    Console.WriteLine("Pass {0} through the loop",
i);
}

Console.WriteLine("After the loop!");

Console.ReadLine();
```

Normally we would try to read the code and figure out what it does before running it to confirm our understanding, but for this case we are going to do this backwards. Go ahead and run this program and observe the result. Once you have seen it, understanding why things worked the way they did will be easier. (Figure 23)

---

[10] Some old-time programmers might refer to these as a for/next loop, since in many early programming languages the for loop was terminated by a next command.

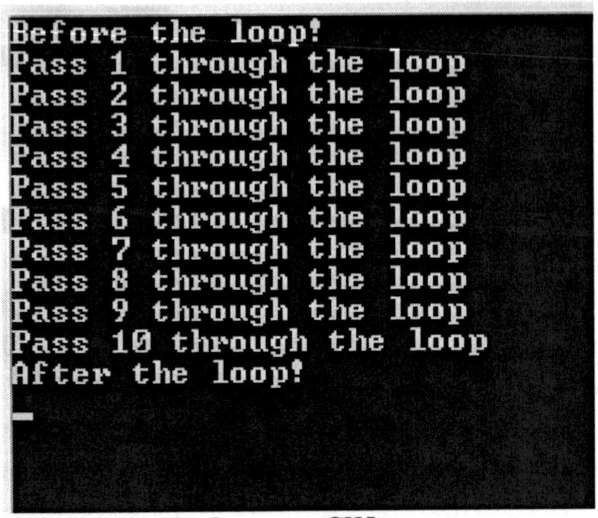

Figure 23: Result of program CH5a

The very first line of code is quite easy. We simply print out a starting message before the loop even runs.

Next is the loop, which does the majority of the work. To set the loop up we have to provide the keyword `for` and then the initialization, which in our code is "`int i = 1`". Take that little fragment out of the loop structure and just look at it on its own. You will find that there is nothing special about it. We simply declare a new variable[11], called `i` and set its initial value to 1.

The next part is the condition (looking very much like an `if` statement) which, in our case, is a simple comparison to see if `i` is less than or equal to 10. As long as this condition is true the loop will continue to run. The next bit of code to run is not the iteration but rather the body of the loop, namely all of the lines of code between the curly braces. In our loop this is just a single line of code that prints out a message, but notice, how in the message we can use the variable `i` and its value. This is perfectly valid and in fact is one of the major benefits of this kind of a loop.

After the code block is completed, the `for` loop finally jumps to the iteration part (`i++`), which simply increments the value of `i` by one. Again, if you pull this little bit of code out and examine it on its own, there is nothing special about it.

---

[11] Using `i` as a variable name in a for loop is rather ugly from the perspective of using proper variable names, but it is sort of traditional going back to some of the earliest days of programming. Many programmers will use this name in their loops.

The loop once again jumps into the code block to execute the prescribed action. Control then reverts to the condition and back to the iteration. This continues for as long as the condition remains true – in our case it will continue until i is incremented to 11, at which point the condition finally becomes false and the loop ends.

The code to execute after the completion of the loop is that last WriteLine, which just announces to us that we are out of the loop. As always, we end our program with a quick ReadLine so the output stays on the screen for us to examine.

Now an interesting tidbit here that most people do not realize – none of these three parts of a for loop is required, you can provide all of these elements yourself manually. In fact this loop is perfectly valid and will compile without any errors at all:

```
for ( ; ; )
{
    <do something>
}
```

Of course without anything in the for loop it just runs forever with nothing to stop it – by all accounts a "Very Bad Thing". While leaving a for loop totally blank like this is quite uncommon, setting up the initialization outside is done occasionally. This code below will generate the exact same output as before:

```
int i = 1;

Console.WriteLine("Before the loop!");

for (; i <= 10; )
{
    Console.WriteLine("Pass {0} through the loop",
i);
    i++;
}

Console.WriteLine("After the loop!");

Console.ReadLine();
```

One very important item to notice here, is that even though I left out both the initialization and the iteration parts of the `for` loop, I still had to put two semicolons in there. Normally, you are better off to let the `for` loop structure take care of all these functions, but there is one case where having the variable declared outside the loop is critical. That is, if you want to use the value of the loop variable ("i") after the loop ends. This involves something called the scope of a variable, which we have not talked about yet, but will.

One question that might have come to mind is this: Since I can use the value of the `for` loop's counter variable within the loop code block, what if I mess with its value? For example, what if I add or subtract something from it while inside the loop body? Yep, you can certainly do that, but be careful! If you end up changing the value in a way that the condition is never able to become false and thereby stop the loop, you will end up with an infinitely running loop, again a "Very Bad Thing".

As a safe experiment, instead of reducing the value of the counter, try to manually increment it. Add this line into the loop block, after the `WriteLine` statement.

```
i++;
```

Run it and notice what happens. The loop still starts at one, but gets incremented twice, once by the `for` loops' own iteration code and once by your code within the loop block itself. In other words, the loop now increments by 2 each time it runs, giving you only the odd numbers.

Now, having a loop increment in some fashion other than by one is perfectly legal and it is quite a common thing to do. You can actually put pretty much anything you want into that iteration section, such as i += 2, i *= 2, etc. You can even run this loop backwards, decrementing the value instead of incrementing it. Change your `for` loop to look like this (Figure 24):

```
for (int i = 10; i >= 0; i--)
```

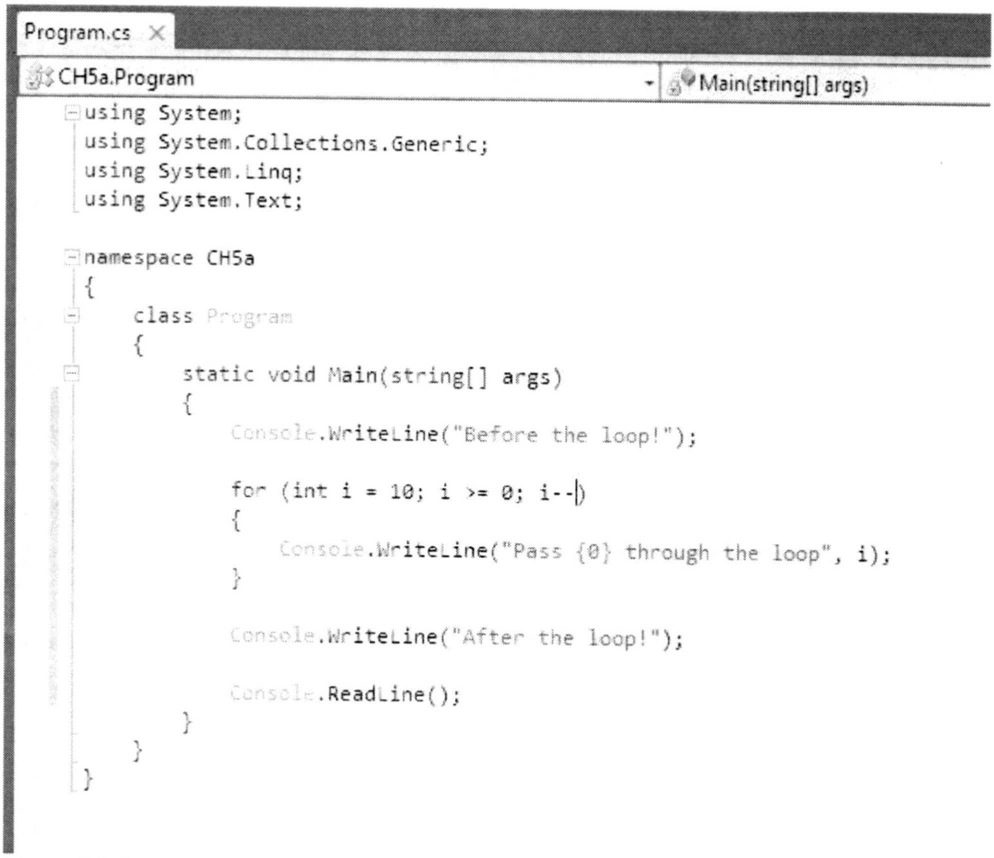

```
Program.cs  ×

CH5a.Program                                    ▾  Main(string[] args)

using System;
using System.Collections.Generic;
using System.Linq;
using System.Text;

namespace CH5a
{
    class Program
    {
        static void Main(string[] args)
        {
            Console.WriteLine("Before the loop!");

            for (int i = 10; i >= 0; i--)
            {
                Console.WriteLine("Pass {0} through the loop", i);
            }

            Console.WriteLine("After the loop!");

            Console.ReadLine();
        }
    }
}
```

Figure 24: Instead of just counting up, a `for` loop can also count down

Now when you run your program the loop starts at 10 and works down until it reaches -1. Of course you could also subtract by any other value than just 1, just as you could increment by any value.

Other Loops

As a child my mother once put a plate of lima beans in front of me, which I of course, refused to eat. In typical Mom fashion, she made the universal suggestion of "Try one, you'll like it!" As any kid can tell you, this is not really a suggestion but rather an order, in which you are stuck having to eat at least one spoonful. As an adult if I don't like the look of something, I can simply push the plate away, never having to take even a single bite! What does this have to do with loops? I'm so glad you asked...[12]

Besides the `for` loop, which is probably the most commonly seen, there are two other common looping mechanisms. They are the `while` and the `do while`[13] loops. Both are quite similar, with the only real differences as to when the decision is made to stop the loop. Basically, with the `while` loop you are not guaranteed even a single pass through your looping code, whereas with the `do while` loop you are definitely going to get at least one pass through your code. (In other words, the `do while` loop means you have to eat at least one spoonful of the lima beans, but with a `while` loop you are free to push that plate away immediately!)

This is because with the `while` loop the condition is at the top of the structure, meaning it gets evaluated before anything else, but the `do while` loop puts the condition at the bottom, so it does not get evaluated until at least one pass through the loop code. Let me show you the two side by side to demonstrate:

```
while (<condition>)              do
{                                {
    <do something>                   <do something>
}                                } while <condition>
```

See the similarity? Unlike the `for` loop, when using either the `while` or `do while` loops, you need to have a condition which can change over time in order for the condition to eventually evaluate to false and stop the loop. The most common way is to define a variable outside of the loops, initialize it and within the body of the loop increment (or decrement) as needed. We can test both of these looping methods by rewriting the same code we used with the `for` loop, but instead using these two new statements instead. First the `while` loop:

```
int i = 1;

Console.WriteLine("Before the loop!");

while (i <= 10)
{
```

_____

[12] My apologies for this analogy if you *actually* like lima beans!
[13] Some languages call the do while loop an "until" loop, since in those languages the until keyword is used at the end.

```
        Console.WriteLine("Pass {0} in the loop", i++);
    }

    Console.WriteLine("After the loop!");
```

Now the exact same thing, but using the do while loop instead.

```
    int i = 1;

    Console.WriteLine("Before the loop!");

    do
    {
        Console.WriteLine("Pass {0} in the loop", i++);
    } while (i <= 10);

    Console.WriteLine("After the loop!");
```

Very similar, the only difference being the location of the conditional statement (while). Before going any further, take a look at the WriteLine statement within the loop body, specifically at my use of the i++ incrementor. Think back to when we discussed the difference between having the ++ (or the -- for that matter) before or after the variable. By putting the unary operator after the variable, the compiler will first use, or return, the current value of the variable, and then increment it. I could have just as easily put i++; on a line of its own and achieved the same result.

So far, both of our examples accomplish the same goal. In fact, based on this example, you could very well ask why there is a need for these two different ways of making a loop. To answer that, let's take a look at this pair of code blocks, first using a while loop:

```
    int i = 10;

    Console.WriteLine("Start!");

    while (i > 10)
    {
        Console.WriteLine("Loop {0}", i--);
    }
```

```
Console.WriteLine("End!");
```

Now the same thing with the do while loop:

```
int i = 10;

Console.WriteLine("Start!");

do
{
    Console.WriteLine("Pass {0} in the loop", i--);
} while (i > 10);

Console.WriteLine("End!");
```

At first glance, both of these programs appear to be designed to do the same thing, namely count down from 10 printing a line as they go. But take a careful look at the condition lines for both. The loop can only run as long as i is greater than 10. However, when initializing the variable i, it got set to 10, meaning it could never be larger than that value. This means that, for both code fragments, the condition will be false the very first time it is evaluated. Because of that, each loop will behave a little bit differently.

In the case of the while loop, the first thing to be executed is the condition, which being false will immediately abort the loop, meaning the WriteLine inside the loop body will never get executed. This is different for the do while code, where the first thing to be executed is the loop body, so the WriteLine in the loop body gets to print immediately after which the condition is evaluated, found to be false and the loop never repeats.

If you try this same example but using the for loop method, you will find that the for loop behaves much like the while loop does. Just as with the while loop, the for loop evaluates the condition before running the loop body and with the values setup like this that condition will fail immediately.

Manually Controlling the Loop Flow

So far, it has been up to the various loop methods to control when we run through the loop body and when we do not. However, you can take more control and manually force the loop to either terminate early or to skip a complete iteration. To demonstrate this concept, we are going to start up a new project in Visual C#, calling it "CH5b". Once you are ready, please type in the following code:

```
Console.WriteLine("Start!");

for (int i = 1; i <= 10; i++)
{
    if (i == 5)
        break;

    Console.WriteLine("Pass {0} in the loop", i);
}

Console.WriteLine("End!");

Console.ReadLine();
```

This should seem quite familiar by now since it is a variation of the same counting example we have been using with all of our previous loops. However, there is a chunk of extra code in here, namely that `if` statement, and it is an important bit of code.

As our loop happily runs along, within the code block, there is an additional check on the value of the loop's counter. When that counter hits 5, the `if` statement becomes true and the keyword `break` gets executed. So what does `break` do? Run the program and take a careful look at the output – notice something missing? Actually quite a lot is missing! (Figure 25)

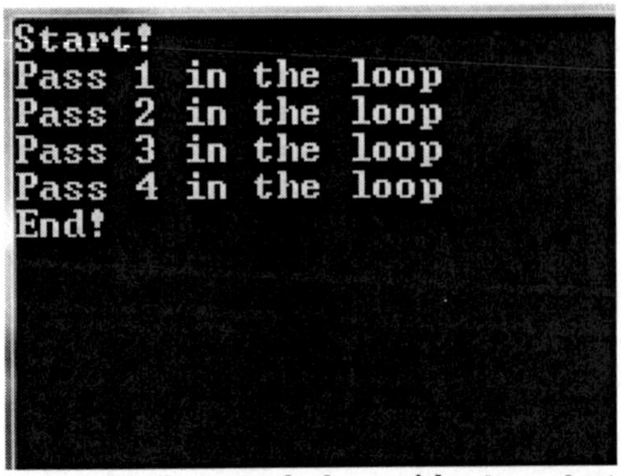

Figure 25: Output of a loop with a break statement

Even though the loop is supposed to run for 10 iterations it gets stopped when it hits 5. The `break` command has a very simple but powerful action, namely it causes the loop to stop immediately and the program to jump outside of the loop. Since in our example the `if` statement is before the `WriteLine` command, the fifth line never gets printed.

Remember the `switch` statement from Chapter 3? At the end of each `case` block we used the same `break` keyword to stop execution of the block. The `break` command works the same way here that it did in the `switch` block.

There is one other way to cause the flow of a loop to change and that is the keyword `continue`. In your code change the word `break` to `continue` and then run your program. (Figure 26) Take a careful look at the output – notice something missing? Even though the loop goes through its full 10 iterations there is no output for line 5! That is due to the `continue` statement taking effect.

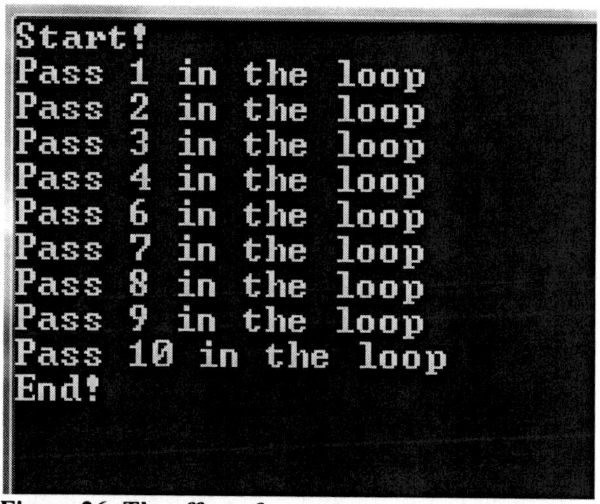

```
Start!
Pass 1 in the loop
Pass 2 in the loop
Pass 3 in the loop
Pass 4 in the loop
Pass 6 in the loop
Pass 7 in the loop
Pass 8 in the loop
Pass 9 in the loop
Pass 10 in the loop
End!
```

Figure 26: The effect of `continue` on a `for` loop

Unlike the `break` command, which causes execution of the loop to immediately stop, the `continue` command does something a little less drastic. Just like the `break` command, it gets the current loop to stop, but instead of dropping completely out of the loop it simply tells the loop to jump to the next iteration.

While in our example I used a `for` loop to demonstrate what the `break` and `continue` commands do, these two commands also work with the `while` and `do while` loops as well.

Loops within Loops

Surprisingly, one of the most common questions I have received regarding loops relate to what kind of code can be entered into the loop body. While, so far, in all of our loop examples we have had relatively simple code inside the loop body, there are no limits or restrictions on what you add into the body of a loop. Complex `if/else` or `switch` statements, other loops, etc. are all perfectly normal and quite common inside a loop.

Probably the other most common question with regard to loops have to do with how much code can be inserted into the loop body. Again, there are no real restrictions, you can use as much or as little as you need or want. However, as the amount of code within the code body becomes very large it also becomes much more difficult to read. In that case you are encouraged, but not required, to find other ways to organize your code for the sake of readability. Most of these solutions involve moving some of your code into methods – something we are going to cover shortly.

Points to Ponder

- Loops allow the same statement or set of statements to be executed multiple times
- Loops can be made to run a fixed number of times (`for`) or until some condition becomes true (`while` or `do while`)
- All loops need some mechanism which stops the loop, otherwise it will run forever, locking up your system
- Loops can count either up or down
- `For` loops are by far the most commonly used loop mechanisms
- A `while` loop checks the condition before executing the loop body, meaning if the condition is false the body may never be executed
- A `do while` loop checks the condition after the body has been executed at least once
- The keyword `break` will cause execution of the loop to stop
- The keyword `continue` will abort the rest of the loop body from completing and jumps control to the next iteration of the loop

Challenge

1) Create a loop that prints out the first 10 positive numbers. Make three different versions of this using the `for`, `while` and `do while` looping methods. Do not use the `break` or `continue` keywords in the loop.
2) Do the same thing as challenge 1, but this time count down from 20 to 0, displaying only the odd numbers. Again try to accomplish this with each of the three looping methods. Do not use the `break` or `continue` keywords in the loop.
3) Using any of the looping methods you prefer, count from 0 to 20 displaying a short message for each line. If the counter is evenly divisible by 5, display a special message.

4) Using the continue keyword, modify the loop from challenge 3 to only display the lines that are divisible by 5
5) Create a program that asks the user for a number and checks to see if the number is a prime. Print an appropriate message whether the number is a prime or not. (A prime number is a positive integer that is divisible only by 1 and itself. For example, 1, 2, 3, 5 and 7 are all prime numbers.)
6) Write a program that accepts a number from the user and prints the following output (assume the user has entered 5):
```
*****
****
***
**
*
```

Review Quiz

1.) You have the following code below.

```
for (int i = 1; i <= 10; i++)
{
    Console.WriteLine("Pass {0} in the loop", i);
}
```

Which code segment is the initialization?
  O a. `int i = 1`
  O b. `i <= 10`
  O c. `i++`
  O d. `Console.WriteLine();`

2.) How many times will the loop in the follow code iterate?

```
for (int i = 1; i <= 10; i++)
{
    Console.WriteLine("Pass {0} in the loop", i);
}
```

  O a. 0
  O b. 1
  O c. 9
  O d. 10
  O e. 11
  O f. Infinite

3.) What does the break statement do?
  O a. If causes the loop to start over at the beginning of the loop block.
  O b. Ends the loop and execution continues after the loop block.

4.) What type of loop runs at least once even if the condition is initially false?
  O a. `for` loop
  O b. `do` loop
  O c. `while` loop

Notes

Chapter 6 – Intermission

Yep, it is now time for a break… as when you go and see any kind of a live performance, there is always time set aside for at least one intermission, perhaps even two if it is long enough. Not only does this give a chance for everyone to visit the bathroom, but also provides a chance to pick up refreshments, stretch the legs and so on. But to me, the most interesting part of the intermission has always been the chance to talk to others who have seen the exact same thing you just have but have a different take on it. There will always be some small nugget that you might have missed that somebody else did not, or the way you interpreted a scene could be different from that of another. No matter, at the end of the intermission you are refreshed and have new insight into what you have been experiencing.

So, I thought I would try to do the same, or at least as close to it as you can get with a book. For our intermission the purpose is not to run to the restroom (though by all means if you have to go then go!) but rather, to take a break from the coding and cover a few areas that did not quite fit into the chapters so far.

By the way, here is an interesting tidbit you might enjoy. Even though this book is about C# in particular, I did mention earlier that all of the C-based languages have a lot in common. While there have been a few C# specific items already mentioned, nearly everything we have learned so far would be the same regardless of which flavor of C you might be using! So, the next time somebody hands you a bit of C or C++ code, don't worry! Using the skills learned here, you will be able to make sense of a vast majority of what you will find in that code and the rest you will be able to make logical guesses about.

Care to Comment?

One of the things we have not talked at all about, so far, is comments within our code. While you should always write your code in a way to easily allow another developer to be able to read it and make sense of it, there will be times when additional information could be critical. Before you think to yourself that you will never share any of the code you are planning to write and think "so who cares about another developer", you could be that other developer! No matter how intimately you know the code you are working on today, in six months or a year when you need to revisit it, you are going to be scratching your head trying to remember why you did what you did! So, be generous in your comments, and use them whenever you think additional help would be of benefit[14].

There are two primary ways of putting comments into C# code, each of which uses a different notation. The first is the double forward slash (//) which is used to mark that anything else following this symbol to the end of the line is a comment. If you have a longer comment, one that will span multiple lines, you could either put // before each line, or use the /* and */ multi line comment symbols. For this style of commenting, anything between the start comment symbol (/*) and the end comment symbol (*/) is ignored by the compiler. Let me give you some examples of each:

```
// This is a single line of comment.
// It can be on a line of its own,
int myNum;        // or follow a line of code

/*
 * However you can also put in much longer
 * multi-line comments without having to
 * put a symbol on each line
 */
```

Notice how there is a star at the beginning of each line within the multi-line comment block. I actually did not put those there, but rather the Visual Studio editor did. Technically, they are not required, but it does make the comment stand out a lot better and are frankly best left there. Also, I put the start and end comment symbols on lines of their own, which is optional but is considered a more elegant way to do it.

There are a few common mistakes that people make with comments. First, with the single line comment method, once you start a comment using the // notation, that's it! In other words you cannot have some code, put in a comment and then have more code after it. By definition the // comment symbol means that from that point to the end of the line is all considered a comment.

---

[14] Of course you can go overboard with comments as well. I once had a computer teacher in high school who wanted one line of comments for every line of code. Needless to say that gets quite old real fast, but there are times when you are working on something so complex that having an abundance of comments is warranted. Just use your best judgment!

Now if you really must have some code, a comment, and then more code – generally an ugly idea, – you can do that with the /* */ style of comment markers, but really consider if you must:

```
int /* integer */ ct /* stands for counter */ = 25;

// My counter (ct) variable, defined as an integer
int ct = 25;
```

The first line has embedded comments, which makes reading the code quite difficult to do. The second example has the comment and the code line separate, but the same information is conveyed and the entire thing is easier to read.

The second common comment related error has to do with comments within comments. What I mean by that is, if you have a block of code with comments within it, and you want to comment the entire block out using the /* and */ tags. You can do this, but only if there aren't any other /* */ marked comments within the block.

The reason for this is quite simple. The compiler will assume that anything between the first start comment symbol (/*) it sees and the first end comment symbol (*/) is the range of the comment. If after the first start comment symbol there is another one, it will not notice it since all of that is already commented and is therefore ignored. However as soon as it sees the first end comment symbol the comment block will end, leaving anything else exposed. If you must block out a section which already has comments in it, make sure that those embedded comments are only marked using the single line comment symbol.

This is hard to explain, so let me demonstrate with a bit of pseudo code, with line numbers:

```
1. /*
2. <real code>
3. <real code>
4.      /*
5.      * comment within existing code
6.      */
7. <real code>
8. <real code>
9. */
```

Imagine if the original code are the lines 2 through 8. Within this block of code you already have a multi-line comment (lines 4-6). For some reason, you wish to comment out this entire block, so you simply put a begin comment (line 1) and an end comment (line 9) around the entire block. So how do you think the compiler is going to interpret this?

As the compiler starts to read the lines of code, it sees the first begin comment symbol on the first line. It then reads each line one by one, ignoring everything except for the end of comment marker, which it will find on the line 6. We know that the end of comment mark on line 6 is supposed to end the comment that started on line 4, but remember the compiler has been ignoring everything since it saw the begin comment marker on line 1, so it never saw the second comment start on the fourth line. This means that lines 7 to 9 are now "exposed" and the compiler will attempt to execute them.

The Debugger

Ah, the debugger – without doubt your best friend when you click that run button, your program starts and all of a sudden something bad happens and everything falls apart. Obviously you did not make any syntax coding errors, since those would have been caught by the compiler, so where did you go wrong? Most likely you have a logic error – something that made perfect sense when you wrote it, but when executed just doesn't add up. Debugger to the rescue!

Without question the most useful benefit of an IDE programming environment is having an embedded debugger. While its purpose is simple, in practice what it does is almost magic. Think of a debugger like the ability to run a movie one frame at a time. If you have ever seen how a cartoon is made, you know that each frame is just a little bit different than the one before it, but when put together those little changes become motion – the same concept is true in programming.

As the processor executes each line of code, values in variables are changed and based on those values various paths through your code are followed. But what combination of values caused your error? Using a debugger you can step line by line through your code and see the value of any given variable, equation, function, etc. at that particular frozen frame. Trust me; it is worth its weight in gold!

While I could explain the process of using the debugger for pages and pages, this is something best learned through example. For that we need some code to step through, so let's start up a new project and get working! Launch your Visual C# program, start a new project and call it "CH6a". Once ready please paste this code in. You are welcome to run it when you are done, to see what it does, but if you spot the logic error in the loop (as based on my comment), please do not fix it – yet!

```
int firstNum, secondNum, answer;

Console.WriteLine("Starting program.");

firstNum = 5;
secondNum = 11;

answer = firstNum + secondNum;

Console.WriteLine("{0} plus {1} equals {2}",
    firstNum, secondNum, answer);

for (firstNum = 1; firstNum < 5; firstNum++)
{   // I want five iterations of this loop
    Console.WriteLine("Loop {0}", firstNum);
}

Console.WriteLine("Ending program.");

Console.ReadLine();
```

We have our code and we can verify that it runs. However, even though the green button on the toolbar that we use to run our programs is labeled as "Start debugging", just by clicking on it there is no debugging – it just runs our program like always (Figure 27). That's true, but only because to get the debugger to kick in we have to tell it when we want it to do so. We do that but selecting a line and setting a breakpoint. What is a breakpoint? It does pretty much what it sounds like, which is to cause the computer to break, or in our case, pause when it gets to that spot and allow us to examine the state of our program. But how do we do that?

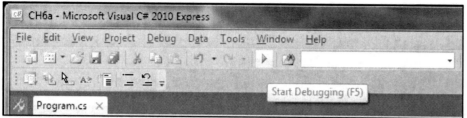

Figure 27: The green arrow (or the F5 key) will run your program in debugging mode

As with many things in modern software, there are actually multiple ways to accomplish our goal, specifically three. First highlight the second line of code (`Console`.`WriteLine`(`"Starting program."`)`;`) and from the Debug menu choose "Toggle Breakpoint". Notice the large red dot that showed up to the left of our line of code (Figure 28).

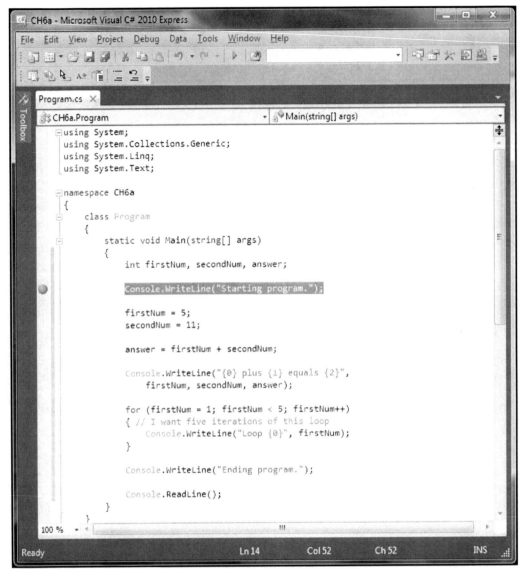

Figure 28: The red dot represents a breakpoint at that line of code

That big red dot signifies the location of our breakpoint. Besides choosing this option from the debug menu, we can also press the F9 key to accomplish the same thing. If your cursor is still on that first line of code and you press F9, the breakpoint will get removed. To put it back, just press F9 again. There is one more way of toggling a breakpoint, and that is by clicking on the breakpoint's red dot icon if it is already there, or in the blank spot where it would be if not already there. Personally I like using the F9 button, but it is up to you.

Ok, so now we have some code and we have placed a breakpoint right at the very beginning. Now what? Just as you normally would, press F5 or click the green arrow on the toolbar (Figure 27), to launch your program.

Right away you will notice a pretty major difference. Instead of the console window coming up, we are right back in the Visual C# environment – but there are some very important changes to notice. Refer to Figure 29 as we cover these differences.

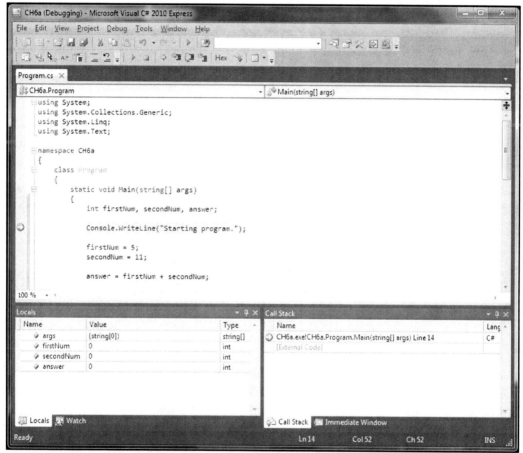

Figure 29: The breakpoint halts your program execution on the highlighted statement

The first thing to notice are two half-screen width sections sitting next to each other at the bottom of the screen. The one on the left is labeled as "Locals" while its neighbor is called "Call Stack". For now we are not going to deal with the Call Stack information, since that is for dealing with how we move among different methods, something we have not covered yet. However, the "Locals" box is quite interesting and is at the heart of what the debugger is all about. Before we get into that, let's see what other differences we can spot.

Up in the main area of the screen you can see your code but the first line is highlighted by a yellow box and there is also a yellow arrow at the left edge of the screen. Remember I mentioned how the debugger lets us step through our code? Think of it like stepping through a movie frame by frame. The yellow highlight and yellow arrow indicate the frame of the movie (or in our case the line of code) we are about to experience.

Now, let's see just how sharp your eyes are. There is one more difference, but it is quite subtle – a new toolbar has showed up. If you carefully examine Figure 29, on my screen this toolbar showed up on the second toolbar row, right at the very left edge of the screen. It has ten buttons on it by default, starting with Continue, Break All, Stop Debugging and Restart. The next button is Show Next Statement and just past it are two buttons you will become very familiar with, Step Into and Step Over. Remember where these are since we are going to need them very soon. I've highlighted the new toolbar in Figure 30.

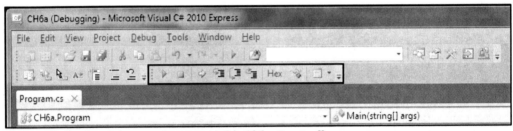

Figure 30: During debug mode, you get this 10 button toolbar

There is one final difference but it is not on the Visual C# screen that you are looking at. Rather this difference is to be found on the taskbar of your Windows OS. Look at the taskbar (Figure 31) and notice there is a button there for our console application (it will have a title that will start with "file:///" and contain the path to where your program is being executed from). This is the window that if the debugger had not stopped our program, all of our output should have shown up in. In fact that is exactly what will happen, as soon as we let our debugger get to a line where something is supposed to show up.

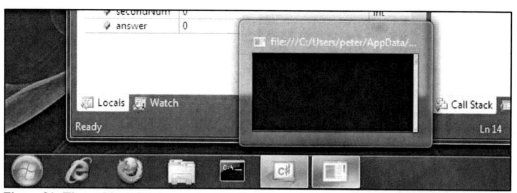

Figure 31: The taskbar shows your program running as File:// and the path of the assembly

If you are lucky enough to have a second monitor attached to your computer, you can drag this console window to your other monitor and as we step through the code you will see our various lines of output show up. However if you do not have a second monitor, don't worry it will still work normally. We just are going to have to click on it to bring it to the front before we can see the output.

All right, let's get back to the Visual C# window and the debugger. Once again, go ahead and examine the Locals window at the bottom left of your screen (Figure 32).

Name	Value	Type
args	{string[0]}	string[]
firstNum	0	int
secondNum	0	int
answer	0	int

Figure 32: The locals window shows you the current values that is variable is set to

Take a look at the entries in this box – look familiar? In our code we have defined three variables, firstNum, secondNum and answer, each as type int. Each variable is listed in this window, along with its value and type. Currently they all have a value of 0, since the line of code that sets them has not been run yet. There is one other variable listed, args, which we did not define.

This variable has a very special purpose and is defined within the Main method's parameter list. We will cover the purpose of this variable, what it contains and how to use it in a later chapter. So for now please ignore it.

Ok, enough talk, let's start running our code and see what happens. When in the debugger you use the Step Into (Figure 33) and Step Over (Figure 34) buttons from the Debug toolbar to control execution of your code. The difference in what they do is only visible if you have methods that you wrote and which need to be executed. Since we have not reviewed methods yet, we cannot demonstrate that difference, but we will as we proceed further. For now, you can treat both buttons as completing the same task; however, get into the habit of using the Step Into one primarily. With that said, go ahead and click on the Step Into button once or press F11.

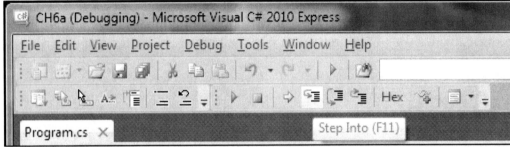

Figure 33: This button, or F11, will step into one statement

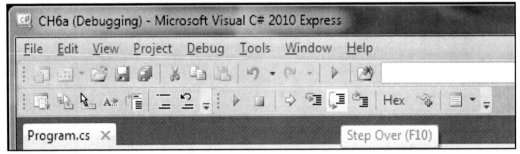

Figure 34: This button, of F10, will step over one statement

Notice how both the yellow highlight that was on the first line of code, as well as the yellow arrow on the left edge, has moved to the next line (Figure 35).

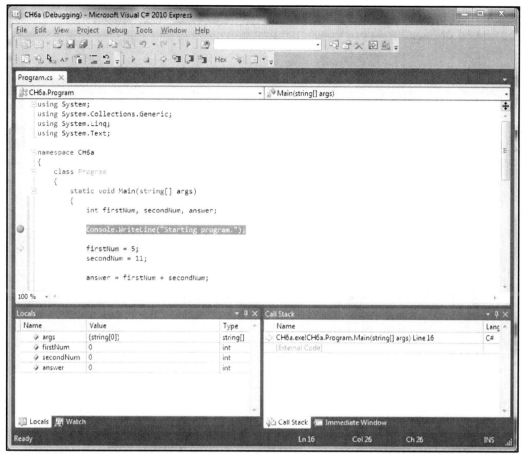

Figure 35: Hitting F11 moves your execution by one line, so the yellow highlight is now past the breakpoint

Even though the debugger has now processed the first line, the breakpoint highlight remains on that row. This is a marker that we placed and only we can remove, so the debugger leaves it alone. In fact, when we finish this debugger session, the breakpoint we placed will still be there.

This brings up an interesting question; can we add or remove breakpoints while in the debugger? Absolutely! This program is quite small so we only set a single breakpoint, but you can actually set as many as you need. While the primary way of using the debugger is to step through the code line by line, you might get to an area which you know is good, so instead of having to step through that as well, you can just set another breakpoint past that point, click the Continue button (or press F5) and have the code execute normally. As soon as the new breakpoint is reached, the debugger will once again kick in. This sample is quite small so we are not going to do that, but as our programs get larger we will be doing more advanced debugging where that will come in handy.

So the first line has executed, but what has happened so far? If you examine the Locals area nothing appears to have changed, the three variables are still showing a value of 0, so what did happen? Well, what was that first line that we have so far executed supposed to have done? Ah, it is a WriteLine, which means that it should have printed a line of text to our console. To check it, click on the console icon on your task bar (or if you have a second monitor and moved it over you can just glace at it). Yep, our line got printed but that is all that has shown up since we have not allowed the rest of the lines to execute – yet. Let's move on!

The highlight should be on the line "firstNum = 5;", but it has not been executed yet so the value of firstNum is still 0. By the way, besides looking at the different variables in the Locals window, there is one other way to check the value of a variable. Move your mouse so the pointer is hovering over the word "firstNum" in the highlighted line of code. Notice the little dropdown that comes up and displays the current value of this one variable (Figure 36).

```
class Program
{
    static void Main(string[] args)
    {
        int firstNum, secondNum, answer;

        Console.WriteLine("Starting program.");

        firstNum = 5;
        sec   ● firstNum  0  ▱

        answer = firstNum + secondNum;
```

Figure 36: When you hover over a variable in debug mode, you can see its present value

Now it's time to execute this next line. However, as you press F11 (or click Step Into), I want you to keep your eye on the Locals window, specifically the Value column for the firstNum variable. Ready? Go for it! Did you notice the change? As soon as the line executed, the variable was set to 5 and immediately the Locals window updated. But it also shows the new value of the `firstNum` variable in red (Figure 37).

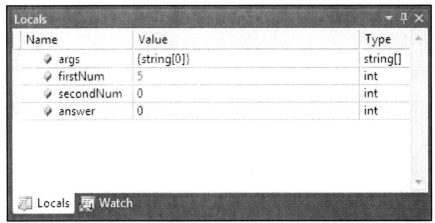

Figure 37: The number shaded in red represents a value that was changed by the last statement

Whenever a variable changes its value, the Locals window displays the newly changed value in red. This is an indication that due to the line just executed this (or these) variable(s) just had their value(s) changed. Again our code sample is quite small, but the line we just executed could be quite complex and as a result multiple variables could have had their values changed. So this highlight helps you pinpoint which variables were affected. As before, you can also see the new value for `firstNum` by hovering over it with your mouse within the code.

The next line to be executed is again highlighted (`secondNum = 11;`) and the debugger is waiting for us to tell it what to do. We know that this line is also going to change the value of a variable, this time the `secondNum` variable. Just as we did with the previous line, keep your eyes on the Locals window as you press F11 to execute this next line. (Figure 38) Compare the two local windows and notice the difference.

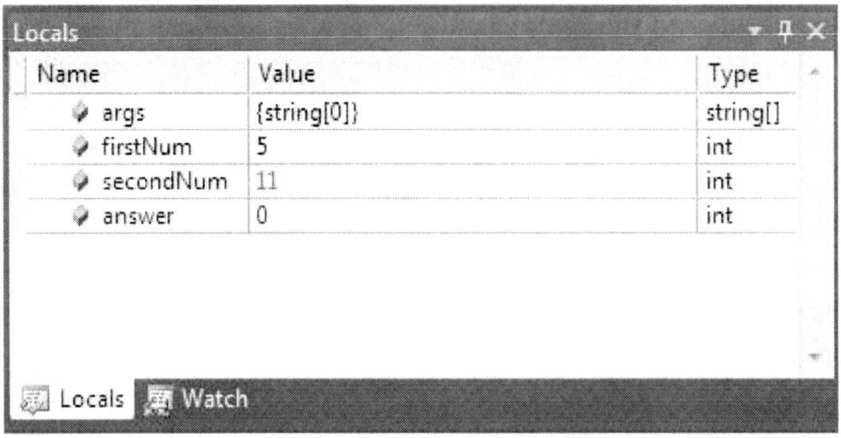

Figure 38: Change to Locals window after executing the second line of code

This time the value for secondNum was updated in the Locals window and its Value column entry set to red, since this is the variable changed due to the execution of the last line. Did you notice the Value column entry for the firstNum variable? It is now displayed in black, which indicates that its value has not been changed due to the execution of the most recent line.

As before, the next line is highlighted and the debugger is waiting. I think you are starting to understand how this works, so execute the next two lines of this program using the Step Into button (or by pressing F11). After the next WriteLine statement has been executed, verify that its output has shown up in the console window by clicking on it in your Task Bar.

The next line of code to be executed is the for loop, so the debugger has it highlighted. But notice how only a part of this statement is actually highlighted (Figure 39).

```
Console.WriteLine("{0} plus {1} equals {2}",
    firstNum, secondNum, answer);

for (firstNum = 1; firstNum < 5; firstNum++)
{ // I want five iterations of this loop
    Console.WriteLine("Loop {0}", firstNum);
}


Console.WriteLine("Ending program.");
```

Figure 39: The `for` loop is made up of three statements. The debugger will highlight only the piece to be executed next

The debugger is smart enough to understand that a `for` loop is made up of three different part. In effect, the debugger treats this as if it was on three different lines and highlights only the part that is going to be executed next. We know that the execution order of a `for` loop starts with the initialize section, which is highlighted, followed by the condition, the loop body, then the incrementor and then back to the condition. As we step through the different parts of this loop, keep an eye on which parts of code are highlighted by the debugger.

Now we are reusing the `firstNum` variable here, mostly so I can show how the value of this variable is going to get changed in the Locals window. This kind of variable reuse is fairly common, but potentially it can also be the source of some problems later on. Especially if you expect this variable's value to not have gotten changed by the process in which you reused it – just a warning to be careful. For now we are aware of the issue and this code is small enough that we do not need to worry. Go ahead and press F11 to run this small chunk of code.

Verify that the Locals window has updated the value of `firstNum`, and colored it red to indicate that it just got changed. As expected the debugger has highlighted the next part of the `for` loop to be executed, which is the condition statement (Figure 40).

```
Console.WriteLine("{0} plus {1} equals {2}",
    firstNum, secondNum, answer);

for (firstNum = 1; firstNum < 5; firstNum++)
{ // I want five iterations of this loop
    Console.WriteLine("Loop {0}", firstNum);
}


Console.WriteLine("Ending program.");
```

Figure 40: The condition of the `for` loop is the next to be executed and is highlighted here

Gotta love it when things work as you expect them to! If you hover over the `firstNum` variable in the code window, or take a look at its value in the Local window, it will currently be set to 1. Since 1 is less than 5, we know this condition is true and therefore the loop can being the first pass through its body. Press F11 to execute the condition and to have the highlight move to the only line of code in the loop body. Ah, but wait that's not quite what happened, is it? The debugger actually highlighted the curly brace pair that encompasses the loop body (Figure 41).

```
Console.WriteLine("{0} plus {1} equals {2}",
    firstNum, secondNum, answer);

for (firstNum = 1; firstNum < 5; firstNum++)
{ // I want five iterations of this loop
    Console.WriteLine("Loop {0}", firstNum);
}


Console.WriteLine("Ending program.");
```

Figure 41: The opening curly brace is highlighted next, to indicate the loop body is next to be executed

This is a strange bit of behavior that is caused by the unique way that the C# compiler treats a block of code surrounded by curly braces. Just as the `if` statement executes only the next line of code when its condition is true, the `for` loop also only executes the next single line while its condition is true. Since we could, and more often than not do, have more than a single line we want looped, the solution is to enclose it in a pair of curly braces. This causes the compiler to see and treat this block of code as if it was just a single line, and the debugger knows that. So it actually highlights what it thinks is the next line of code. Yeah, it is weird but hey, aren't we all?

We just need to live with it and get in the habit of pressing F11 one more time to actually jump to the first line of code within this block and get it to execute. Go ahead and step through the rest of the loop by pressing F11 whenever ready until the firstNum variable reaches the value of 5 (Figure 42). When it gets to that value and the debugger highlights the condition statement, let's stop and discuss what has happened and what is about to happen.

Before we go any further, click over to the console window and verify that the for loop has worked and four lines of text have been displayed (it had better!). Once you have seen the four lines of output, click back to the debugger window. Notice my comment in the for loop, the one that says that I want 5 iterations of this to run? So far we have had four iterations, hence the four lines of output.

The for loop has incremented the firstNum variable to 5, as expected, but the condition is now being evaluated as "5 is less than 5". Hmmm, that does not sound like it is true and I'm pretty sure the compiler will agree with us. In fact let's check to see what the compiler thinks of this condition. If you hover your mouse over the condition, but be careful not over the firstNum variable's name, the debugger will display the expression being evaluated as well as its result – see Figure 42.

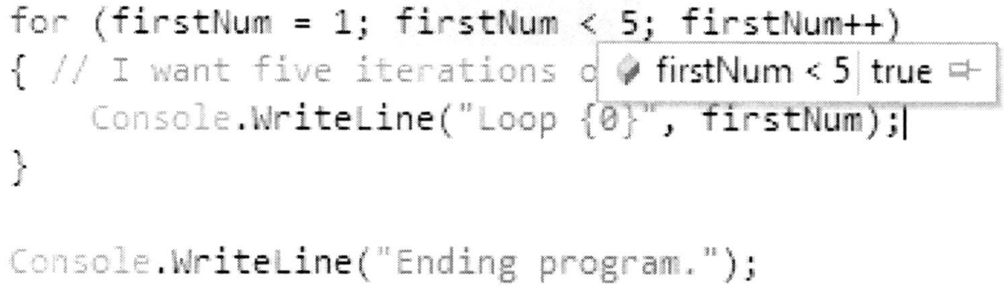

```
for (firstNum = 1; firstNum < 5; firstNum++)
{ // I want five iterations o ⬤ firstNum < 5  true ⇦
    Console.WriteLine("Loop {0}", firstNum);|
}

Console.WriteLine("Ending program.");
```

Figure 42: If you hover over an expression, you can see if it is true or false

Yep, the compiler shows that this is false, in other words I am not going to get my fifth iteration, am I? This is a classic logic error, where what I told the computer to do is quite correctly expressed as far as the C# syntax goes, but is not correct with what I wanted to happen. What I should have said was "firstNum <= 5". For this kind of problem, and many, many more, the debugger is a great tool.

So if we press F11 to execute the condition what will happen? Of course we know it is false, so the loop body does not get executed again therefore the next line to be processed is our final WriteLine and that is what gets highlighted. Go ahead and press F11 to execute it, and if you wish, check the console window to verify that it actually got printed out. Our last line to be executed is the ReadLine command which is going to sit there waiting for an input before it can continue.

For this line to be fully executed some user intervention is required, so the focus will jump to the console window and it should pop to the front and be waiting for you to press enter. (If you do have two monitors and the console window has been on the second one, the focus will change to it but that change may be too subtle to notice. Just be aware that you need to be on the console widow, and to press enter before this line is successfully executed so that the debugger can move on.)

After you press Enter in the console window, the debugger moves to the last line but the focus does not change to the Visual C# program – instead the icon for it in the task bar will flash to indicate that it is ready for you to continue on with it. Click on the Visual C# icon to bring it up to the front, and notice how the debugger has the final curly brace of the Main method highlighted as the next line to be executed. (Figure 43) Press F11 on it for it execute and for your program to finish. With that the debugger windows (Locals and Stack Trace) go away and you are back in the Visual C# environment ready to continue working on your program.

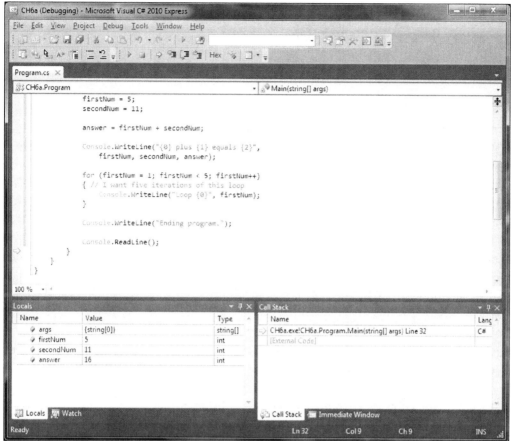

Figure 43: The last curly brace of the program is highlighted to indicate the end of the program. Pressing F11 will end the program execution and quit the debugger.

As I mentioned before, even though we have finished with the debugger, the breakpoint is still set on the first line. The next time you press F5 to execute your program, the debugger will once again launch and halt your program at the breakpoint. If you do not want that to happen, just put your cursor anywhere on that line and press F9 to toggle the breakpoint off. What if you did forget but did not want to go through the whole debug process? One of the commands you can give the debugger when it is waiting is the F5 button, which just tells it to resume running the program normally. Go ahead and try it!

That's it for the debugger for now. As we get into more advanced parts of C#, we are definitely going to be using it again. I will also introduce more advanced functions of it, but for now, this will let you step through your programs as needed. Feel free to use the debugger anytime. In fact, I strongly recommend that as we introduce new functions and methods of C#, you use the debugger to see how and in what order various parts of things get executed. The `for` loop is one of the best examples of this, as you saw how the debugger highlighted only the parts of it that were about to run.

Do you Have to be so Contrary?

Have you ever found yourself in an awkward situation where you and your significant other just could not get away? Last time this happened to me, my wife said "Well, that was fun" in a sarcastic tone as we were driving away. Obviously she did not mean that sentence literally, but in fact meant exactly the opposite. Sometimes it is easier to say the opposite of what you mean, but in a way that indicates to everyone around you that you really mean the opposite of what you are actually saying. This can also be true for programming languages, but since we cannot program in a sarcastic way, we have to find another way to indicate that we mean the opposite.

So far with all of the conditions of our various loops, if and for statements, we have said that things will continue for as long as the expression remains true. There is a way to make things flip around, and to actually run while the condition is false. Anytime you put an exclamation mark in front of a condition it turns its state from true to false or from false to true. For example:

```
if (!(myNum > 5))
```

This would be read as while "not myNum is greater than 5", or logically as "while myNum is less than 5". So if the value of myNum is 1, then the condition would be false since 1 is not greater than 5, but the ! [15] mark negates that and turns this currently false condition into a true one, so the if statement is happy and runs its code block.

Compile but not Run

While the compiler cannot help you with logic errors, it will most certainly spot any syntax errors, missing parentheses, curly braces, etc. Of course, each time you press F5 to run your code the compiler goes through it. However what if you

---

[15] Weird computer tidbit. In the Unix word the exclamation mark is commonly referred to as "bang".

do not want to run your code, but still have the compiler check it out? Easy! Instead of using F5, press F6 to have your code compiled but not executed. The F6 key is the shortcut for the command "Build Solution" under the Build menu. Should there be any syntax errors in your code, the compiler will spot them and give you a list of all the errors it finds in the "Error List" window.

Personally, I like to sometimes get a compile of what I have written to verify everything is where it is supposed to be, but am not ready for it to be run yet.

Points to Ponder

- There are two kinds of comments:
  1. Single line comment, which are started by two forward slashes (//) and go to the end of the current line
  2. Multi line comments, which start with a /* and end with */
- Be careful of nesting comments within comments!
- The debugger allows you to run through your code one line at a time, examining the value of your variables as the program runs
- You use the F10 (Step Over) and F11 (Step Into) keys to step through your code one statement at a time
- You can see the value of the variables by looking at the list in the Locals window, or by hovering the mouse over the name of the variable in the code window
- Putting an exclamation mark in front of a statement negates that statement. In other words !True == False and !False == True
- The F6 key will compile your program, and save any modified files in the process, but will not execute it

Review Quiz

1.) How do you comment out a single line in C#?
- O a. /
- O b. //
- O c. --
- O d. /* ... */

2.) How can you get your program to stop at a given point in order to aid in debugging?
- O a. Insert a Watch Window
- O b. Insert a breakpoint
- O c. Start the program by hitting ctrl-F5 during the program run

3.) While stepping though the code during run time, you can alter the variable values in the Watch window?
- O a. True
- O b. False

4.) Using the code fragment below

```
if (!(n == 5 || n > 7))
{
    Console.WriteLine("Block Run");
}
```

What numbers will cause the console to say "Block Run"?
- ☐ a. 4
- ☐ b. 5
- ☐ c. 6
- ☐ d. 7
- ☐ e. 8

5.) You want to build your application without running it. What F key will do this?
- O a. F5
- O b. F6
- O c. F9
- O d. F10

Notes

Chapter 7 – Arrays

Can multiple values all refer to one specific object? As an example from the real world, think of an Olympic figure skater. After they complete their routine, they will go to the center of the ice and look up at the judges. Each judge will present his or her score – each score is an individual number belonging to that one judge, but as a whole they all make up part of the skaters' score.

Until now, all of our variables have been individual values, with no connection to any other variable. However, there are times when instead of just a single value, you need a whole set of values, all of which are related to each other. Examples of this in the real world can be something like lottery numbers, a set of coordinates, the tire pressure for each tire of a car, and so on. Of course each of these elements are complete individual numbers in their own right, but when looked at as a whole, they take on a more significant meaning. An array is a construct by which you can link a series of values to a single variable name. Any variable type can be turned into an array.

Line them Up!

As an easy mental metaphor, think of an array like an apartment complex. When you want to visit your friend, you need two pieces of information; the physical address of the apartment complex, and his or her individual unit number. The address only gets you to where the structure is physically located, but the unit number gets you to the specific individual's location. An array works in a very similar way. As with all variables, the array has a name, but it also has an index value, which is the "unit number" of the individual element of the array that you are looking for. To specify this index you use square braces, "[]". For example if the name of the array is lottoNumbers and you are trying to set the second number of this array you would code that like this:

```
lottoNumbers[1] = 19;
```

No, that is not a typo. I know that I said we are trying to access the second element of the array, yet I used a 1 for the index. All arrays start counting at 0, which means the second element is 1. Be careful of this! Having an off-by-one error when dealing with arrays is very common!

Ok, so using an array is fairly straightforward, but what about declaring an array? After all, just as with any other variable before you can use it, you need to declare it. Once again we use the square braces to indicate that we are defining an array, but here is where things get a little bit funny. Let me show you:

```
int [] myArray ...
```

Yes, the ... means more has to come there, but I don't want that to distract us quite yet.

Notice how the square braces are not after the name of the array but rather are put after the type. This is a little backwards from other programming languages, so if you have done work with other programming languages, be very careful of this!

This tells the compiler that I am defining a variable called `myArray`, which is to be an array of type `int`. So far so good, but the compiler still needs more information before it can setup this array in memory. Specifically what it needs to know is the size of the array, as specified in the number of elements the array will have. Think about that sentence carefully. It means you cannot just create an empty array with an undefined number of elements and just add them as needed!

There are two ways to give the compiler this information. The first method requires that you know the values you want to store in each element of the array. For the second method you just tell it how many elements you want, but without giving it the values. Let me show you both methods:

```
// Method 1: Using known element values
int [] myArray1 = { 1, 1, 2, 3, 5, 8 };

// Method 2: Specify how many elements, without
values
int [] myArray2 = new int [6];
```

Both of these lines create an array with six elements, but after they are executed, `myArray1` will have the six numbers I specified within the curly braces assigned to the six elements, while `myArray2` will have six elements but with no values assigned yet (in other words each element will be set to 0).

In the second method, I manually specified 6 within the square braces to indicate the size of the array. C# would also have allowed me to use a variable in there, so I could have written it like this:

```
// Method 2: Specify how many elements, without
values
int arraySize = 6;
int[] myArray2 = new int[arraySize];
```

Both are perfectly legal. Now that we know how to define an array, let's put this new skill to use. This next program is going to combine a number of the skills we have learned so far, in order so it can ask the user for six numbers, which are going to be stored in an array and then displayed back to the user.

Ready? Start your Visual C# program and start a new project called "CH7a". As always, here is the code:

```
int[] myLottoNums = new int[6];

Console.WriteLine("Please enter this week's lotto
numbers:");
for (int i = 0; i < 6; i++)
{
    Console.Write("Number {0}: ", i + 1);
    myLottoNums[i] = int.Parse(Console.ReadLine());
}

Console.WriteLine("Thank you!  You entered:");
for (int i = 0; i <= 5; i++)
{
    Console.Write("{0} ", myLottoNums[i]);
}

Console.ReadLine();
```

Ah, so short yet so full of neat things to find and examine! Go ahead and run the program and play with it to see what it does. (Figure 44) Now that you have seen it, let's examine a few key areas in more detail.

Figure 44: Result of running project CH7a

Of course we start off by defining our array, but since we do not know the values each element will hold we use the second method. After a quick instruction to the user, we setup a `for` loop to go from 0 to 5. Hmmm, to 5 – I thought we had six elements to gather? True we do, but remember arrays start counting from 0, which means instead of the `for` loop going from 1 to 6, it has to go from 0 to 5. Were you to type out these six numbers, you would end up with 0, 1, 2, 3, 4, 5.

Now computers may like to start counting at 0, but for most humans that is rather confusing. In order to prevent the user from seeing the prompts from 0 to 5, notice how there is a +1 put into the `Write` line after the `i` variable. This simply increases the element counter by 1 so the users never see a 0, but we did not assign the result of this back to our counter variable, so the array will still see 0 to 5.

After the user has entered all six values, we start another loop, again from 0 to 5, but this time we display the array members. Ah, but even though the loop still runs from 0 to 5, this time I wrote it a bit differently. In the first loop the condition was `i < 6`, which means once `i` hits 6, it is no longer true and the loop ends. The last time the condition was true, the value of `i` was still 5, giving us the valid upper range for the array. For the second loop the result is the same but the condition is now written as `i <= 5`. Why, is there an advantage with either method? Actually there is no advantage either way – it is totally up to you. Regardless of which method you prefer, be familiar with both since other developers may prefer to write the logic differently in order to get the same results as you do.

Of course this is a really simple example to demonstrate the way arrays work, so we know the size of the array and our output loop can count correctly. But in many cases you might not be the one who defined the loop and may not know the size of it, yet you still have to iterate through it. So how can you write a loop when you do not know how high you can go up to? There are actually two solutions to this problem. Once an array has been defined, its size is fixed and the compiler will keep track of it. You can get this information out by accessing the length property of the array. For example, that last loop could have been written line this:

```
for (int i = 0; i < myLottoNums.Length; i++)
{
    Console.Write("{0} ", myLottoNums[i]);
}
```

While I may not know what the winning lottery numbers are going to be from week to week, I do know that in my state, it will always be six numbers. Six is not the winning number, but is the length of my number selection. If you were to print out the value of myLottoNums.Length, or use the debugger to look at it, it would return a 6, which is the size of the array as we defined it. In fact the debugger can even show you the values of each of the array's elements. Go ahead and put a breakpoint onto WriteLine just before the second for loop. Run your program, enter in six numbers and when the debugger pops up take a look at the Locals window (Figure 45).

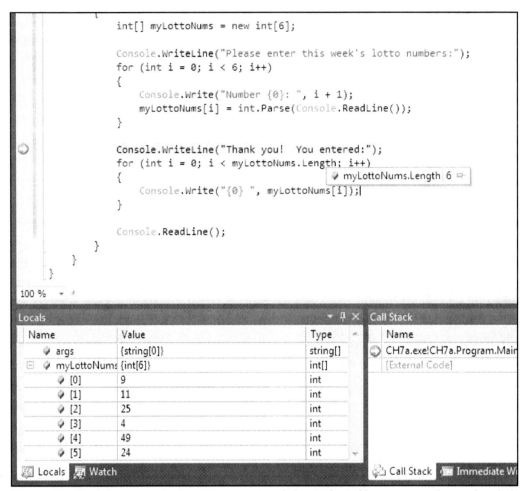

```
            int[] myLottoNums = new int[6];

            Console.WriteLine("Please enter this week's lotto numbers:");
            for (int i = 0; i < 6; i++)
            {
                Console.Write("Number {0}: ", i + 1);
                myLottoNums[i] = int.Parse(Console.ReadLine());
            }

            Console.WriteLine("Thank you!  You entered:");
            for (int i = 0; i < myLottoNums.Length; i++)
            {                                        myLottoNums.Length  6
                Console.Write("{0} ", myLottoNums[i]);
            }

            Console.ReadLine();
        }
    }
}
100 %
```

Locals			▼ ╫ ×	Call Stack
Name	Value	Type	▲	Name
✓ args	{string[0]}	string[]		⊙ CH7a.exe!CH7a.Program.Main
⊟ ✓ myLottoNums	{int[6]}	int[]		[External Code]
✓ [0]	9	int		
✓ [1]	11	int		
✓ [2]	25	int		
✓ [3]	4	int		
✓ [4]	49	int		
✓ [5]	24	int	▼	
🗗 Locals 🗗 Watch				🗗 Call Stack 🗗 Immediate Wi

Figure 45: Hovering over the length property of the myLottoNums array shows that it is holding 6 numbers

If you click the small + sign next to the myLottoNums variable name in the Locals window, it will expand and show you the values of each element. Also in the figure, notice how my mouse is hovering over the myLottoNums.Length value in the second for loop and the small pop-up is showing that the length of this array is 6 elements.

So we can get the size of the array out of the system and setup a loop accordingly. But there is another way, one where we do not actually care how many elements there are, we just want to step through them all. There is a method for this and it is called the foreach loop. Using this method, that second loop could be rewritten like this:

```
foreach (int x in myLottoNums)
{
    Console.Write("{0} ", x);
}
```

It looks rather strange at first glance, but as with many other things in programming, once you understand it, it actually becomes quite simple! As always, it starts off with the foreach keyword followed by some parameters inside a set of parentheses. There are actually three parameters in there, separated by the keyword in. The first two are a variable declaration and variable name (the int and the x). The variable name is required, but the declaration is not, as long as the variable has been defined outside of the loop. (This is similar to how you can define the variable that a for loop uses outside the for declaration.)

After the keyword in is the third parameter, which is the name of the array we wish to step through. The way this loop works is that for each iteration of the loop, the foreach command pulls out the next element's value and copies it into the variable specified before the keyword in, or x in our case. We can then use that new variable within the loop body to display the value or process it in any other way we wish.

Go ahead and rewrite the second loop in your Visual C# project with the new foreach loop and run the program. It should work exactly the same way as before, but with less work on our part. If it helps, run this new loop through the debugger and see how the compiler steps through each part of the loop and notice how the variable x is updated, for each iteration.

Arrays are quite useful when you need to store and work with a sequence of identical data types, but since nothing is ever perfect, there is a pretty major limitation. For example we buy eggs by the dozen and knowing this the cartons are designed with 12 round slots for the eggs to sit in. If I decide that I wanted to put 13 eggs into one carton, the standard carton design would not work. I would have to create a 13 egg sized carton before being able to buy 13 eggs in a single carton.

I alluded to this earlier but at the time I did not want to get sidetracked, so we did not go into detail but I think now it is time. During the declaration of the array you have to specify its size, either explicitly or implicitly. By explicit, I mean you specify the number of elements (like 12 or 13) within the square braces, while if you give all the values inside curly braces then you have implicitly set the size.

After the declaration the array size is set and you cannot add additional elements to it nor remove them.

Because of this you need to think your program's needs out in advance and make sure you get your arrays sized large enough when you declare them. To offset this limitation, arrays offer one advantage – they are fast. Since the size is known when it gets declared, the compiler is able to set aside a chunk of contiguous memory at that time, so all the elements are going to be nicely lined up making for quick access.

So what can you do if your array is already set, but find that you have an extra item or two to add into it? There is only one option, which is to declare a whole new array at the new larger size, copy all the elements of the old array into the new one and then destroy the old array. Not a pleasant task to consider, is it? There is a better solution, but that is for another day...

What Else can we do with an Array?

It turns out that arrays have a number of built-in functions, such as sorting their values, reversing the array order, clearing out all members, and so on. There are many other functions, but they require that you supply additional code before they work and we are not ready for that yet, we will cover that much later on. For now let's just examine two common array functions, sorting an array and reversing its order.

Both of these methods work the same way, only the command is different. For example, to sort our myLottoNums array we would use the following line:

```
Array.Sort(myLottoNums);
```

Notice how we are using the Sort method of the Array object and giving it the name of the array that we want sorted, in our case myLottoNums. If you want to try this, enter this line just before the second for loop then run your program. Enter in a bunch of numbers in random order and notice how you get a nice ordered output (Figure 46).

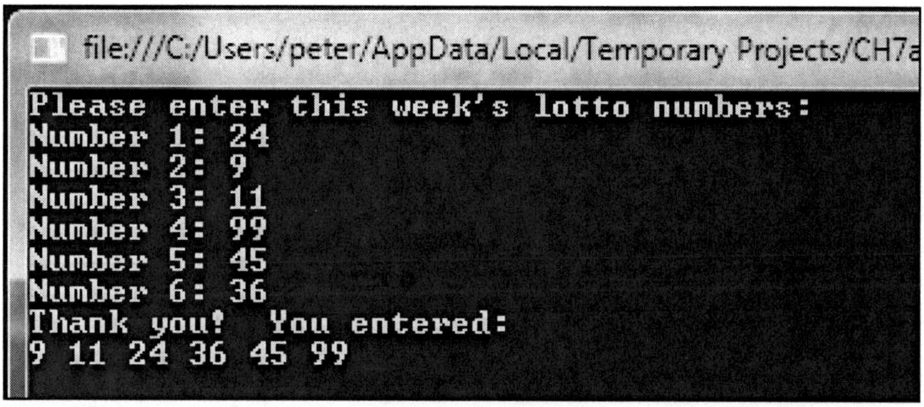

Figure 46: Array values were entered in random order, but the Sort method put them in order

Writing your own sort routine is actually quite complex, so having this sort function built-in can save you tons of time.

I also mentioned a reverse function. This works the same way, just change the Sort line to reverse, like this:

```
Array.Reverse(myLottoNums);
```

Run your program and again enter in some numbers. When the output shows up notice how the order is reversed.

Multi-dimensional Arrays

The arrays we have looked at so far have all been one dimensional arrays, meaning they were just a sequence of elements. C# also supports multi-dimensional arrays. The easiest way to explain a two dimensional array is to think of it as a spreadsheet. This time you not only have numbers going across (columns) as you do with a one-dimensional array, but you also have rows giving you that second dimension. To define a multi-dimensional array you have to provide both the width (columns) and height (rows) of the array. For example to define a simple 3x3 array you would enter:

```
int[,] myArray = new int[3,3];
```

Just as with a one dimensional array, this initializes all of the elements of the multi-dimensional array with 0, but you could also specify values as well. For our 3x3 array that would look like this:

```
int[,] myArray = {{1, 2, 3}, {4, 5, 6}, {7, 8, 9}};
```

Notice the usage of the curly braces around not just the entire array range, but around each individual "row" of data. This would create an array in memory that would look like this on paper:

	0	**1**	**2**
0	1	2	3
1	4	5	6
2	7	8	9

Of course the height and width of your array does not have to be the same, you can make arrays like 3x5, or any other shape. Addressing each element of a multi-dimensional array requires two values, one for the column and the second for the row. For example to address the cell with the number 6 in it, you would use:

```
int myNum = myArray[2, 1];
```

You can go deeper and create arrays with even more depth, such as 3, 4, 5 or even more[16]. For each additional depth just put another comma between the square braces. Therefore the definition of a four dimensional array, with each level made up of three elements, would look like this:

```
int[, , ,] bigArray = new int[3, 3, 3, 3];
```

With two (or more) dimensions the length property of an array returns the total number of elements across all dimensions. With our 3x3 example above, the length property will return a 9. While that can be useful, more often you are looking for the length of a given dimension of the array, such as the number of rows or columns (assuming a two dimensional array). For this there is another property, GetLength, which takes an integer parameter. This parameter is the number of the dimension whose size you are trying to get.

---

[16] Multi-dimensional arrays are quite a complex subject, so other than mentioning that they exist, we are not going to cover them in any further detail.

With our 3x3 example, valid values for GetLength would be a number from 0 to 1 (remember 0 based counting) and each would return 3. That is because we have three rows and each row has three columns.

	0	1	2
0	1	2	3
1	4	5	6
2	7	8	9

GetLength(0) = 3

GetLength(1) = 3

This array has two dimensions, which in real world terms we would call height and width. Each dimension contains three elements, so both return the same answer.

Since we created this small array, we know that it has two dimensions – but what if we did not create it? There is another useful property of arrays, called Rank, which can help you. The Rank property returns the number of dimensions that the array has, but with a twist. Even though computers count from 0, and for GetLength I have to specify the dimension I am interested in, using 0 based counting; the Rank property returns the answer in human terms. What does that mean? Simple, for our sample array above, the Rank command would return 2! Take a look at the small code sample and its output in Figure 47.

```
class Program
{
    static void Main(string[] args)
    {
        int[,] myArray = new int[3, 3];

        Console.WriteLine("Rank: {0}", myArray.Rank);

        Console.ReadLine();
    }
}
```

```
file:///C:/Users/peter/AppData/Local/Temporary Projects/C
Rank: 2
```

Figure 47: Output of the Rank method on a 2 dimensional array

Points to Ponder

- An array is a like a series of variables, all the same data type, linked together
- The size of the array (how many elements it can contain) if set when you define the array and cannot be changed
- All elements of the array must be of the same data type
- An array is defined by typing in the data type of the array, followed by empty square braces, followed by the name of the array
- After defining an array, you must initialize the space in memory by using the new keyword
- You access the individual elements of an array by using square braces [] and the index value
- Arrays are 0 based, meaning the first element is 0, the second is 1, the third is 2, and so on. So if an array has 10 elements, the index will go from 0 to 9.
- You can use the foreach keyword to step through all member of an array without having to know how many elements the array has
- Arrays have a number of built-in methods, such as sort
- Multi-dimensional arrays are defined the same way, but for each dimension you need, you enter a comma between the square braces. For example a two dimensional array of integers would be declared like this:
  `int[,] myArray;`

Challenge

1. Ask the user to enter 10 numbers and store these in a one dimensional array. Get one additional number from the user and then search the array to see if any of the elements is equal to this additional number. If you find it, display a message that you did and if not display another one that it could not be found.
2. Modify the previous program so if the number being searched for is found multiple times, you can display a count of the times it was found
3. Write a program to store the days of each month in an array. Ask the user for a number, which is to represent a month (for example 1 for January). Have the program return the number of days in that month. If the user enters an invalid month number, display an error message.

Review Quiz

1.) How do you initialize a declared array of strings named student?
 O a. `string[] student;`
 O b. `string student[];`
 O c. `student = new student[3];`
 O d. `student = new string[3];`

2.) How would you declare an array of integers named Apple?
 O a. `Apple int[];`
 O b. `int[] Apple;`
 O c. `Apple = new Apple[3];`
 O d. `Apple = new int[3];`

3.) An Array size of [5] would have what index for its first or initial element?
 O a. [0]
 O b. [1]
 O c. [4]
 O d. [5]
 O e. [6]

4.) An Array size of [5] would have what index for its last element?
 O a. [0]
 O b. [1]
 O c. [4]
 O d. [5]
 O e. [6]

5.) Assume your array is populated in the following way. What would be the values of the following properties?

```
int[,] BOAComboLock = {{17,55,93,29}, {99,40,19,59}};
```

 a. Length: _____
 b. GetLength(0): _____
 c. Rank: _____

6.) If the index of the final element in your array is [7] then what is the length of your array?

   O a. 6

   O b. 7

   O c. 8

7.) What are two ways to iterate through an array?

   ☐ a. `for`

   ☐ b. `new`

   ☐ c. `foreach`

   ☐ d. `IndexOf`

8.) Which of the following are true about initializing an array that will be populated later? (Choose all that apply.)

   ☐ a. The size must be specified before the array can be filled.

   ☐ b. All elements must be of the same type.

   ☐ c. You can specify size during the declaration.

   ☐ d. You can specify the size when initializing.

   ☐ e. The first element in your array always starts with [0].

   ☐ f. The first element in your array always starts with [1].

Notes

Chapter 8 – Strings

So far we have only used numeric variables in all of our samples and demonstrations. However C# also has support for string variables, which allows us to store alphanumeric[17] sets of characters. Nearly everything we have done with numeric variables so far, such as declaring and initializing variables and arrays, all work the same way when using strings. A few other operators, such as +, behave a bit differently.

An overview with strings

Let's just jump right in with an example program that uses many of the subjects we have covered so far, but with a focus on strings instead of numbers. Start a new console project, naming it "CH8a". When ready type this code into the Main method:

```csharp
string userName;

Console.Write("What is your first name? ");
userName = Console.ReadLine();
Console.Write("Hello {0}! ", userName);

Console.ReadLine();
```

Go ahead and run this code. This is a pretty simple example, and not all that different from some of our earliest programs, except we are now using a string for our variable data instead of a number. Let's expand on this. Please modify your program using the code below:

```csharp
string userName;
string[] jobTitles = new string[5];

Console.Write("What is your first name? ");
userName = Console.ReadLine();
```

---

[17] A fancy word which means both characters and numbers.

```
Console.WriteLine("Please enter a list of the top 5
job titles.\n");

for (int ct = 0; ct < 5; ct++)
{
    Console.Write("Enter job title #{0}: ", ct + 1);
    jobTitles[ct] = Console.ReadLine();
}

Console.Clear();

Console.WriteLine("Choose which title you like the
best:\n");

for (int ct = 0; ct < 5; ct++)
{
    Console.WriteLine("\t#{0}: {1} {2}", ct + 1,
jobTitles[ct], userName);
}

Console.Write("\n\nYour choice: ");
int theChoice = int.Parse(Console.ReadLine());

Console.Clear();

Console.WriteLine("Introducing {0} {1}!",
jobTitles[theChoice - 1], userName);

Console.ReadLine();
```

Wow, that may be the longest program we have written so far! Go ahead and read through it, then run it to see what it does. Ah, welcome back Mr. President!

While not a very complicated program, it does have a number of new concepts in it besides just using strings for the first time. Of course the very first difference we find is right on the first two lines, where we are defining a string variable and a string array. Notice, except for the new keyword string, this is done the exact same way we have done it in the past.

The next two lines are simple Console.Write commands, which we have used in the past, and a Console.ReadLine to get the user input. The only difference between its usage here and how we used it before is, the lack of the Parse function wrapping the Console.ReadLine. Whenever we get user input back using the ReadLine method of Console, the result is always a string. Previously, we would have had to parse this result in order to see the numeric value. This time, we are expecting back a string, the name of the user, and then putting that directly into a string variable. No parsing is required. Hey, less to type – what's not to like about that?

The next line is also a fairly straightforward Console.WriteLine statement, but there is one new item at the end of the string. Notice the last two characters within the string to display are "\n". Now, when you ran the program did you actually see the backslash and the letter 'n' character being displayed? Of course not! Unlike with numbers, there are a number of nonprinting characters that cannot be typed directly, such as a new line, form feed, tab, or backspace. For these special characters we have something called an Escape Sequence that we can use instead.

An Escape Sequence is always made up of two characters, the first of which tells the compiler to treat the following character not as a literal value to display but rather as a code for something special instead. In C#, as in many other languages, the Escape Sequence starts off with a backslash, which is the character that causes the compiler to treat the following character as something special. Since the compiler knows that this is the start of a set of characters with meaning only when taken together, it does not display the backslash character. In our example the next character is the letter n, which stands for a new line, otherwise known as a carriage return. By the way, the most common Escape Sequence is the \n and you will see it quite a bit. Of course there are others, and I will give you a list of them in just a bit.

After displaying our message, the next thing in the code is a simple for loop that repeats 5 times. Each iteration of the loop will cause two lines of code to run. The first of which displays a request for the user to enter a job title and the second actually grabs and stores that entry. Notice how we have to add one to the variable ct to display from 1 to 5 to the user, even though the loop actually runs from 0 to 4 (remember, arrays start with 0, not 1).

Once we have our five job titles safely stored in our string array, the next line of code does something we have not seen so far, but I'm willing to bet you could make a pretty good guess as to what that will be. The Clear method of the Console object simply clears the screen. A very simple task, that is very useful in keeping the screen from getting too cluttered.

After clearing the screen, we display another heading (notice the use of the \n Escape Sequence again) and run through another loop. Within this loop we use a single `WriteLine` command to display each job entry with the name of the user appended to it. Included in that `WriteLine` string is another Escape Sequence, the \t. The \t sequence is interpreted as a tab character, causing our output to be offset from the left edge of the screen – just a nice visual arrangement to make the list stand out.

Finally, we ask for a numeric input, clear the screen again, and display a final message, using the user's preferred title with their name.

Go ahead and run through this a few times, use the Debugger if it helps, to understand how each line works and why the program behaves the way it does. There is a lot here, but by now all of it should be familiar and easy to understand.

Escape Sequences

Earlier on when I was explaining how an Escape Sequence works, how many of you caught that bit about the backslash not actually getting displayed? Of course it should not get displayed, since its purpose is to warn the compiler that the next character is to be treated as an indicator of something special and not as a regular character. What if you actually wanted to display a single backslash character? For example, if you wanted to display "Ready to begin? (y\n)"? In this case you really want the "\n" to be displayed using exactly these characters to the screen.

If you just enter a single backslash the compiler will not display it, but rather will read the character following it and try to interpret it as an Escape Sequence. If the next character is not a valid Escape Sequence character, the compiler will actually give you an error. For example \N (capital N) is not recognized, but \n is a valid escape sequence. If by some luck, it is a valid sequence then it will execute the escape sequence. However, that is not what you intended.

The solution is a special Escape Sequence whose purpose is to simply display a single backslash character. That sequence is "\\" – yep two backslashes in a row. What if you wanted to display two backslashes in a row? Simple, for each individual backslash you want displayed, simply type in two backslashes. So if you really wanted two backslashes displayed you would enter "\\\\".

So what is the list of valid Escape Sequences? There are not many, in fact only 13, most of which are rarely used. Here is the complete list:

Escape Sequence	Result
\'	Single Quote
\"	Double Quote
\\	Single Backslash
\0	Null
\a	Alert (aka beep)
\b	Backspace
\f	Form Feed
\n	Newline
\r	Carriage Return
\t	Tab
\v	Vertical Tab
\uXXXX	Unicode character XXXX
\UXXXX	Unicode character XXXX as a hex value

In actual practice, the \a and \v sequences are hardly ever used. The \f sequence is also quite rare, and it tends to be paired with \r. The effect of the pairing of \f and \r is equivalent to \n. You might ask why even have \f and \r if they are hardly even used and together they are the same as \n? A lot of it has to do with historical reasons as well as to deal with other operating systems. All Windows based operating systems use the combination \f\r in order to get the cursor down one line and back to the beginning, but other OS' (such as all variations of Unix), only need \r to accomplish the same task.

To explain the difference between form feed and carriage return, think back to a typewriter. To get the paper in the typewriter so the typing head is over the first character of the next line, you first have to roll the paper, aka the form, down to the next line. However, the typing head is still positioned at the same location it was before, so you also need the carriage return to actually move the paper, attached to the carriage, to the far left edge of the paper. If you want to test this on a computer screen, try this line of code and see what the result is:

```
Console.Write("this is the first line\fthis is the
second line");
```

Finally, the last two Escape Sequences, \uXXXX and \UXXXX are also a bit strange and rarely used. As you may know, all font tables are made up of 255 characters. Normally we can only type a small subset directly from the keyboard. Some of the other characters which we cannot directly type are international characters used by other languages, which on their localized keyboards might have dedicated keys. If we happen to know the Unicode value for these characters (in either decimal or in hex), then we can use these Escape Sequences, followed by the right number, to display them. Again, rarely used, but helpful if you ever happen to need them.

One more trick if you want to display characters without them being interpreted as an escape sequence. Take the string "Are you sure (y\n)" as an example. If we try to print this directly, the "\n" will be interpreted as the new line escape sequence, and you will not get what you are looking for. As we saw above, the solution is to escape the backslash, by using two backslashes. In other words:

```
Console.WriteLine("Are you sure (y\\n)");
```

This works great, but could get rather ugly if you have a whole set of slashes to escape. There is another solution, which involves the use of the @ symbol before your string. This symbol tells the compiler to not examine the following string for escape sequences, but rather to print every character as displayed. This means that I can achieve the same results with this line of code:

```
Console.WriteLine(@"Are you sure (y\n)");
```

Concatenation

Here is a trick question for you... If 1 + 1 is equal to 2, what is a + b equal to? Ah, you think a and b are variables so they must have a numeric value. Nope, a and b may just be strings, so I probably should have written this as "a" + "b". So what are two strings equal to, when added together?

Hmmm, the plus sign means to add two numeric values together, so how can you add two strings? Well you cannot, so if you think of this mathematically then this cannot make sense. Turns out that the + sign has multiple meanings depending on what values are on either side of it. In C# terms, this means the operator has been overloaded. We are going to cover the concept of overloading later on, since it is a very important concept in C#.

All this means is that if the + sign sees numeric values around it then it does a standard math addition function on them, but if it sees string values it does something called concatenation. This fancy word, which personally I can never pronounce correctly, simply means to take the two string values, stick them next to each other and return it as a new value. Take this code fragment as an example:

```
string var1 = "a", var2 = "b";
string var3 = var1 + var2;

string var4 = "4", var5 = "5";
string var6 = var4 + var5;

Console.WriteLine("{0}", var3);
Console.WriteLine("{0}", var6);
```

What do you suppose the value of var3 is when it gets displayed? If you answered "ab", then you are correct! But what about var6 – it is made up of var4 and var5, both of which have numbers in them (Figure 48)

Figure 48: Using + with strings will concatenate the values

Even though var4 and var5 contain numbers, they are declared as type string, which means it is treated as a string and not as a numeric value. Since they are just strings, the + sign simply did what it does with all strings. It sticks them together and returns the result. If I had really wanted to add 4 to 5 and get a 9 as a result, I would have had to first parse these strings into a numeric data type and then I could add them up as numbers. This is actually a fairly common mistake, so be careful when dealing which numeric input stored as a string.

String Data Types

Actually, there are only two data types that deal with strings, the first of which, `string`, we have already used. The other string data type is called `char` and calling it a string data type is sort of giving it too much credit, since it can only hold a single character at a time.

This leads to the obvious question – if a `char` can only hold a single character, just how much can a `string` hold? It is a logical question, since until now all of the data types we have looked at had some kind of an upper limit. Turns out that `string` is rather unique, in that it has no fixed limit! Once you have declared a variable as a type `string`, you can stick as much text into it as you want. As it gets bigger, the compiler will just use up more and more memory to store what you put into that variable.

Just as with any other data type, before you can use a variable of type `char`, you need to declare it. After declaring the variable you can use it, but be careful. Take a look at this code fragment and try to figure out what is wrong with it. (Trust me, if you try to compile this it will fail.)

```
char test = "x";
```

Looks pretty good, doesn't it? We know that a `char` type can only hold a single character, so we are assigning it exactly one character. However the problem comes in the fact that we are using the double quotes symbol around our single character. To the compiler, anything surrounded by double quotes means a string, regardless of length. Since it knows that a `char` type cannot hold a string, it gives you a conversion error (Figure 49).

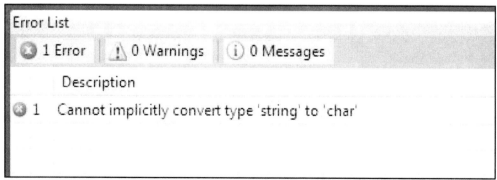

Figure 49: Error when trying to assign a string to a variable of type char

The solution is rather easy, though maybe not obvious. If the double quotes symbol means a string, then you need another symbol whose meaning is character. Luckily for us C# has such a symbol, it happens to be single quotes. So, if we change our line of code to look like this, then all of our problems go away!

```
char test = 'x';
```

Ah, much better! Be careful of the single vs. double quote issue. In the same way that the double quote always means a string to the compiler, the single quote always means a character. This means that, when assigning a string to a string variable, you cannot use single quotes to surround the string – you will get an error that the literal is too long.

We have Reached a Milestone!

Believe it or not, by covering `string` and `char` we have covered all of the native data types that C# has! From here on out, all of our variables will have to be one of these numeric or character data types that we have described so far, or, be based on them. Yes, it is possible to create new data types and data structures that can hold multiple and different types of data. Even these user defined data types will be based upon the native data types covered so far. As a review here is the complete list of data types that C# recognizes:

Alias for	Type	Range	Bits	Bytes
bool	System.Boolean	True or false (aka 0 or 1)	1	1
byte	System.Byte	0 to 255	8	1
sbyte	System.SByte	-128 to 127	8	1
decimal	System.Decimal	$\pm 1.0 \times 10^{-28}$ to $\pm 7.9 \times 10^{28}$	128	16
double	System.Double	$\pm 5.0 \times 10^{-324}$ to $\pm 1.7 \times 10^{308}$	64	8
float	System.Single	$\pm 1.5 \times 10^{-45}$ to $\pm 3.4 \times 10^{38}$	32	4
int	System.Int32	-2,147,483,648 to 2,147,483,647	32	4
uint	System.UInt32	0 to 4,294,967,295	32	4
long	System.Int64	−9,223,372,036,854,775,808 to 9,223,372,036,854,775,807	64	8
ulong	System.UInt64	0 to 18,446,744,073,709,551,615	64	8
short	System.Int16	-32,768 to 32,767	16	2
ushort	System.UInt16	0 to 65,535	16	2
char	System.Char	One single character	8	1
string	System.String	A sequence of characters, any amount	8/char	1/char

String Manipulation

Once you have a string in hand there are a number of things that you can do with it, such as convert the case of its letters, get the length of the string, and so on. A number of these are fairly advanced and we are going to cover them later, but there are a few which are easy to understand and common enough that we should try them here.

Before we go on, we need to think about what a string really is. Unlike a numeric value, which simply has a single meaning regardless of its size, a string is actually a collection of discreet components – those components being chars. Let me put this in another way. If I have an int variable and I assign it the value of 1, 100, 1000, or higher, it is still just an int. It still takes up the same amount of memory (32 bits or four bytes). No matter how long the number is when I write it out on paper, it is still handled as a single value. Even a char behaves this way, since it has a limit of a single character. A string, on the other hand, is quite a bit different since it has no such limit.

While to us a string is an easily understood and dealt with concept, computers do not really work that way. To a computer a string is actually treated not as a single entity but rather as an array (sequential set) of chars. Once we can get our brain wrapped around this idea and start treating strings like giant arrays, all kinds of interesting options become possible. Take a look at this example.

```
string myString = "This is a test";

Console.WriteLine("{0}", myString[5]);
```

At first glance you might think that this is wrong and will not compile. After all the variable myString is declared as type string, yet in my WriteLine I am using it as an array. Actually this is quite legal and would print out the letter 'i' as the answer (remember arrays start counting at 0, so the sixth letter has to be referred to as 5).

T	h	i	s		i	s		a		t	e	s	t
0	1	2	3	4	5	6	7	8	9	10	11	12	13

Hmmm, so if I can treat a string variable as an array and be able to access the individual elements, can I also change them? For example, could I check each letter in the string for the letter 'I', and change it to another letter. Perhaps even change it from a lower case letter to an uppercase one? Ah, you mean like this:

```
string myString = "This is a test";

Console.WriteLine("Original string: {0}", myString);

for (int ct = 0; ct < myString.Length; ct++)
{
    if (myString[ct] == 'i')
        myString[ct] = 'I';
}

Console.WriteLine("Modified string: {0}", myString);
```

Actually, this is wrong. If you try to compile this you will get an error that the array is read-only and cannot be modified like this (Figure 50).

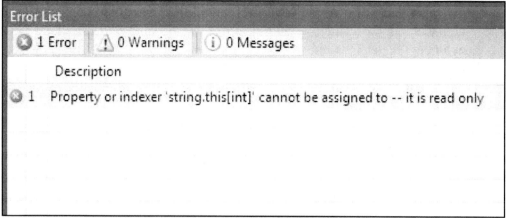

Figure 50: Error message when trying to modify a string using array like syntax

The object `string` supports a number of methods to manipulate it, one of which is the replace function. This function takes two parameters, the first is the character or string fragment to find and the second is the character or string fragment with which to replace it with. So our example from above needs to be rewritten like this:

```csharp
string myString = "This is a test";

Console.WriteLine("Original string: {0}", myString);

myString = myString.Replace("i", "I");

Console.WriteLine("Modified string: {0}", myString);
```

Running this will give you the output as seen in Figure 51.

```
Original string: This is a test
Modified string: ThIs Is a test
```

Figure 51: Using the replace function to modify a string

Besides the replace function, there are other functions that the `string` object supports. The most commonly used of these are:

- Length, which I used in a previous sample, and whose job it is to return the length of the string

- ToUpper and ToLower do what they sound like, namely to convert all the characters in the string to either all uppercase or all lowercase letters. For example "Peter" would become "PETER" if you used the ToUpper method.
- Trim, which removes the specified character(s) from both the beginning and end of a string
- TrimEnd and TrimStart are specialized versions of Trim, which only work on either the end of or the beginning of a string

TrimEnd and TrimStart operate the same way as Trim does, in that as a parameter to the function, you need to provide the character(s) they are to look for and remove. However, Trim is a bit smarter than that. If you just use Trim by itself, it will automatically remove whitespace from both ends of the string, but if you give it an optional character as a parameter, then it will look for and remove that character instead of a space. Whitespace is commonly defined as spaces, tabs and return characters.

There is one more common string function I would like to cover, though there are many more. I cannot cover them all here, but this next one I would like to describe in detail.

The function is called Substring, and is used to pull out a part of a string. This is great if you want to use only a small part of the whole string somewhere else in your program. One common example would be if you asked the user for their full name, but want to pull out just their first name.

This brings us to the next point about Substring. It takes two parameters: the first is the start location and the second is the length, or how many characters you would like to return. So using our example from above, we would have to know how long the first name is in order to pull out just the letters which make up the first name. One easy solution would be to first walk through the string and find the space which separates the first name from the last name.

Actually the length parameter is optional; if you leave it off it will grab everything from the start location to the end of the string. Now before we look into using this function, how did I get this information? Actually the Visual C# environment told me, through IntelliSense. Specifically, as soon as I type the name of a string and press the period, a dropdown shows up with all of the methods that this object supports (Figure 52).

```
class Program
{
    static void Main(string[] args)
    {
        string myString = "This is a test";

        Console.WriteLine("Original string: {0}", myString);

        myString = myString.|

        Console.WriteLine("M                              ng);
                         Skip<>
        Console.ReadLine();    SkipWhile<>
    }                          Split
}                              StartsWith
                               Substring       string string.Substring(int startIndex, int length)  (+ 1 overload(s))
                               Sum<>            Retrieves a substring from this instance. The substring starts at a specified character position and
                               Take<>           has a specified length.
                               TakeWhile<>
                               ToArray<>        Exceptions:
                                                  System.ArgumentOutOfRangeException
```

Figure 52: IntelliSense shows the parameter options for any method of the object

As you use the up and down arrow keys to move through this popup list, a small description box shows up for each item. As you can see in Figure 52, I have the Substring method highlighted. In the box to the right it shows the method and its parameters (first line), a description (second line), and a list of exceptions that this function can generate at the bottom. (Exceptions have to do with capturing and dealing with errors, which we are going to cover very shortly.)

Notice how at the end of the first line it has "(+1 overload(s))" displayed. Hmmm, what could that mean? Function overloading is a very important concept in C#, one which we are going to cover in some detail in an upcoming chapter. For now it just means that there are different ways of calling this method. To show you all these options, you need to actually type in the name of the method as well as the first open parentheses of the parameter list. Once you do that another popup will display with the parameters that it expects, and if there are overloads (other ways to call this method) you can see those as well. Take a look at Figure 53, in which I have grabbed the two methods that the Substring function supports.

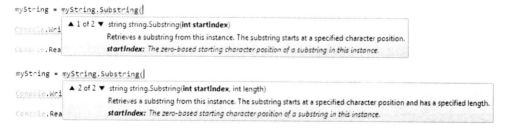

Figure 53: There are two ways to call Substring. Both require a startIndex, but the second choice (the overload) allows you to also specify a length.

As you can see, the first method just needs a single parameter, which is the startIndex, or the location within the string where you want to start to pull characters from. In this use of the method, Substring will return all characters from the startIndex to the end. However if you give it two values, the second way to use this method, the startIndex just as before, but this time also a length value, or how many characters from startIndex to grab, Substring will return a string as long as the length value starting from startIndex in the string being worked on.

IntelliSense is a very powerful tool that makes the C# language (as long as you use the Visual Studio set of tools) almost self-documenting. Feel free to examine the rest of the methods that the `string` object supports and read what they do.

Now that we know how to use Substring, let's see how that would look in actual code.

```csharp
string myString = "Peter Bako";

Console.WriteLine("Full name: {0}", myString);

string firstName = myString.Substring(0, 5);
string lastName = myString.Substring(6);

Console.WriteLine("First name: {0}", firstName);
Console.WriteLine("Last name: {0}", lastName);

Console.ReadLine();
```

To keep this example simple, I am hard coding the length of the first name (5) and the starting point for the last name (6). If this were real code, I would have to provide some mechanism to find the location of the space, in case the name entered would have a first name that is not 5 characters in length. If we run this, we get the following output (Figure 54):

```
Full name: Peter Bako
First name: Peter
Last name: Bako
```

Figure 54: Using Substring to split a string

Points to Ponder

- String variables can store alphanumeric text – both numbers and characters
- The ReadLine method, which we have used in the past, returns a string, so parsing it is not required if you are expecting a string value
- An Escape Sequence is a two-character command which allows us to "display" special characters, such as carriage returns, tabs, etc.
- The first character in an Escape Sequence is always a backslash and the second character specifies what special output we want
- Two backslashes in a row will display as a single backslash
- When used with numeric variables, the + sign will add the values together mathematically. When used with string variables it will concatenate the strings together (in other words attach them to each other).
- Strings can be thought of as an array of characters
- You can access the individual characters of a string with the same notation as you would for an array, namely with square braces []
- Strings have a number of useful properties and methods, such as Length, Trim, ToUpper, etc.

Challenge

1) Ask the user for their first name and their last name. Store these in two different variables. Declare a third string variable called fullName, and use the value of the first name and last name to fill this variable. Don't forget a space in the middle! Display the user's full name along with a greeting.
2) Ask the user to enter in a sentence. Display the sentence back to the user, then also display how long the sentence is and how many times they used the letter 'e'.
3) Expand upon the challenge from step 2, and count how many times all the vowels were used. Hint, use a `switch` statement. Check your program – does it count both upper and lower case vowels?
4) Create a program to store the names and birthdays of five of your closest friends. Ask the user to enter a name, then look up that name in your list and display their birth date. Hint: Use a multi-dimensional array to keep the friends name and birth date linked.

Review Quiz

1.) How would you make the following output?

I am "With it" today!

```
O a.) System.Console.Write("I am "With it" today!" );
O b.) System.Console.Write("I am \"With it\" today!" );
O c.) System.Console.Write(@"I am "With it" today!" );
O d.) System.Console.Write(@"I  am  \"With  it\"  today!"
     );
```

2.) How would you make the following output? (Choose all that apply)

Are you in (yes\no)?

```
☐ a. System.Console.Write("Are you in (yes\no)?");
☐ b. System.Console.Write("Are you in (yes\\no)?");
☐ c. System.Console.Write(@"Are you in (yes\no)?" );
☐ d. System.Console.Write(@"Are you in (yes\\no)?" );
```

3.) You have the following code.

```
string myString = "This is a test";
```

You want to pull out the letter 'a' from this string. What code will do this?

```
O a.) Console.WriteLine("{0}", myString[5]);
O b.) Console.WriteLine("{0}", myString[7]);
O c.) Console.WriteLine("{0}", myString[8]);
O d.) Console.WriteLine("{0}", myString[9]);
```

4.) You have the following code.

```
string myString = "This is a test";
```

You can convert any lower case letter 't' to an uppercase 'T'. When done, your string should look like this: "This is a TesT". Which code will achieve this result?

```
O a.) myString = myString.Replace("t", "T");
O b.) myString = myString.SubString(11,14);
O c.) myString[11] = 'T'; myString[14] = 'T';
```

Notes

Chapter 9 – Fun with Variables

We have been using variables of different data types since the beginning, but until now, we have just treated them as simple containers of values. True, by definition that is the purpose of a variable – however, there is much more to know and understand about them in order to utilize their full powers.

Data Conversion

Think of a variable as a container, such as a pitcher, or a glass. If we know that the pitcher is empty but the glass is full, then we also know that we can pour the contents of the glass into the pitcher without any fear that the pitcher will overflow. What about if the situation is reversed? If the pitcher is full but the glass is not, can we pour the entire pitcher into the glass and not have the glass overflow? Probably not, since a pitcher is larger than a drinking glass. But there is an exception to this, which is, that we can look at the pitcher and if we see that the amount of water in it is smaller than the empty part of the glass then we can pour away without fear of making a mess.

In the world of C#, we talk about variables and their size limits instead of pitchers or glasses. We know from our data type chart that a variable of type int can hold a value from about negative 2 billon to about positive 2 billion, but that a byte only goes from 0 to 255. Think of the int as our pitcher and the byte as our glass. In the same way that the glass (byte) can fit into the pitcher (int) without any problems, so can any possible value of a byte fit into the int. Let's put this into a code fragment.

```
byte myGlass = 192;
int myPitcher;

myPitcher = myGlass;
```

Yep, this works great and the compiler will make the conversion without any trouble. This kind of a conversion, where the "source" variable is of a type smaller than the "destination" variable, is known as an Implicit Conversion. Ok, now let's try to reverse this situation and try to assign the value of an int to a byte variable.

```
byte myGlass;
int myPitcher = 192;

myGlass   = myPitcher;
```

Oh boy, that compiler sure did not like that! (Figure 55)

Figure 55: Error when trying to assign a larger variable into a smaller one

So, what is this error trying to tell us? We know that an implicit conversion is one where the source data type is smaller than the destination data type. The error says that it cannot make that implicit conversion since our data types are the wrong way around. What is needed is an explicit conversion, done through something called a cast – in fact, the second sentence of the error message tells us exactly that.

Before we go into an explicit conversion, let me answer the question that I bet all of you are asking right now. "Wait, the variable myPitcher is set to 192, which is well below the range of the myGlass variable, why is it still not working?" Ah, now you are giving the compiler way too much credit. While we can read the code and know that the value in the myPitcher variable would fit quite nicely into myGlass, the compiler does not actually know what value it holds.

All it knows is the data type to the right of the equal sign is way bigger than the data type of the variable to the left of the equal sign. Now it's true, the compiler could have been written to be smart enough to understand the code. In a case like ours it could realize that the values are within range of the destination variable, but what if this value is not set at compile time? What if the value held in myPitcher is calculated based on some externally provided numbers, or entered by a user during run time, which could potentially exceed the size of that byte? The compiler could not possible know that, so it simply gives you this error.

As we write our program, we could ensure that the value of `myPitcher` would not exceed 255 regardless of how it was presented or calculated, thereby ensuring that the conversion could take place. To force the compiler to take our word for it, we have to do something called an Explicit Conversion, which is done by a cast. All a cast does is to promise the compiler that regardless of the data type on the right hand side of the equal sign, its value will never exceed the type to which we are going to cast it. To do this, simply put the data type you wish to convert into before the larger variable, surrounded by parentheses. Applied to our little code fragment that would look like this:

```
byte myGlass;
int myPitcher = 192;

myGlass = (byte)myPitcher;
```

With this cast in place, that error message we saw in Figure 55 does not show up and the compiler happily accepts our code. But remember, a cast is nothing more than a promise and we know that promises can be broken. So, what happens if somehow the value in `myPitcher` does end up getting bigger than 255? That will cause the program to break, aka cause an exception, otherwise known as a crash. But all is not lost! There is a way we can capture exceptions and deal with them, but that is to be covered in just a bit.

Overflow and Underflow

If the time is 12:58, and you move it forward by two minutes, what time would it be? It becomes 1:00, which is a smaller number! Does that mean that time just went backwards? Of course not – the clock simply maxes out at 12:59, so when you go past that time (or overflow), the clock simply starts over with the lowest number, which is 1:00.

In the previous section I told you how the compiler will not let you put more into a variable than its data type will allow. However, there is a way to create a situation where you are able to go past the upper limit of a variable. Imagine a variable of type `byte` that currently has 254 assigned to it. If we add one to this variable we would expect the value to become 255, which is still within the range of a `byte` variable. What happens if we add one more to our variable? It cannot become 256, since that is larger than the max value of a byte, so what will happen? Better yet, what would you expect to happen?

Before we answer that question, let's flip this problem around. Imagine another byte variable, but this time its value is 1. If we subtract one from it, we know the variable will now become 0 – exactly as we would expect. Great, now let's subtract one more from it! From a mathematical point of view the answer is -1, but we know a byte goes from 0 to 255 – negative numbers are not allowed. So what will happen?

These two examples are what are known as overflow and underflow situations. (Sounds like a bad plumbing problem, doesn't it?) Officially defined, an overflow is when you increment the value of a variable beyond the upper limit of its data type, and an underflow is when you decrement a value below the data type's lower limit. Traditionally when this happened, the program would crash, or at the very least throw an error which our program would have to deal with. C# can also behave this way, but its default setting is to be a bit more forgiving. Before we go on, let's confirm that your environment has not had its default settings changed – otherwise, our next examples are likely to behave differently then described.

The change we are about to look at is set on a project by project basis, so before we can even check on its current status we have to start a new project. As usual, please create a new console application named "CH9a". Once your project comes up, please choose "CH9a properties" from the "Project" menu. (Please note the name of the project before the word "properties". If you named your project something different than "CH9a", your menu item will be different than my example.) We are not going to go into detail about the various settings available here. Frankly, there are too many to cover now, plus a lot of them have to do with things which we are not ready to deal with. For now, we are only interested in one very specific setting. On the left hand side of the Properties page are a set of sub-option headings. Of these, the second one from the top is called "Build", so please find it and click on it. When it comes up, look for the "Advanced" button at the bottom of the window (Figure 56) and click on it.

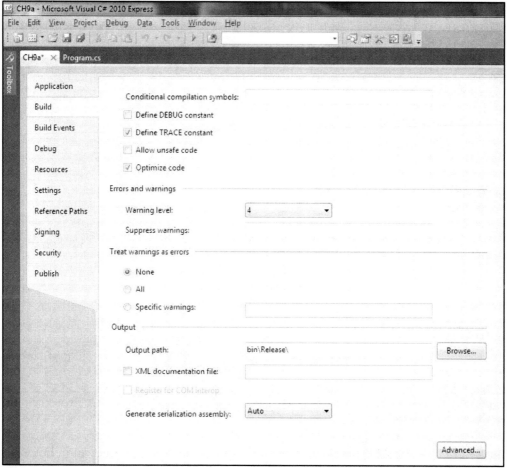

Figure 56: The Project Properties has an Advanced button that can pull up the overflow options

When the advanced options dialog displays (Figure 57), note the checkbox labeled as "Check for arithmetic overflow/underflow".

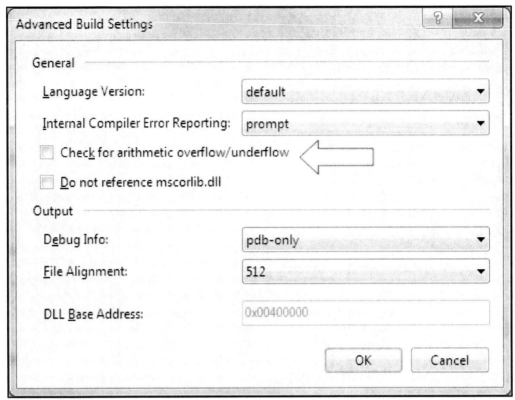

Figure 57: If the "Check for arithmetic overflow/underflow" is not checked then the numbers overflow without raising an error

Make sure this checkbox is unchecked, such as in the figure above, and click OK. This returns you to the Build page of the project's properties. Since all changes take effect immediately, there is no Save or Cancel button. You can leave this page open, or close it via the little X at the top right of the pages tab.

Now that we have our project and set the options as needed, let's put some code into Main!

```
byte num1 = 254, num2 = 1;

Console.WriteLine("Before: Num1 = {0}", num1);
num1 += 2;
Console.WriteLine("After: Num1 = {0}", num1);

Console.WriteLine("Before: Num2 = {0}", num2);
num2 -= 2;
Console.WriteLine("After: Num2 = {0}", num2);
```

```
Console.ReadLine();
```

This is very simple code, and by now, every line should be perfectly understandable, so I am not going to go into any detail on them. Before we run the program, let's try to guess what results we expect. Both variables are of type byte, so they have a valid range of 0 to 255. In the first example, we set num1 to 254 and then increase its value by 2, which normally would be equal to 256 – a value that is above the range of our byte sized variable. The second example is similar, but with a starting value of 1 and then we subtract from it 2, which normally would leave us with a result of -1 – again, outside of the range of a byte variable.

So, what will C# do with these examples? When I first saw this presented to me, my reaction was simple; the program will crash as soon as we try to exceed the value of the data type. "Nope", my teacher said, "it will not". Ok, my second guess (and boy, was it a guess this time!), was that the variable will just get maxed out and remain there. In other words, I guessed that num1 would become 255 and num2 would become 0; the thinking being since the data type byte cannot exceed those values, it has to stop there. Ok, enough guessing, run the program and see what pops out!

Wait, what was that? How did num1 become 0 and num2 become 255?! Before we go into that, modify your program: Add 3 to num1 and subtract 3 from num2. Run your program and check out these results. Hmmm, now num1 ends up at 1 and num2 at 254! Ok, that is strange.

Well, yes it is, but it is also considered normal. What happened is that the byte data type got respectively over-, and under-flowed. Think of the data type's range as if it were a clock. What happens to the clock when it goes from 12:59 to 1:00? We simply have reached the end of our valid range of values and we started all over again. C# does exactly the same thing. Instead of going from 12:59 to 1:00, it went from 255 to 0 and then up from there (known as an overflow) or from 0 to 255 and down from there (an underflow). (Figure 58)

Figure 58: Think of a byte like a clock with 255 numbers. If you tick past 255, you then overflow to the first number, or 0.

Now, this kind of behavior is quite strange for anyone that has programmed in another language; or even for the C# folks from before the 2005 version of Visual Studio. All other languages would generate an error instead of allowing this overflow/underflow situation. The default setting for Visual Studio, before 2005, was to also treat this as an error.

If you prefer, or need, for this to still remain a checked error condition you have two options. The first is in that dialog box I showed you under the Project properties menu (Figure 57). By turning this checkbox on, your current project will no longer allow a variable to flip around like this but will rather cause an error. Go ahead, change this setting in your properties page and run your program again. If you do, you will get the following crash and error message (Figure 59).

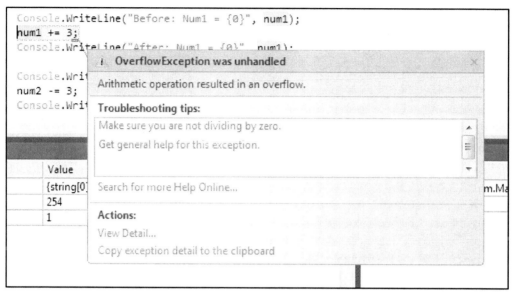

Figure 59: Error message for an overflow with the "Check for arithmetic overflow/underflow" flag turned off

Notice how the line where we attempt to overflow the variable is highlighted and the error tells us that an "Overflow Exception" has occurred.

Now, as weird as it sounds, there are cases when having an overflow/underflow not generate an error is a good thing; but, you might have one special case in your program where it is not such a good thing. Turns out, there is a way to ask the compiler to ignore the project overflow/underflow setting within a specified area in your code. Before I show you, return to your project's properties and turn off the overflow/underflow error checking (see Figure 57 for a reminder). Once you have made that change, run your code and verify that there is no error generated. Good. Now we want the overflow for num1 to not crash, but we do want the underflow for num2 to cause an error. Change your code to look like this:

```
byte num1 = 254, num2 = 1;

Console.WriteLine("Before: Num1 = {0}", num1);
    num1 += 3;
Console.WriteLine("After: Num1 = {0}", num1);

Console.WriteLine("Before: Num2 = {0}", num2);
```

```
checked
{
    num2 -= 3;
}
Console.WriteLine("After: Num2 = {0}", num2);

Console.ReadLine();
```

Notice the change? I put in the keyword "checked" and then wrapped the line(s) that I want overflow/underflow to be enforced on in a set of curly braces. If you run your program now, the error will occur only when we try to underflow num2, but the overflow of num1 will not get so much as a peep from the compiler. So, if the keyword "checked" causes an overflow to be dealt with when it would normally be allowed, what about the opposite? What if the project already is set to check for and not allow overflow/underflow, but there is one location where I am ok with it happening? For this, use the keyword "unchecked" and wrap the line(s) you do not want to be overflow/underflow checked with curly braces!

Variable Lifetime (aka scoping)

So far, we have converted our data types and dealt with overflow and underflow situations. What else do we need to know or worry about with regard to variables? Ah, we saved the best for last!

On the TV show, "*Star Trek: The Next Generation*", they had something called the holodeck. It was a room which acted like a 3D projection reality video game, where the computer could create any environment you wanted. You could find yourself on a ship full of pirates or walking through a meadow, depending on which program you loaded in. In one episode, the door to the holodeck was opened up while the program was still running and one of the projected people tried to walk outside. As soon as they went past the range of the projection system, they disappeared. For them, the holodeck was their only scope, the only place where they could exist. Real people could go anywhere in the ship, both in and outside of the holodeck, so their scope, that of the entire ship was much larger.

Let me ask you something. How long does a variable last? Nope, this is not a trick question. If you answered "for as long as I need them", then, based on our examples to date, you would be right. However, as with most things in life, the rules are not that simple. Actually, variables have very specific lifetimes, or scope, as they are officially known. Simply put, a variable exists and is available only within the block of code in which it was defined and any child blocks within. Such a simple statement contains so much potential for problems, if not understood fully.

Until now, all of our programs have been small and have been written between the curly braces of the Main method, so this problem has not come up. As we move outside of the Main method, the concept of variable scoping will become very critical. While I am not ready to delve into methods yet, it turns out that we can create the variable scoping situation from within Main.

Let's start a new project, called "CH9b", and use the following code. Please, be careful, this code will have a lot of extra curly braces and they are all important! If you miss just one, the compiler will give you all kinds of errors! In fact they are so important that instead of just showing you what should go into Main, as I normally have done, I am going to type in all of Main. I have also put in comments to show the start and end of each block of code. You do not have to type the comments in, but it might help to understand having these block elements visually marked.

```
static void Main(string[] args)
{ // start of Main block
    int a = 5;
    Console.WriteLine("Block 1: a={0}", a);

    { // start of 2nd block
        int b = 6;
        Console.WriteLine("\tBlock 2: a={0}, b={1}", a,
b);

        { // start of 3rd block
            int c = 7;
            Console.WriteLine("\t\tBlock 3: a={0}, b={1},
c={2}", a, b, c);

        } // end of 3rd block
    } // end of 2nd block

    { // start of 4th block
        int d = 8;
```

```
        Console.WriteLine("\tBlock 4: a={0}, d={1}", a,
d);

    } // end of 4th block

    Console.ReadLine();
} // end of Main block
```

To confirm your code, take a look at Figure 60.

```
Program.cs ×

CH9b.Program                                              ▼  Main(string[] args)
    using System.Text;

    namespace CH9b
    {
        class Program
        {
            static void Main(string[] args)
            { // start of Main block
                int a = 5;
                Console.WriteLine("Block 1: a={0}", a);

                { // start of 2nd block
                    int b = 6;
                    Console.WriteLine("\tBlock 2: a={0}, b={1}", a, b);

                    { // start of 3rd block
                        int c = 7;
                        Console.WriteLine("\t\tBlock 3: a={0}, b={1}, c={2}", a, b, c);
                    } // end of 3rd block
                } // end of 2nd block

                { // start of 4th block
                    int d = 8;
                    Console.WriteLine("\tBlock 4: a={0}, d={1}", a, d);
                } // end of 4th block

                Console.ReadLine();
            } // end of Main block
        }
    }
```

Figure 60: Several code blocks are nested inside other code blocks, giving different scope lifetimes to your variables

Yep, that is a lot of curly braces! Let's carefully step through all of this, since there are some very critical concepts here that, if you do not fully understand, will cause you a lot of errors and grief in the future.

By the way, besides the comments I put in to mark the start and end of each code block, Visual Studio also can be quite helpful. Whenever you highlight either the starting or ending curly brace, Visual Studio will automatically highlight its corresponding pair. For example, if you click on the opening curly brace right under the Main declaration, notice how both it and the curly brace at the end of the Main block get highlighted. Try this with some of the other curly braces as well.

For our program, the main parent code block is the one defined by the curly braces that make up the Main method and which I have labeled as the start and end of the Main block. Within this block, live two additional code blocks, specifically the second and the fourth code block. What about the third code block? Ah, that one is the child of the second block. Each block of code can define its own set of variables that the block(s) outside it cannot see. So, the variable c, which is defined within the third block, is unknown to any of the other blocks of code. Since the third block has no child blocks, any variables it defines are only visible to the third block itself.

Now take a look at the second block. This block of code defines a variable called b which it can see, but is also visible within the 3rd code block. Why? Simple, the third code block is a child of the second code block – children inherit the variables of their parents. Ah, in that case the second code block, which is a child of the Main code block, is able to see variable a, which is defined in its parent, and variable b, which it defined itself, but cannot see variable c, since that one comes from its child block.

What about the fourth code block? That block of code is within the Main block, so it inherits variable a from there, and of course can see variable d which is defined within the fourth code block itself. Can the fourth code block see any of the variables defined in the second code block; after all, they are both children of the Main block? No, while it is true that they are both children of the Main code block, they cannot see the variables of other code blocks at their level. (Think back to the holodeck example from Star Trek.) Think of the second and the fourth block as siblings, and as those of us with siblings know, we do not share our toys! The projected people in holodeck A will never have access to the projected people on holodeck B.

Of these code blocks, the one which has access to the most variables is the third code block, which can see its own variable (c), the one of its parent (b) and of its grandparent (a).

All of the above can be nicely summed up by three simple one-liners:

1. Children blocks can see variables of their parent blocks
2. Parent blocks cannot see children block variables
3. Siblings cannot see each others' variables

Once you understand the rules about which variables are visible to which block of code, another element arises that can be both beneficial and, if not dealt with carefully, very confusing. While within a given block of code you cannot have two variables with the same name, you can use the same variable names in blocks which do not have access to each other. So, in the fourth code block I could have create variables b and c without any problems. However, a variable named a would not be allowed, since that name was inherited from its parent.

While our example is forced in order to show this concept, there are cases when something like this does actually happen. Think of the for, while, and do while loops that we have already covered. Each of these loops uses curly braces to hold the code to be looped, thereby creating a child code block. Any variables we define in these blocks are not visible outside of them and therefore not usable.

This is most easily demonstrated using the for loop, which commonly defines a new variable to handle the loop count. While the for loop is running, the counter variable is visible and usable, but once the loop ends and you are outside of the code block, that variable and its value are gone. Try it! Here is the code in which I first demonstrated the for loop back in Chapter 5.

```
Console.WriteLine("Before the loop!");

for (int i = 1; i <= 10; i++)
{
    Console.WriteLine("Pass {0} through the loop",
i);
}

// the variable i cannot be accessed here

Console.WriteLine("After the loop!");

Console.ReadLine();
```

Remember this? Within the body of the for loop, we are able to use the variable i and display its value, but what if we try to print out the value of i in that message after the loop? If you try, you will get an error message that "The name i does not exist in the current context". In other words, outside of the for loop block, the variable i no longer exists and it cannot be used.

This context message deals with what is called the scope of the variable. The scope of the variable deals with when it is in memory, or how long it lives. C# does what is called "garbage collection" automatically. This is a fancy way of saying that when the compiler notices that a variable has gone out of scope, it automatically releases the memory where that variable lived. This allows other processes to use the memory as needed.

With many other programming languages you, as the developer, are responsible for not only declaring a variable before using it (to reserve the memory for it), but also for releasing it when you are done with it in order to free memory. It is a common programming mistake, in such languages, to declare a whole set of variables but forget to release them. This means the memory is held for as long as your program runs.

That's fine for a short program that might run for a few seconds or minutes, but can you imagine a long running program just grabbing memory whenever it needs it and never letting it go? It would not take long before there would not be any free memory left, either for itself or for any other running application, which would cause the system to crash. This is commonly known as a memory leak. Since C# automatically takes care of this as variables go out of scope, memory leaks are quite rare with C# programs.[18]

Struct and Enum

While struct and enum may sound like some exotic and foreign names ("I'd like to introduce you to my uncle, Mr. Enum and his lovely wife Struct."), they are actually C# keywords with the ability to create customized data types. Even though C# has given us plenty of data types to cover pretty much any sort of data you can imagine, there are times when you might need something special.

For example, if you are working on a mapping program, you might have to store coordinates in the form of latitude and longitude. By themselves, both a latitude

---

[18] There are still times when you, as a programmer, can reserve memory in a way that the C# garbage collector cannot clean up after you, but that is for a much later part of this book to deal with.

and a longitude can be expressed as a floating point number[19], but you rarely work with just a latitude or just a longitude value on its own. So, how would you make sure you always keep these two values as a single pair? I suppose that you could use an array, but that would get quite unwieldy after a while.

Instead we can create a `struct`, which is a user defined data type, but one which is made up of system defined data types. You could even throw a string value in there to store the name of the location. Hmmm, I like that idea – let's code it! Please start a new project, named "CH9c".

Normally we would place all of our code between the Main method's curly braces – in fact the code to process the program itself will still go in there. However both the `struct` and the `enum` definitions go outside of Main into the application's Class definition. (We haven't talked about Classes or Namespaces yet, they are just around the corner. So for now don't worry about it and go with the flow!) Therefore, I am going to give you this program in two pieces. This first part, which defines our custom data type, has to go before the Main method's declaration but after the opening curly brace of the Class.

```
struct Location
{
    public string name;
    public float latitude, longitude;
}
```

Finally the actual code of our program goes into the Main method as usual.

```
static void Main(string[] args)
{
    Location myLoc;

    Console.Write("Enter a location name: ");
    myLoc.name = Console.ReadLine();

    Console.Write("Enter latitude: ");
    myLoc.latitude =
float.Parse(Console.ReadLine());

    Console.Write("Enter longitude: ");
```

---

[19] Even though geographic coordinates are normally expressed as degrees, minutes and seconds, there is a way to convert and work with them as a decimal value.

```
    myLoc.longitude =
float.Parse(Console.ReadLine());

    Console.WriteLine("The {0} can be found at {1}
Latitude by {2} Longitude",
    myLoc.name, myLoc.latitude, myLoc.longitude);

    Console.ReadLine();
}
```

If you put all the parts into the right places, you screen should look like this (Figure 61):

```
using System.Text;

namespace CH9c
{
    class Program
    {
        struct Location
        {
            public string name;
            public float latitude, longitude;
        }

        static void Main(string[] args)
        {
            Location myLoc;

            Console.Write("Enter a location name: ");
            myLoc.name = Console.ReadLine();

            Console.Write("Enter latitude: ");
            myLoc.latitude = float.Parse(Console.ReadLine());

            Console.Write("Enter longitude: ");
            myLoc.longitude = float.Parse(Console.ReadLine());

            Console.WriteLine("The {0} can be found at {1} Latitude by {2} Longitude",
                myLoc.name, myLoc.latitude, myLoc.longitude);

            Console.ReadLine();
        }
    }
}
```

Figure 61: The Program class contains the Struct and Main method. Struct is not inside Main!

The first item of interest, in this program, is the `struct` definition. It is a pretty standard construct, the keyword `struct` followed by a name after which there is a list of standard data types which become the members of this struct enclosed in curly braces.

So, what is that whole "public" stuff in front of the data type keywords? Since C# is an object oriented programming language, it has a concept of permissions which defines which elements of an object are visible to the code trying to access the block. We will be covering the different access levels to objects in a bit, but for now, if you leave the keyword public off, when you try to use the members of this struct they will not be available.

Just defining an object does not really mean much by itself. After all, I can describe to you what the perfect Ferrari looks, feels and smells like, but that doesn't mean that you actually own a Ferrari. So, in our Main program we need to define a variable, in this case myLoc, to be an actual instance of the type Location, which is the name of our structure. Notice that there is nothing special about using a user defined struct, it looks just like an ordinary variable declaration. While there is nothing unusual about the way we declare it, there is something a bit different about how we can use it. Since this variable is made up of multiple parts, we need a way to be able to address the individual components, and for that we use the period. This is exactly the same way that we access the Write or ReadLine methods of the Console object.

```
Console.Write("Enter latitude: ");
myLoc.latitude = float.Parse(Console.ReadLine());
```

So, in our code, we are able to write to, or read from, the individual elements of the myLoc structure by putting a dot after the name and then specifying the individual element. In fact, the IntelliSense of Visual Studio is smart enough that after you type myLoc and press the period key, the list that pops up will include each of the member elements! (If you are not seeing the member elements in that list, check that you have the public keyword before each of the declarations in the struct definition.)

Our example struct currently has three members, each of which is a default C# data type. However, the members of a struct are not limited to only the default data types, but can be any data type that C# knows about. Once we define a struct, enum or class, it becomes a known data type and can be used.

The other way to create custom variables is through the use of the enum keyword. This is a little different and its purpose may not be immediately apparent, but it will become so as you progress through your programming skill. Unlike a struct variable which is capable of holding discreet bits of data, an enum actually is data, or if you prefer, it is a way of holding larger bits of data represented by smaller numeric replacements.

Probably the easiest example I can give is to use the months of the year. If you see a date in which the month is listed as 4, you know that they are referring to April. So, why use 4 instead of April? Well for one, it takes up less space to store a 4, just a single byte of data, than it does to store the string "April", which is 5 bytes of data. Wouldn't it be nice if we could get the computer to know that when we say 4 we actually mean April? That is exactly what an enum structure does – it equates a set of larger values to a sequentially incremented list of numbers. Let's put this to code and examine it further.

Start a new project, "CH9d" and enter this enum definition in the same place that we put the struct definition in our previous project.

```
enum Months { January, February, March, April,
    May, June, July, August, September,
    October, November, December };
```

Similar to the struct definition, we start with a keyword, this time it is enum, followed by a name. After the name, we have a set of larger values enclosed by curly braces and separated by commas. No quotes are necessary, since the enum definition assumes all of its members will be strings.

Now for the actual code part inserted into Main:

```
int theMonth;

Console.Write("Enter a number (1-12): ");
theMonth = int.Parse(Console.ReadLine());

Console.WriteLine("Month {0} is called {1}",
                theMonth, (Months)theMonth);

Console.ReadLine();
```

When all done, your screen should look like Figure 62:

```
namespace CH9d
{
    class Program
    {
        enum Months
        {
            January, February, March, April, May,
            June, July, August, September, October, November, December
        };

        static void Main(string[] args)
        {
            int theMonth;

            Console.Write("Enter a number (1-12): ");
            theMonth = int.Parse(Console.ReadLine());

            Console.WriteLine("Month {0} is called {1}", theMonth, (Months)theMonth);

            Console.ReadLine();
        }
    }
}
```

Figure 62: Your enum called Months, can be called on by its numeric position

Pretty simple. We declare a simple int variable, ask the user for a number between 1 and 12 and then display that number and the month name to which it corresponds. To get just the number value out, we simply use the variable name like we have done dozens of times before, but to take advantage of the enum we cast the number to the name of the enum structure. Run your program and enter a number.

Whoa, that can't be right! (Figure 63)

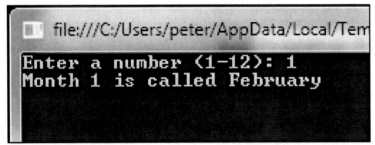

Figure 63: Since structs start at 0, the number 1 entry will show February

I'm pretty sure that the first month of the year is actually January, and a quick check of my code indicates that I did type January in first. So what went wrong? Remember, computers do not count from 1 as we do, they prefer to start at 0. In other words, all of the returned months are going to be off by one number. Luckily, there is an easy solution to this. In the enum definition, we can provide any element with a fixed number and each following element will increase from there. To fix your code, change the enum definition to look like this (notice the = 1 addition):

```
enum Months { January = 1, February, March, April,
    May, June, July, August, September,
    October, November, December};
```

Try your program again. Ah, that's better!

Actually, the enum construct is quite flexible about its numbering. To any of the values within the curly braces, you can assign a specific value. The following values will simply continue to increment from that point on, until they come to the end of the curly braces or to another value assignment. By the way, it is perfectly allowable to assign numeric values to each individual value and in any order you wish.

Quick question. Who is wondering what would happen if I entered a value outside of the range of the enum structure? In other words, I have twelve elements defined, so any number between 1 and 12 will result in a value, but what if I enter 13 or higher? Since there are only twelve values, the cast will not result in any other value and it will simply print out the number as you entered it.

Points to Ponder

- There are two ways to convert data types: implicitly and explicitly
- An implicit conversion is one that can be safely done automatically, such as going from a smaller data type to a larger one. (i.e. byte to int)
- Explicit conversion is one that is forced by you because it cannot be safely done automatically (int to byte)
- Explicit conversion is done by a process called casting
- Going past the upper limit of a data type is called overflow, and going under the lower limit is called underflow
- Depending on the settings of your Visual Studio, an overflow or underflow can either generate an exception error, or the compiler can handle it on its own

- You can use the keywords checked and unchecked to force or ignore overflow/underflow conditions, regardless of the setting in Visual Studio
- Variables only remain in memory until the block of code they live within is finished being executed
- A block of code is delimited by the use of curly braces
- You can make up your own data types by the use of the struct and enum keywords
- Struct, which stands for structure, allows you create a data type which is made up of one or more basic data types
- Enum, which stands for enumeration, is a special data type where you can have a sequence of terms be equated to numeric values

Challenge

1. Create an enum structure with the names of the days of the week, starting at one. Ask the user for a number and convert that number into the actual name of the day.
2. Create a struct to store a person's first name, last name and phone number. Use another struct for the phone number! (In other words, embed one struct within another.) Populate the fields with data then display the result

Review Quiz

1.) Take a look at this code fragment:

```
int I1 = 101;
byte B1;
```

How can you assign I1 into B1?
- O a. B1 = I1;
- O b. I1 = B1;
- O c. B1 = (int)I1;
- O d. B1 = (byte)I1;
- O e. I1 = (byte)B1;

2.) Take a look at this code fragment:

```
byte Ct = 101;
int ttl;
```

What is the shortest way to assign the value of Ct to ttl?
- O a. ttl = Ct;
- O b. Ct = ttl;
- O c. ttl = (int)Ct;
- O d. ttl = (byte)Ct;
- O e. Ct = (byte) ttl;

3.) How do you create an enumeration of months of the year?
- O a. enum Calendar
     {Jan,Feb,Mar,Apr,May,Jun,Jul,Aug,Sep,Oct,Nov,Dec}
- O b. Calendar enum
     {Jan,Feb,Mar,Apr,May,Jun,Jul,Aug,Sep,Oct,Nov,Dec}
- O c. enum string Calendar
     {Jan,Feb,Mar,Apr,May,Jun,Jul,Aug,Sep,Oct,Nov,Dec}
- O d. Calendar string enum
     {Jan,Feb,Mar,Apr,May,Jun,Jul,Aug,Sep,Oct,Nov,Dec}

4.) Using the enumeration from the previous question you have written the following line of code:

```
Calendar myBirthMonth;
```

What are 2 ways you could refer to the month of Feb?
- ☐ a. myBirthMonth = Calendar.Feb;
- ☐ b. myBirthMonth = (Calendar)2;
- ☐ c. myBirthMonth = (Calendar)1;
- ☐ d. myBirthMonth = Calendar(1);

5.) What are two kinds of user defined types?
- ☐ a. int
- ☐ b. enum
- ☐ c. byte
- ☐ d. struct

6.) You want to declare an integer that does not hold negative numbers and will not go beyond 65,535. You decide to declare an unsigned short integer with the ushort keyword. What class is this keyword using?
- O a. System.Int16
- O b. System.UInt16
- O c. System.Int32
- O d. System.UInt32
- O e. System.String

Notes

Chapter 10 – Methods: Part 1

Without doubt, the most important part of any programming language is the ability to create methods[20]. In short, a method is a chunk of code that you can refer to, by name, as many times as needed. An example of a method, in real life, would be like asking your kids to take out the garbage. To actually take out the garbage, you have to first go around the house and empty out all of the garbage cans, pull the garbage out from under the kitchen sink and then carry it all down to the can sitting outside by the side of the house.

Yet, you did not have to specify all of those steps individually (the body of the method), you simply asked for the garbage to be taken out (the name of the method). Of course, before you could ask your kids to take out the garbage you had to first teach them. Once the method has been created (or the kids taught the method), all you have to do is invoke the "Take out the garbage" instruction again and the method will be completed by your kids, without the need for any further instruction.

Methods can operate on their own, take incoming data on which to work, and return a result. While we have not created any methods so far, or even really talked about them, we have actually been using them all along. You can always recognize a call to a method by the parentheses that come after its name and which contain the data upon which you want the method to work. Even if the method does not need or take any incoming parameters, you still need to provide the parentheses. Looking back over all the code we have written so far, every `Write`, `WriteLine`, and `ReadLine` has been a call to a method. In fact, even the Main method where all of our code has gone is a method. However it is called by the C# compiler, rather than by us.

So what does a method look like? Here is the syntax definition of a method:

```
<access modifier> <return type> name([<type>
<name>])
{
    <code to execute>
}
```

---

[20] Known as functions in most other languages, and occasionally referred to as such even in C# circles.

Well, that doesn't look too bad! In fact, if you compare this template to the Main method that we have seen at the top of all of our programs, you will see all of these elements represented. Let's cover all of these elements one by one.

- Access modifier: We have used this before when we declared the member variables for our `struct` and `class` examples. Basically this tells the compiler from where the method can be called. Common values here are "`static`", "`private`", "`internal`", "`protected`" and "`public`". Actually, you may not see `private` very often, since it is the default permission setting, but it is considered good practice to use it. (Technically `static` is not an access modifier, it is a method type, but that is a bit too complex at this stage.)
- Return type: If your method will return a value, the compiler needs to know what that data type is going to be. You can use any of the built-in data types or any other objects the system knows about – yes, this does include any `structs` and classes that you have defined. If your method will not return any value, then you have to use the keyword `void` to let the compiler know that as well.
- Name: This is the name of your method. It is generally recommended to use PascalCasing[21] for method names. The same naming rules apply here as for variables.
- Type and Name: For each incoming parameter, you need to define the data type of the variable as well as a local name. We will talk about this quite a bit.
- Code to execute: Of course a method is pointless without some code to execute, so that follows between the curly braces.

To demonstrate how methods work, let's rewrite our very first program, the Hello World from Chapter 1, using a method. This is not really the most efficient way of doing things, but it does let you see how methods are set up and used. Please start a new project called "CH10a". When ready, mark the ending curly braces for the Main method, the class Program and the namespace CH10a. (Generally, marking the end of your various code blocks like this is frowned upon in the world of professional programming. However, when learning, it helps to keep things in their correct places.)

---

[21] As a reminder, Pascal Casing means you capitalize the first letter of the word(s) which make up your variable name (for example: MyVariable). The other naming convention is Camel Casing, where the first letter of the first word remains lower case (for example: myVariable).

We are going to write this program starting with the method first – the reason for which you will see shortly. Find the curly brace that ends the Main method, put your cursor on the end of that line and press enter twice. Then copy the following code in:

```
static void Greeting()
{
    Console.WriteLine("Hello World!");
} // end of Greeting
```

This is our very short and simple method. Notice how I have the keyword "void" in the front, indicating that this method will not return a value. Also note the parentheses after the method name are empty, meaning no parameters are coming into the method. The keyword "static" at the very beginning is required so we can access this method directly from the Main method, which is also marked as static. (Much more on this later.) When you are ready, type the following lines into the Main method:

```
Greeting();

Console.ReadLine();
```

If you did everything correctly, your code should look like Figure 64.

```
namespace CH10a
{
    class Program
    {
        static void Main(string[] args)
        {
            Greeting();

            Console.ReadLine();
        }

        static void Greeting()
        {
            Console.WriteLine("Hello World!");
        } // end of Greeting
    } // end of class Program
} // end of Namespace CH10a
```

Figure 64: The Main method is calling the Greeting method

So, why did I have you create the Greeting method first? When you were typing in the code for the Main method and started to type the word "Greeting", did you notice how IntelliSense popped up with the Greeting method listed? IntelliSense does not just know about the core syntax of C#, but it also recognizes methods, classes and other objects that you create and they all show up in that little popup dialog. As our methods get more complex and we start putting in parameters, return types, etc., the IntelliSense box will even show those parameters. For now, go ahead and run your program.

Rather underwhelming, isn't it? This may not be very exciting but it does let you see how methods work. When the program runs, the first line of code it sees is `Greeting()`, which tells it to find and call a method by that name. So, the compiler jumps to the Greeting method and executes the line(s) of code it sees there – which in our case is just a simple `WriteLine`. Once all of the lines in the method have finished executing, the compiler jumps back to where it was called and continues on to the next line, which is the `ReadLine` to pause our program. Simple, right?

Method Parameters

A method without any parameters or a return value is quite limited in what it can do. Let's take our Greeting method and modify it to take the name of the user we want to greet, and then use that name within the greeting string. To do this, we are going to have to change two things: first the Greeting method will need the parameter type and local name put inside the parentheses, and second the call to the Greeting method from inside Main will have to be modified to provide this information. Change your program to look like Figure 65.

```
namespace CH10a
{
    class Program
    {
        static void Main(string[] args)
        {
            Greeting("Joe");

            Console.ReadLine();
        }

        static void Greeting(string userName)
        {
            Console.WriteLine("Hello {0}!", userName);
        } // end of Greeting
    } // end of class Program
} // end of Namespace CH10a
```

Figure 65: The Greeting method takes a string parameter and uses it in that block

Now when we call the Greeting method in Main, we need to provide a string value. In our example, I simply typed the value in directly, so the quotes around the name are required. If you leave the quotes off, the compiler will think you are referring to a variable name and will complain when it cannot find it. To receive this value, the declaration of Greeting needs two items inside the parentheses. The first is the data type of which we are going to receive, which we know is a string, followed by the name of the local variable. Think of this as declaring a variable, which we have done quite a few times now, but the assignment of the variable's value comes from an outside source, namely the method call. That variable has a scope of the entire method, so we can use that variable anywhere inside the method. To use it, I just put it onto the end of the WriteLine. Go ahead and run the program to see how it behaves now.

You do not have to provide a value directly when calling a method. In fact the majority of the time, the parameter sent to a method will come from a variable within the calling routine. Let's modify our program to first ask for the name of the user from within the Main method, and then pass that value to the Greeting method for our friendly greeting. Change your code to look like Figure 66.

```
namespace CH10a
{
    class Program
    {
        static void Main(string[] args)
        {
            Console.Write("What is your name? ");
            string theName = Console.ReadLine();

            Greeting(theName);

            Console.ReadLine();
        }

        static void Greeting(string userName)
        {
            Console.WriteLine("Hello {0}!", userName);
        } // end of Greeting
    } // end of class Program
} // end of Namespace CH10a
```

Figure 66: A string variable is passed into the method, which satisfies the string parameter

No changes were needed to the Greeting method; however, we added a few lines to the top of the Main method. We simply prompt the user for their name, declare a new string variable called theName and assign the text entered to it. Pretty standard stuff so far... We then take the variable theName, and use it as the parameter to pass into the Greeting method.

There is a very important concept to understand here, the name of the variable that holds our username in the Main method is theName, but by the time it gets to the Greeting method it is called userName. This is not an error. These two variables are not the same! Let me repeat this point – the two variables are not connected to each other, rather they are completely independent.

When the Greeting method is called from Main, the compiler takes the value of the theName variable and copies it into the variable userName which is defined by the Greeting method. Think of this like a fax machine. When you fax a sheet of paper to a friend, you still have the original paper in your hand, the fax machine has made a copy of it and your friend is holding that copy. Upon receiving the fax, both sheets are identical but each is a separate physical entity. If either one of you makes a change to your respective sheet, you write a comment into the margin for example, that change will not be on the other person's sheet. It is the same here.

This concept is so important that I think we should explore it further. Let's modify our program in both Main and in the Greeting method to demonstrate this. In Main, we are going to display the name the user enters both before and after calling the Greeting method. Inside greeting, we are going to display the name we received from Main, change it, and then display our greeting. Here is what the new Main should look like:

```
static void Main(string[] args)
{
    Console.Write("What is your name: ");
    string theName = Console.ReadLine();

    Console.WriteLine("Main: Before greeting,
theName is {0}", theName);

    Greeting(theName);

    Console.WriteLine("Main: After greeting, theName
is {0}", theName);

    Console.ReadLine();
} // end of Main
```

And here is what the new Greeting should look like:

```
static void Greeting(string userName)
{
    Console.WriteLine("Greeting: Name received:
{0}", userName);

    userName = "Peter";

    Console.WriteLine("Hello {0}!", userName);
} // end of Greeting
```

Run your program. Enter any name you would like, as long as it is not Peter, since we are going to change the userName variable in Greeting to that name. Your output should look like Figure 67:

Figure 67: Changing the parameter value from Joe to Peter does not change the variable

Even though I have changed the value of the variable `userName` in the `Greeting` method, that change did not get carried back to the `theName` variable used in the Main method. Sending of variable values from one method to another like this is called "passing by value", which means we simply copied the value of the variable in the calling method (Main) to a variable in the called method (greeting).

Return Value

The concept of a return value in a method is quite easy to understand. Think of a method like an ATM machine. The inputs of the ATM machine are your debit card, your PIN number and how much cash you would like. Based on these three pieces of information, the ATM gives you the cash, the return value!

Now we know how to send a value into a method, but how about getting a value back? This is both quite simple and very common. The best way to demonstrate this is with a new project, called "CH10b". In this project, we are going to ask the user for two numbers from the Main method, then pass those numbers to a method that will add them and return the result. Back in the Main method, we are going to capture that result and display it to the user.

Once your new project is ready, enter this code into your Main method:

```
static void Main(string[] args)
{
    int firstNum, secondNum, result;

    Console.Write("Please enter the 1st number: ");
```

```
        firstNum = int.Parse(Console.ReadLine());

        Console.Write("Please enter the 2nd number: ");
        secondNum = int.Parse(Console.ReadLine());

        result = Adder(firstNum, secondNum);

        Console.WriteLine("{0} + {1} = {2}", firstNum,
                        secondNum, result);

        Console.ReadLine();
    }
```

Finally, use this code to create a method called Adder (remember to place this method after the closing curly brace of Main):

```
static int Adder(int num1, int num2)
{
    int theAnswer;

    theAnswer = num1 + num2;

    return (theAnswer);
} // end of Adder method
```

If you got everything in the right place, your window should look like Figure 68:

```
namespace CH10b
{
    class Program
    {
        static void Main(string[] args)
        {
            int firstNum, secondNum, result;

            Console.Write("Please enter the 1st number: ");
            firstNum = int.Parse(Console.ReadLine());

            Console.Write("Please enter the 2nd number: ");
            secondNum = int.Parse(Console.ReadLine());

            result = Adder(firstNum, secondNum);

            Console.Write("{0} + {1} = {2}", firstNum, secondNum, result);

            Console.ReadLine();
        } // end of Main method

        static int Adder(int num1, int num2)
        {
            int theAnswer;

            theAnswer = num1 + num2;

            return (theAnswer);
        } // end of Adder method
    } // end of class Program
} // end of namespace CH10b
```

Figure 68: The Main method will call on the Adder method and will expect an integer as the return value

Try your program to understand what it does, and then let's review it.

Most of the code in the Main method is pretty standard; the only new item is the call to the Adder method. Notice how we have the two numbers inside the parentheses, which is what the Adder method expects. Of more interest is the variable result, which is set to be equal to the output value of the Adder method. Hmmm, the method has a value we can assign? Yes, so let's see how that is done.

Check out the declaration of the Adder method. This time, instead of the keyword void in front, we now have int. This tells the compiler that when it is finished, the Adder method will return a value, specifically an int, back to whatever called it. Since we promised the compiler that this function will return something, we had better deliver on it!

Inside `Adder`, the first two lines are pretty standard, but the last line is new. The keyword `return` fulfills the promise that was made to the compiler on the declaration line, namely to return a value, specifically of type `int`. What we are returning is the value inside the parentheses of the keyword `return`, which is the value of the variable `theAnswer`.

Back in the Main method, this return value is handed to the variable `result`. Then it, along with the two user entered numbers, are displayed. Getting a return value out of a method is very useful, but has one very large limitation – you can only return one value per method. There is a solution to this, but we'll save that for another chapter.

Points to Ponder

- A method is a set of commands turned into a single block of named code that can be called from other blocks of code
- Methods are sometimes known as functions
- Methods can take 0 or more incoming variables as input
- Methods can optionally return a single value. The data type of this return value has to be declared during the method's declaration.
- Methods live inside classes
- Methods have an access modifier which determines from where they can be called
- When calling a method, you use the name followed by a set of parentheses. Any parameters to be passed into the method are listed inside the parentheses.
- The values passed into the method are copies, so any changes to them inside the method will not be reflected in the calling routine

Challenge

1. Take your last project and create additional methods that subtract, multiply or divide the two numbers passed into it. In the divide method, check that the second number is not 0, since dividing by 0 is an illegal

mathematical concept. If the second number is a 0, just return back a 0. Call each method with some values and display the results to the screen.

Review Quiz

1.) You want to design a method with as few parameters as possible. What is the lowest number of parameters a method can be designed with?
- O a. 0
- O b. 1
- O c. 2
- O d. 8
- O e. 32

2.) You don't want your method to have a return value. What keyword do you use?
- O a. Empty
- O b. None
- O c. void
- O d. int
- O e. bool

3.) You have the following code:

```
int result;
double Num1 = 7.77;
byte Num2 = 5;

result = Adder(Num1, Num2);
```

The method runs without error. What is the Adder method's return type set to?
- O a. double
- O b. void
- O c. int
- O d. bool

4.) You have the following code:

```
static void Main()
{
    string v1 = "Green Light"
    Greeting(v1);
    Console.WriteLine("Answer is: {0}", v1);}
} // end of Main

static void Greeting(string userMessage)
{
    userMessage = "Red Light";
} // end of Greeting
```

What will be displayed to the Console?
  O a. Answer is: Green Light
  O b. Answer is: Red Light

5.) You have the following code:

```
static int Adder(int num1, int num2)
{
    int theAnswer;

    theAnswer = num1 + num2;
} // end of Adder method
```

You want the method to return the sum to the calling code. Why won't it compile?
  O a. The return type should be changed to void
  O b. The method body needs a return statement
  O c. Change num1 and num2 to a void type
  O d. Delete the word static

Notes

Chapter 11 – Anatomy of a C# Program

In the previous chapter, we went outside of the Main method's structure and added code into the class structure. This means we had better talk about how a C# program is put together, the various parts we need to know about, and why they are there. This discussion will also lead us into our next subject, classes, since the primary place to write methods is in classes of their own.

Namespace

This book you are reading has about 300 pages of text, but it is not 300 pages of just raw text. Instead it is broken down into chapters, sections and paragraphs by the use of spaces, line breaks, and periods. This breakdown does not give you any additional information, but rather organizes the words into logical groups which actually contain the information. This concept is also used in C#. What we call a chapter in a book is called a Namespace for C#.

Put another way, a namespace is a master container into which we put other objects (for example other namespaces, classes, `structs`, `enums` or methods) and the code to form either complete or parts of projects. By splitting a project up into individual chunks, you can make your final project modular. As you get better or learn a new solution to the problem at hand, you can swap out one chunk of code for another.

Even though we have not explicitly mentioned it, we have been using namespaces all along. At the top of all of our programs there has been a declaration for a namespace followed by the name of our project. Within this namespace there has been a definition of a class, normally called "Program", and within that our Main method where all of our code has gone.

There are four other namespace declarations that we have not dealt with or even noticed. Take a look at Figure 69, which is simply the top part of a previous project.

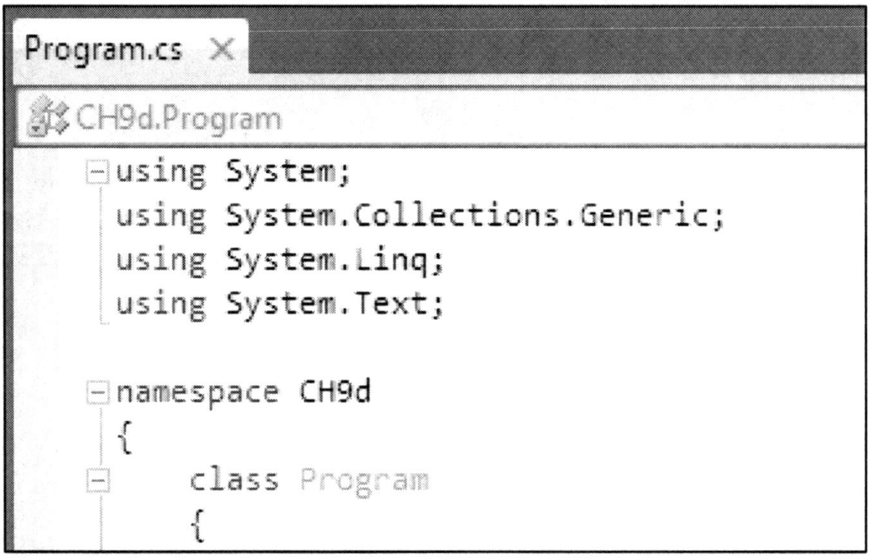

Figure 69: Our Program class is nested inside the CH9d namespace

We can see the namespace declaration followed by the project name and within it the class declaration – just as described above. Where are these other four namespaces I mentioned? See those four lines at the very top, the ones that start with "using"? Each of those four lines refers to an external namespace that we are pulling into our code. But why are we pulling these namespaces, and the code they contain, into our code? Simply put, because without these namespaces our programs would not work!

Let me explain! We have been using `Console.WriteLine` in nearly all of our programs, yet we did not write this particular method, so where did it come from? One of the namespaces that is being pulled into all of our programs is called `System`, and in fact is the very first namespace to be important. This namespace contains a whole set of "built-in" functions, such as `WriteLine`, which we are then able to use. In other words, whenever we have used a method such as `Console.WriteLine` or `Console.ReadLine` we have been calling upon elements of the System namespace.

In fact if we break down the name of these methods, we actually get to see the namespace, class and method names and how they all link up to each other. Let's take a look at `WriteLine` for example. This method lives within the Console class, which in turn lives within the System namespace. Hmmm, so how did I get all that?

Open up any of our past projects and find one of the `Console.WriteLine` statements. Right click anywhere within the word "WriteLine" and from the popup menu select "Go To Definition". This opens up the file in which this method actually lives. Scroll up and notice how this method, along with many others, is all contained within a class called Console. Note that this class is within the System namespace. The `Using` keyword imports this namespace into our program so we can call upon these objects by specifying only the class and method name we want.

Without that imported namespace we would have to use the Method's complete name in order to use it. For example, below is the project CH9d, with the `using` `System` line commented out. This forces me to use the full name for all objects that live within this namespace.

```csharp
//using System;
using System.Collections.Generic;
using System.Linq;
using System.Text;

namespace CH9d
{
    class Program
    {
        enum Months { January = 1, February, March,
            April, May, June, July, August,
September,
            October, November, December};

        static void Main(string[] args)
        {
            int theMonth;

            System.Console.Write("Enter a number (1-
12): ");
            theMonth =
int.Parse(System.Console.ReadLine());

            System.Console.WriteLine("Month {0} is
called {1}", theMonth, (Months)theMonth);

            System.Console.ReadLine();
```

```
            }
        }
    }
```

Notice that we had to put the `System` namespace in front of every statement that says `Console`. The program will run just fine, but we sure have a lot more typing to do. As we get better at C#, we are going to be writing programs of our own and then importing the namespace in which our methods live into other programs. This concept of being able to share and access other code sets is one of the basics of Object Oriented programming.

While namespaces are the top level containers of code and other objects, we actually will spend much more time segmenting our code into different Classes.

Classes

If we think of a namespace as a house, then you can think of classes as the individual rooms inside that house. Assuming we are already inside the house, I would never ask anyone to meet me in the living room of my house. I would just say let's go to the living room. On the other hand, if I were with a friend in a café would I say "Come over to the living room of my house?" No, that would be unnecessarily specific; I would just ask him to come over to the house.

So, the house, or the namespace, is the master object within which all the important stuff lives. However, the actual things I want to do are done in the rooms of my house, or in the classes of the namespace. For example, how I use my guest room is totally up to me, and it is likely to be different than the guy's next door. I could turn the guest room into an office, library, or a kids room – it all depends on my situation and need at the time. Classes do the same things. By themselves they are just empty containers. Depending on what I put into them, their behavior will change dramatically.

Just as with a room, a class can be customized for all kinds of purposes. The "furniture" elements of a class, members as they are referred to in C#, are primarily made up of fields and methods. If we ignore the methods for a minute, then the layout of a Class is quite similar to a `struct`. In other words, the fields of a class are simply defined data types, both declared and accessed in the same way that we would access members of a `struct`.

However, what makes a class truly unique and powerful is the ability to also include methods. These methods are able to access the internal fields of a class, take external values, and return other values. If you structure these elements of your class in the right way, you can create a very strong object which has explicit control over how data comes into it, goes out of it and how it is handled within the methods of the class.

When guests come over to my house they can enjoy the snack bowl(s) that I leave out. In fact, they do not ever have need to ask to take something from them, since by putting it out I have indicated that they are for everyone to enjoy. However, if they want a soft drink from the fridge, they need to ask me for that, since the fridge is not open to all. However, I could tell them to help themselves to the fridge. This does not make the fridge open to all, only to those that I have given the right to access it. However, nobody would ask to look through our jewelry box, since that is private. Actually, they do not even know if we have a jewelry box or not, so asking to look through it might not even make sense. Basically, these objects in my home have different levels of access associated with them.

So, how do we control the access to the fields of this class? Remember when we created our `structs`, we had to put the keyword `public` in front of our member declarations? Classes also use this keyword to allow fields to be directly accessible from outside the immediate structure. However, if you make these members private, then they can only be accessed through methods for which you can control the outside exposure.

Let's create a new class, put some members into it and play with the access modifiers needed to directly access these members. We are going to use the same situation that we did with our `struct` example, namely an object that stores decimal values for latitude and longitude, as well as a string for the name of the location. Initially this may not appear to be any better than using a `struct`, but as we continue on through the following few chapters we are going to expand upon this example and you will see the true power and abilities of a class.

Start a new project called "CH11a". Once you have your project created we need to start by making a new class. (Usually each new class gets its own C# code file, but for the purposes of our examples we are going to keep everything together.)

Figuring out where to put a new class in the namespace can be tricky, so here is a technique that you can do to help yourself out. Remember how earlier I told you that Visual Studio's IntelliSense will highlight the corresponding curly brace when you highlight one? Use that trick, find the closing curly brace for the Main method, the Program class and the CH11a namespace. After each curly brace, put a comment marking what section each curly brace closes. This will help you in keeping track of what links to where (Figure 70).

```
namespace CH11a
{
    class Program
    {
        static void Main(string[] args)
        {
        } // end of Main
    } // end of class Program
} // end of namespace CH11a
```

Figure 70: The ending curly brace of each level is marked with a comment

To create a new class, put your cursor after the curly brace that closes the Program class, press enter a couple of times and type in the keyword "class" followed by a name. This can be any name of your choosing, but most programmers follow the same rules as for variables. The idea is to keep it something that will make sense to the purpose of this class. Since this class will store geographical information, let's call it Location. After giving the class a name, press enter again and put in an open curly brace and then on the next line a closing curly brace. If you want, put a comment after the closing curly brace to identify where it belongs (Figure 71).

```
namespace CH11a
{
    class Program
    {
        static void Main(string[] args)
        {
        } // end of Main
    } // end of class Program

    class Location
    {

    } // end of class Location
} // end of namespace CH11a
```

Figure 71: Just before the end of the namespace we put a class called Location

We now have the structure in place for our new class – all that's missing is the code to actually make it do something useful. Inside the curly braces of the Location class, please enter the following lines of code:

```
public string name;
public float latitude, longitude;
```

That's it! If you compare this to our `struct` sample, you will note that these are the same lines that went into the `struct` definition. Just as before, we are also using the keyword "public" to allow these member fields to be accessible to processes outside of the class.

All of this typing still has not resulted in a program that will actually do anything. To use this new class, we need to put some lines of code into Main. Since we are basing this on the `struct` example, the code will be quite similar – however, there is one major difference. Please enter this code into your Main method.

```
Location myLoc = new Location();

Console.Write("Enter a location name: ");
myLoc.name = Console.ReadLine();

Console.Write("Enter latitude: ");
myLoc.latitude = float.Parse(Console.ReadLine());

Console.Write("Enter longitude: ");
myLoc.longitude = float.Parse(Console.ReadLine());

Console.WriteLine("The {0} can be found at {1}
Latitude by {2} Longitude",
myLoc.name, myLoc.latitude, myLoc.longitude);

Console.ReadLine();
```

Notice the first line of code inserted into Main. In the past whenever we declared a variable, all we had to do was enter the data type followed by a name for the new variable – this was even true when using a `struct` as the data type. When using a class, things are a little bit different. Actually, you can just type the name of the class followed by a variable name, which technically will create a variable.

When creating an instance of a new class, you need to use the `new` keyword, which you do not need to use with a `struct`. If you don't use the new keyword the compiler will give you an error, specifically "Use of unassigned local variable". What the heck does that mean? Instead of thinking of a variable as a container which can hold a value of a specific data type, think of the variable as an address to a spot in memory.

When you declare a variable with a known data type, say an `int` for example, the compiler knows exactly what an `int` is and how many bytes of memory are needed to store it. Thus it can create a spot of that size in memory. Since a `struct` is always made up of standard data types, the compiler can do the same for a `struct`. It simply adds up the memory needs of each individual member and puts them next to each other in memory. A class, however, is very different. Even though in this current example we are using the class in the exact same way that we would a `struct`, there is one very important difference.

All regular data types and `structs` represent a single instance of given data. However, a class is not actually a holder of data! Rather, it is a template for an object, which can itself store data. Because of this template-like nature of a class, we have to instantiate a copy of it in order to use it. If it helps, think of it like this. A blueprint of a house is not an actual house but rather a template for it. I cannot live in the blueprint, but have to find a physical location for the house and then build it using the blueprint. Once my house is built, I can use the same blueprint and build another one, however, the two houses are not the same.

Using this metaphor, declaring an `int` (or any other regular data type) variable is more like renting an apartment. I do not have to build the apartment, the building has been built by somebody else and I am just renting one "unit" of this pre-built structure. A `struct` would be like renting multiple apartments.

Instantiating an Object of a Class

To actually turn our blueprint into a house, or using C# terms, make an instance of a class, we have to use the keyword "`new`". So, think of that first line of new code in Main like this. The variable name "`myLoc`" is the address of the place in memory where the compiler will build a new copy of the structure defined by the Location class. No matter how we fill in the fields of this new structure, if we instantiate another instance of this class, the values contained in this second instance will be separate (in memory) from the values contained in the first. This is true even if the values are identical.

As you can see in the program, we access each field of this instantiated class using the same notation with which we addressed the individual elements of a `struct`. Specifically, we use the variable name, followed by a period, and finally the name of the field. Before we go on, please run your program to see what it does.

Of course, so far this class is nothing more than a holder of some data – hardly exciting – so let's work on that! Unlike a `struct`, classes can also contain methods which can do a variety of tasks. Right now, we actually use the code in the Main method to place values into our instantiated class, to pull them out, and to display them to the user. Let's give the class a method that can display its own values. First we need to update the class by writing this new method. Please add the following code into the Location class, just below the field declarations.

```csharp
public void ShowInfo()
{
    Console.WriteLine("The {0} can be found at {1}
Latitude by {2} Longitude",
name, latitude, longitude);
}
```

Notice how this method's single line of code is nearly identical to the `WriteLine` we currently have within the Main method. The big difference is that when I wish to show the values I do not have to put anything in front of them! Since this method lives within the class, it is able to see and access the fields of the class and therefore does not need any additional information, as we needed in Main.

Now that we have put a method into the class to display its information, we might as well use it! In the Main method, remove the `WriteLine` there and in its place put the following line of code:

```csharp
myLoc.ShowInfo();
```

As before, we access the method within the class by first putting in the variable which holds this instance of the class, followed by a period and finally by the name of the method. Run your program to verify that it all works as before. If you need to, put a breakpoint onto the first line of code in the Main method and step through the program using the debugger.

While this is a great demonstration of a very simple class and its method, the really impressive thing is when we make another instance of this object. For the sake of brevity, instead of asking the user for the name and coordinates of a location, let's hard code those values into Main – like this:

```csharp
static void Main(string[] args)
{
    Location myLoc1 = new Location();
    Location myLoc2 = new Location();

    myLoc1.name = "Eiffel Tower";
    myLoc1.latitude = 48.858001709f;
    myLoc1.longitude = 2.29460000992f;

    myLoc2.name = "Statue of Liberty";
    myLoc2.latitude = 40.689201355f;
    myLoc2.longitude = -74.0447998047f;

    myLoc1.ShowInfo();
    myLoc2.ShowInfo();

    Console.ReadLine();
} // end of main
```

Notice the letter "f" at the end of the coordinate values? That simply tells the compiler to treat this value as a float and is a shortcut to putting (float) in front of the value.

Go ahead and run the program. Notice how you get the information for the two locations displayed, even though in both cases we used the exact same method. The beauty of a class is that each instance is totally independent and the methods within them only operate on that particular instance of the method!

Static vs. Non-Static

Technically, my last sentence is not 100% accurate – actually, there is a way for a method within a class to apply not to just the current instance but to the entire class as a whole. Remember the first time we used methods (Chapter 10), when we put them within the Program class we also had to put the keyword "static" in front? That is what the static keyword does – it creates a method which is able to ignore the individual instances of a class and instead applies to the class itself.

If it helps, use this analogy to picture the differences. Imagine an organization with a large number of employees. Within their HR software, the code creates an individual instance of a class called "employee" for each individual. Within this class, there are fields that are unique to each person, such as name, age, SSN and so forth. However, the organization also has certain information with regard to employees that are not individually specific but rather apply to the whole set. One such bit of information might be a government mandated tax rate.

If this information, common across individuals, were to be stored as a non-static field of the instance, each individual instance would have to have this value set. Should the government ever change this value, the program would have to update each individual account one by one – if this organization is large enough that could be thousands of updates! Instead, this value can be made static and stored within the class itself and referenced in a central fashion. This way, if the government does change this value, the program only has to update it in one location.

To show this, we are going to modify our program by giving our class two static elements – one will be a single static field and the other will be a static method. Once these are in place, we can use both of these new additions and see how they differ from the non-static fields and method already in place. So, please update your Location class to look like this:

```
class Location
{
    public string name;
    public float latitude, longitude;
    public static int locationCount;

    public void ShowInfo()
    {
```

```
        Console.WriteLine("The {0} can be found at
{1} Latitude by {2} Longitude",
            name, latitude, longitude);
    }

public static void ShowLocationCount()
    {
        Console.WriteLine("The count is: {0}",
locationCount);
    }

} // end of class Location
```

For both our new static field and static method, the keyword "public" is still required in order to be able to access them from outside of the class. Do note the order of the keywords, they are important and the compiler will complain if they are not in the right place.

Now that we have a couple of static items, we need to actually do something with them, otherwise they have no purpose. (If you run the program at this point, you will see that there has been no change to the output.) These changes will be in the Main code block, where we are going to increment the value of the locationCount each time we add a new instance and at the end to display that count. Though, to make this happen, we only need to add three lines to the Main method, I think it would be easier to just show the entire code block.

```
static void Main(string[] args)
{
    Location myLoc1 = new Location();
    Location myLoc2 = new Location();

    myLoc1.name = "Eiffel Tower";
    myLoc1.latitude = 48.858001709f;
    myLoc1.longitude = 2.29460000992f;

    Location.locationCount++;

    myLoc2.name = "Statue of Liberty";
    myLoc2.latitude = 40.689201355f;
    myLoc2.longitude = -74.0447998047f;
```

```
Location.locationCount++;

myLoc1.ShowInfo();
myLoc2.ShowInfo();
Location.ShowLocationCount();

Console.ReadLine();
} // end of main
```

Go ahead and run your program to see the new output. Once you are ready, go through it and understand the difference in the usage of the static and non-static elements.

The first two lines of the code declare and assign two instances of the Location class (aka object) into the variables myLoc1 and myLoc2. The next three lines then take the first instance, myLoc1, and assign values to the three fields that the object supports – so far no changes from the original code. The next line, however, is new. On this line we access the static field of this object in order to increment its value by one.

Notice how we do not refer to this using either of our instantiated objects (for example myLoc1), but rather refer to the class name directly. This is because this field is a static field, and does not exist within the instantiated objects. To test this, try this little experiment. Anywhere in the Main method after the two declaration lines, type the name of either instantiated object and press period. Look through the list that comes up and notice that the static field (LocationCount) is not listed (Figure 72)!

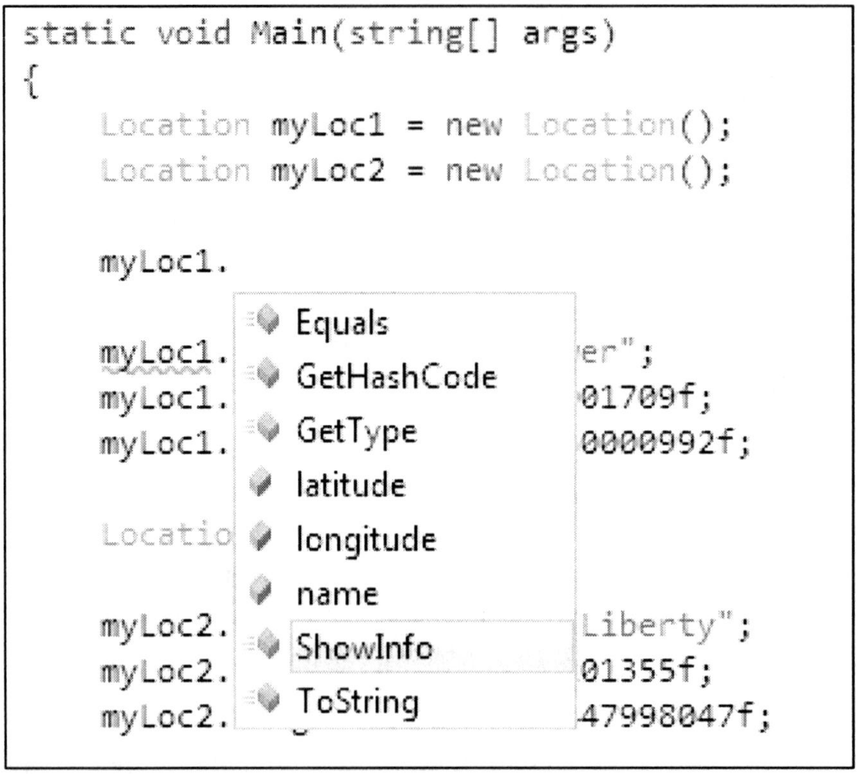

```
static void Main(string[] args)
{
    Location myLoc1 = new Location();
    Location myLoc2 = new Location();

    myLoc1.
```

	Equals	
myLoc1.	GetHashCode	er";
myLoc1.		01709f;
myLoc1.	GetType	0000992f;
	latitude	
Locatio	longitude	
	name	
myLoc2.	ShowInfo	Liberty";
myLoc2.		01355f;
myLoc2.	ToString	47998047f;

Figure 72: The non static members of a Location instance appear in you IntelliSense

On the other hand, the opposite is also true. If, instead of typing the name of an instantiated object, I type the name of the class itself and press period, only the `static` fields will show up (Figure 73).

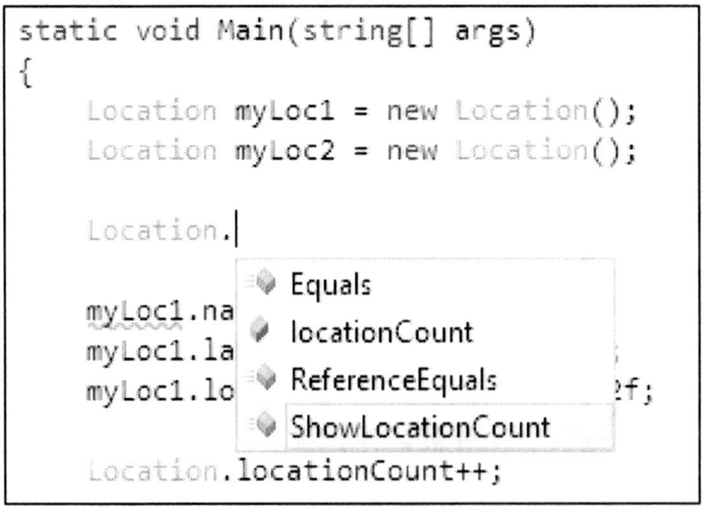

```
static void Main(string[] args)
{
    Location myLoc1 = new Location();
    Location myLoc2 = new Location();

    Location.|
```

myLoc1.na	Equals	
myLoc1.la	locationCount	
myLoc1.lo	ReferenceEquals	f;
	ShowLocationCount	

```
    Location.locationCount++;
```

Figure 73: The static members of the Location class show up in your IntelliSense

IntelliSense is smart enough to understand the definition of a class's members and fields and will only show the appropriate items in these little dropdown lists. Of course, you do need to be careful. Sometimes an item that you expect to show up does not. Check the permission level! If you do not mark a field or method as `public`, IntelliSense will assume that it is a private member and not display it from any code block outside of the class itself! (There is a whole set of permission levels, but that is for another time. For now, just to keep things simple, we are going to mark everything as `public`.)

Let's get back to our program. The next three lines take the second instance of our Location object and assign it some values, followed by a line that once again increases the `static` field's value by one. Since these four lines are identical to the four we just covered, I'm not going to go into any additional detail.

Following this are the two lines where we call on the instantiated objects' `ShowInfo` method. This is again like our previous example, so its behavior should not be a surprise. The important thing to remember here is that the method will only show the values assigned to the particular instance of the object against which you call this method.

Finally, we have the call to the object's `ShowLocationCount` method. Since this is a `static` method, it is called against the class's name and not against either of the instantiated objects (`myLoc1` or `myLoc2`).

Even though this is a pretty simple example of `static` vs. non-`static` fields and members, the basic concept is one you are likely to run across quite often. Keeping count of how many instances of an object have been created is a very common and quite useful system to have in place. Our implementation does have a few flaws – for example, since the counter is publicly accessible, it could very easily be messed with either by accident or on purpose. Also, by having to manually increment it each time an object is created, there exists the chance that you might forget to take care of incrementing the counter. There are solutions to all of these issues and we will cover them as we get further into objects.

When to use Static Methods over Non-static Ones?

Looking at our sample program, you might be asking yourself why you would ever write a non-`static` method if calling and using a `static` method is so much easier and faster. Actually, this is a fair observation and there are times when speed and efficiency are the primary consideration in deciding what type of a method to write. Basically, this boils down to two issues.

First, are the method(s) you are providing meant to be general purpose methods which are independent of external data? Examples of this would be methods that provide general purpose calculations, string manipulations, or other non-individual object specific functions. In such cases `static` methods are the way to go. These would be types of methods that you could easily call and retrieve results from without having to go through the hassle of creating an object instance first. Excellent examples of such `static` methods within the system are the system provided `WriteLine` and `ReadLine` methods we have been using all along. Both of these methods are `static` methods within the `Console` class, as provided by C#.

The second issue deals with data. Whenever you create an object with data which will need manipulation by internal routes, then writing non-`static` methods, i.e. class instance specific methods are the way to go. Using the example from earlier on, the Employee class for our company might contain routines to change the last name of an employee, modify pay rate, calculate vacation hours, and so on. Each of these examples is specific to the data for that one instance of the Employee class, in other words to a single employee at a time. These methods will never need to operate across the class modifying multiple users, so they are best left as non-`static`, instance specific methods.

Speaking of a collection of generic `static` methods, the recommended solution is to create a class dedicated to a set of related methods, which are then called within your code as needed. This way all of the methods are to be found together, probably in their own .cs file, which makes them easy to find and troubleshoot as necessary.

Adding Additional Files to a Project

Most applications are made up of many small files that work together. For the purposes of learning the C# keywords and syntax, all of our sample programs have been quite small – this makes it easier to understand and troubleshoot if necessary. In the real world, things are rarely quite that simple or small. Major software projects can be large with from hundreds of thousands to millions of lines of code. Can you imagine trying to put that much code into a single .cs file? A single file would have two obvious drawbacks: Only one person could work on the file at a time, and all programs need maintenance. It would be an overwhelming job to find the code segment(s) needing changes!

Most of us are familiar with Microsoft Office. When you open up Word and type a letter, you have the spell checker to help you out. If you make a PowerPoint presentation, you again have a spell checker. In fact all of the Office applications have spell checking. Are there five spell checkers that ship with Office, or is this code shared with all of the applications of the Office Suite? If some of your code is generic enough that you would like to share it with another project – how would you share part of a file? The solution is to segment your code into manageable chunks, each written into its own C# file. Now you can have different developers working on different files that are part of the same program. Also your common code can be copied into other projects just by sharing a file or two.

You may remember that in our last code example we put two classes into one .cs file. You can put as many classes into a single file as you want. However, one of the best practices in C# programming is to write each Class definition into a .cs file of its own. Not only does that make it easy to share individual classes, but keeps individual chunks of code smaller and easier to manage. As a practice, let's take our last project, CH11a and add to it a new .cs file – into which we will move the Location class code.

If you have already closed down your CH11a project, please launch Visual C# and open the project. Feel free to review the code before we make any changes to it. The first thing we need to do is add a new C# file to the project. As with many other common tasks there are actually multiple ways of making this happen. If you prefer to work with menus, then you can go to the Project menu and select "Add new item". The other way is through the Solution Explorer window, which you have probably shrunk down to the right side of your screen. Hover your mouse over the Solution Explorer tab, wait for it to expand, then right click on name of your project and from the popup menu select "Add". This will bring a sub-menu out, from which you can select "New Item" (Figure 74).

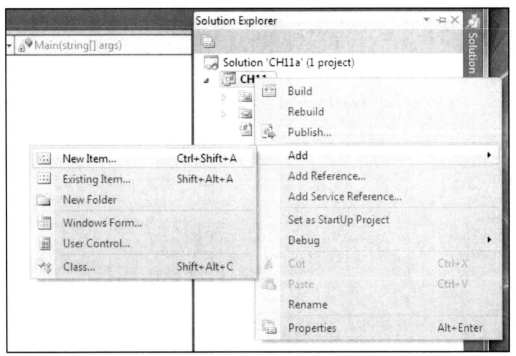

Figure 74: Right clicking the CH11a project, gives you the choice to add a new item to the project

No matter which method you choose, the result for both will be the same: the "Add New Item" dialog box will pop up (Figure 75).

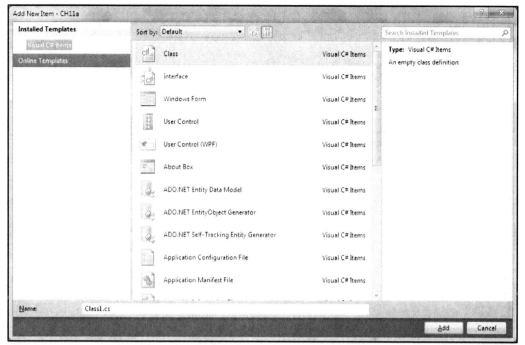

Figure 75: The "Add New Item" dialog box gives you many options of what can be added to this project

There are many options to choose from, most of which we have not discussed yet. All we want is a new C# file into which we can put our Location class. If you look through this list, two items look promising. First is the icon labeled as "Class" and the second is labeled as "Code File" (scroll down a bit if you cannot see it). They both sound good. The one called "Class" is almost too easy of a choice, but that is exactly what we want!

So, what is the difference between these two options? In a fundamental way they both really accomplish the same thing, which is to add a new CS file to your project – the difference is the "Code File" option just gives you a totally blank new file into which it is up to you to write everything, while the "Class" option actually prepares the file for you. It does this by linking in your project's namespace and creating an empty class container. I'm always good with programs preparing things for me, so please click on the "Class" icon. Notice the name box at the bottom defaults to "Class1.cs" – a good starting name, but I think we can do better. Let's call this file after what it will contain, so change the name to say "Location.cs" and then click Add.

As soon as you click Add, the new file is created, added to your project and opened up within the editor for you to start working with (Figure 76).

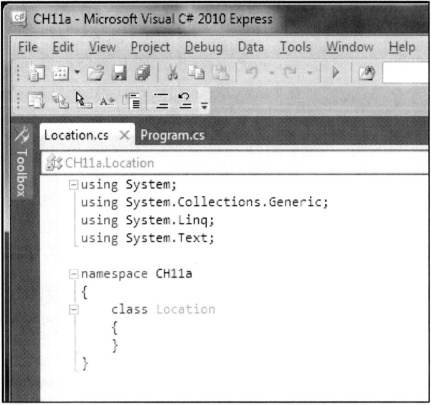

Figure 76: Your Location.cs file is added and contains an empty Location class

Those of you with really sharp eyes might have noticed that when we added this new file we chose the "Add New Item" option, but there was also an "Add Class" option as well (Figure 74). Turns out that the adding of a new class file is so common, that a shortcut was made within the Visual Studio products to make this action easier and faster. Choosing the Add Class brings up the same "Add New Item" dialog, but it already has the "Class" icon selected. Maybe not a major saving of time, but every little bit helps...

Before we examine the contents of the new file, let me quickly "show" you something else. Notice the tabs at the top, of which you should have two – Location.cs and Program.cs (Figure 76). Just as with any multi-document editor, the tabs refer to the various files you have open. You can just click on a tab to move to that file. By default, all new files are opened with a tab in the left most position but you can move the tabs into any order that you find logical. Simply drag the tab to where you would like it. Personally, I like the file with the Main method (Program.cs) at the leftmost position and all other files after it; so, I would drag the Location.cs tab to a position after the Program.cs tab – go ahead and try it!

So, now we have our file in place and it already has some code in it – or more precisely, it has some structure into which code may be placed. These two different classes in the two .cs files are part of the same Namespace. Notice the namespace declaration refers to the same namespace as in our Main file, "CH11a". But wait, isn't the namespace in both the Main file and this new file fully enclosed? In other words, after the keyword `namespace` we have an open curly brace and after the code area there is a closing curly brace. It would appear that we have two completely defined, but identically named, namespaces.

That would seem to be a problem. After all, you cannot have two structures with the same name! However, the compiler is smart enough to understand that all code tagged with the same namespace is logically grouped together. Since you are allowed to have multiple code files, it takes all of these individually completed namespaces with the same name and at compile time merges them into a single entry!

If you can have a namespace split into multiple files, what about a class? Can I have the class Location defined in both the Program.cs and now the Location.cs file? Ah, unfortunately not[22]. In fact if you try to build your program now, you will get an error that this class has already been defined (Figure 77).

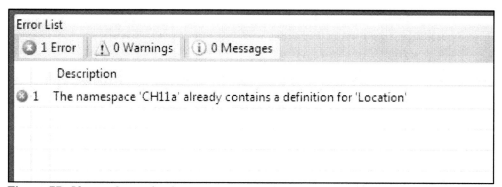

Figure 77: If two classes in the same namespace are given the same name then you get a compiler error

Well, we should fix this problem. Since we started this off by trying to move the Location Class out of our Main code file into this new one, I think it is time to do

---

[22] Actually, there is a way to split a class into multiple files, using the keyword `partial`, but let's not jump ahead of ourselves!

so! Copy all of the code that is currently within the Location class definition in the Program.cs file and paste it into the Class Location definition inside the Location.cs file. When done, delete the Location class from the Program.cs file, otherwise you are going to get this error again. Build your program and make sure you are not getting any errors. Once done, run your program and verify that it still work as before.

Points to Ponder

- A C# program is organized by the use of namespaces and classes
- A namespace is a set of code that can be logically grouped together
- Your program can import other namespaces into, such as the System namespace, which are provided by the C# environment
- A namespace can contain other namespaces and classes
- A class contains any combination of fields, parameters and methods
- Before you can access a class, you need to instantiate it. This creates a space in memory where that particular instance of the class will reside.
- You can make as many copies (instances) of a class as you need. These instances are independent objects that will not "see" each other.
- Static methods of a class can be accessed without having to instantiate the class
- Static elements apply to the class itself, whereas non-static elements apply to particular instance of the class that you are working with
- A C# program does not live within a single C# code file. Normally you want to put each class into a separate C# file

Challenge

1. We have been talking about an Employee class, so I think we need to actually create it! Create this class (in a file of its own) with fields for a name, address (street, city, state, and zip), year of birth, and hourly pay rate. Since a class is useless by itself, write a program inside Main which asks the user for the information needed to fill in an instance of the Employee class.

2. Write a method within the Employee class that takes the year the person was born in, subtracts it from the current year (hint: System.DateTime.Now.Year), then prints how old the employee is.

3. Create another method that calculates and prints out how much the Employee's annual pay rate is based on their hourly rate (hint: multiply by 2080).

Review Quiz

1.) What keyword do you use to import a namespace?
   - O a. importing
   - O b. namespace
   - O c. using
   - O d. System

2.) How many namespace imports can you have?
   - O a. 1
   - O b. 2
   - O c. One for each class
   - O d. As many as you need

3.) What access modifier is used to allow members of the class to be accessed from any calling code?
   - O a. public
   - O b. private
   - O c. protected

4.) What access modifier is used to allow only the class itself to access the member?
   - O a. public
   - O b. private
   - O c. protected

5.) Which is the fully qualified way for calling the `WriteLine` method?
   - O a. `System.Console.WriteLine();`
   - O b. `Console.WriteLine();`
   - O c. `WriteLine();`

6.) What keyword will import a namespace to allow you to use the short names?
   - O a. using
   - O b. with
   - O c. import
   - O d. virtual

7.) What is true about namespaces? (Choose all that apply)
- ☐ a. You can nest them with a dot notation. i.e. Name1.Name2
- ☐ b. They will be at the beginning of any fully qualified name
- ☐ c. They are considered a better way to organize your classes for large assemblies
- ☐ d. The same namespace can be declared in more than one .cs file in the same assembly
- ☐ e. You can declare namespaces as private

8.) If a member of a class does not have an access modifier what becomes its default?
- O a. public
- O b. private
- O c. protected

9.) When do Name clashes occur?
- O a. When too many class prefixes are present
- O b. Anytime two namespaces have the same class name declared
- O c. When two or more classes have the same name in a namespace

Notes

Chapter 12 – Methods: Part 2

Although we have worked with methods quite a lot already, there is always more to learn! All of the examples we have seen so far have used methods in a very simple manner – either without any inputs, or with a very simple, pre-set number of incoming parameters. In C#, you can create a second method with a very different set of parameters that still uses the same name! This concept is called overloading and gives your methods some very powerful abilities. These methods can also deal with the outside world in some very direct methods. In fact, if done the right way they can affect the value of variables outside of their own scope!

Overloading

When I was learning C#, it was this concept that I got the most kick out of. In every programming language I have ever learned, seen, or heard about, the number one cardinal rule has been that all items, from variables to functions, must have unique names. C# takes this rule and doesn't quite break it but certainly bends it quite a bit.

An easy way to think of overloading is to imagine a checkout line at a grocery store. Once all of your items have been rung up, you need to pay, but the store gives you the option of paying with cash, check, or credit/debit card. The end result is always the same, once you pay for your items you get to leave with them. To the cash register how you pay does not matter, only that it has been told by some method that you actually paid. If you paid with cash or a check, the message noting that you have paid will come from the cashier in the format of pressing the appropriate buttons. However if you pay with a credit or debit card, this message will come from the credit card machine.

In C# terms, the method would be called something like ProcessPayment, but the input to this method will be different based on the payment option you used:

```
ProcessPayment(cash Amount)
ProcessPayment(debit Amount)
```

The method is the same, but has two (or more) different sets of parameters.

The reason this is possible is due to the way C# defines the "signature" of a method. Instead of just relying on the name to define a method (as nearly every other programming language does), it also takes into consideration the data types of the parameters. It also looks at whether the method is static or non-static, and finally if the parameters are passed by value or reference (next section). These considerations combined form a signature. As long as the signatures of two methods do not match, they can have the same name. Instead of getting further into the definition of a signature, let's just code a couple of examples – we'll come back to signatures in just a bit.

Imagine a simple method whose job in life is to take two int values as input parameters, add them up and return the result as another int. As long as you only have int type values to add this method will work just fine – but what if you also have floats, doubles, and so on? Sure, you could cast the variables before passing them into the function and cast the result out, but that is messy – and possibly, you could even lose data as you convert between ints and floats or doubles. Casting, while a normal part of programming, can easily be forgotten when typing code and it could lead to issues later on. Rather you can just take your function and make different versions of it, all with the same base name, but different return values and incoming parameters.

Allowing the same method name to have different possible parameter signatures is called Overloading. While this is all very cool, the best part is still to come! Since IntelliSense understands the concept of overloading, as soon as you type the name of your overloaded method and press the opening parenthesis good things happen. You get a little drop-down with the name of the method, its incoming parameter list, and a set of up/down arrows with which you can see the set of available overloaded methods! As you choose each option, the updated parameter list shows up to give you a hint of what data types this flavor of the method expects!

This is too cool to just talk about, so let's put it into practice so you can see it for yourselves! Please start a new console project, "CH12a". When ready, create a new class called "MyMath" and enter the following code to create the Adder method.

```csharp
public int Adder(int num1, int num2)
{
    return num1 + num2;
}
```

This is a very simple method whose function you should have no problem understanding. About the only thing different in here, from our past usage of a method, is how I have the addition directly on the return line. This is not a requirement; you are most certainly welcome to declare a new variable, add the values into that, and then return the result variable. However, there is no real need for that. This just keeps the method nice and short.

Great, we have our first Adder function, but it will only work for int type of data. Go ahead and cut and paste two more versions, replacing the data type from int to double and then from int to a float. When done your MyMath method should look like Figure 78.

```
class MyMath
{
    public int Adder(int num1, int num2)
    {
        return num1 + num2;
    }

    public double Adder(double num1, double num2)
    {
        return num1 + num2;
    }

    public float Adder(float num1, float num2)
    {
        return num1 + num2;
    }
} // end of class MyMath
```

Figure 78: Three methods with the same name, each having its own unique parameter signature

Of course, I could have gone further and created additional methods for other data types, but for the purposes of this example, these three will be enough. Though if you wish, you are welcome to create additional ones.

As always, a class and its methods are of little use unless we call upon them from somewhere else in our program. The next step is to write something into Main to do just that. Since we are just trying to show the concept of overloading, we are going to keep our Main program short. We will assign the values directly instead of asking the user for the numbers. To start off, declare three variables called `value1`, `value2` and `answer`, all of type `int` for now. Before we can use the methods in the `MyMath` class we have to instantiate it since we did not mark the methods as `static`. Call this instance of the `MyMath` class "calculator". So far your code should look something like this:

```
int value1 = 5, value2 = 6, answer;
MyMath calculator = new MyMath();
```

Now let's get a value into `answer` using the Adder method in our class. Start by typing "`answer = calculator.Adder(`" and then stop. Take a look at the little dropdown that IntelliSense is displaying (Figure 79).

```
static void Main(string[] args)
{
    int value1 = 5, value2 = 6, answer;
    MyMath calculator = new MyMath();

    answer = calculator.Adder(|
                  ▲ 1 of 3 ▼  double MyMath.Adder(double num1, double num2)
}
```

Figure 79: When calling the Adder method during design time, your IntelliSense shows you have three different choices

For one little line, there sure are a lot of things to notice here! First take a look at the bolded part of the parameter list. This is the next bit of information that IntelliSense expects you to enter, which is the first of the two parameters that this overload of the method supports. It also shows the data type that it expects, which is a `double`. Hmmm, didn't we also write a version for `float` and `int`? Where are those? Good questions! To find those additional versions of this method, take a look at the very beginning of this hint line.

Do you see the "1 of 3" there, surrounded by the up and down arrows? Go ahead and click the down arrow to get the "2 of 3" version of this method and you should see the `float` version of our method displayed (Figure 80).

```
static void Main(string[] args)
{
    int value1 = 5, value2 = 6, answer;
    MyMath calculator = new MyMath();

    answer = calculator.Adder(|
                ▲ 2 of 3 ▼  float MyMath.Adder(float num1, float num2)
}
```

Figure 80: IntelliSense showing the second of three overloads to the Adder method

Click once more and the int version will also show up. Odd, didn't we write the int version first, followed by the double and finally the float? We did, but IntelliSense is displaying things in alphabetical order, so int comes last.

Now there is one common misconception that a lot of new developers get here. We know that the values we are about to pass to the Adder method are going to be a pair of ints, yet the hint line is asking for doubles. Does that mean we have to click the down arrow twice for the int version to show up before we can type this line? Absolutely not! These hint lines are just that – hints to help you remember the parameter list and their data types to call the method correctly. What you type in will be checked by the compiler against the method at compile time. If there are multiple versions of the method, as long as one version matches, you are good to go!

To get our program working, go ahead and finish this line of code, then using a WriteLine print out the results (Figure 81). Once it is working, change the data type of the three variables, assigning them appropriate values, then run the program again.

```
class Program
{
    static void Main(string[] args)
    {
        int value1 = 5, value2 = 6, answer;
        MyMath calculator = new MyMath();

        answer = calculator.Adder(value1, value2);
        Console.WriteLine("The answer is: {0}", answer);

        Console.ReadLine();
    } // end of Main method
} // end of class Program
```

Figure 81: We passed two int values to the Adder method and showed the answer variable with a WriteLine

To really prove to yourself that the right method is being used, use the debugger to step through the code with the data type of the three variables different for each pass.

One more final note – all three of our overloaded Adder methods are very similar. Each took two input parameter values and returned a single value. This extreme similarity between overloaded methods is not required, I could have just as easily given one of these methods a third parameter, or made one a void return type and used a WriteLine to display a message. All that is required to overload a method is to make the signature of the method different from that of any other method of the same name.

As promised, let's return to the subject of method signatures for just a bit. Since it is the signature of the method that has to be different for it to be overloaded, it is worth making sure that these differences are well understood. Here are the primary elements which make up a signature.

1) Static vs. non-static methods
```
static void MyMethod(...)
void MyMethod(...)
```

If one method is static and the other is not, all other differences are immediately ignored – meaning even if they have the exact same parameter list, they are still considered to have different signatures.

2) Data type of parameters
```
void MyMethod(int x)
void MyMethod(string x)
```

Each method has a different data type for its parameter, so they are considered to be different.

3) Amount of parameters
```
void MyMethod(int x)
void MyMethod(int x, int y)
```

If the number of parameters does not match, even if they are all of the same type, then the signatures are different.

4) Order of parameters
```
void MyMethod(int x, string s)
void MyMethod(string s, int x)
```

Ah, this one is tricky. Even though these two methods have the exact same parameter data types, the order does make a difference, making them different.

5) By value vs. reference parameters
```
void MyMethod(int x)
void MyMethod(ref int x)
void MyMethod(out int x)
```

The next section is going to talk about what passing by value vs. passing by reference means, but for the purposes of method signatures we do need to cover this. The first example is passing by value, while the last two are both passing by reference. This means the first method can be paired up with either of the last two, but the last two are considered to have the same signature.

Notice how we did not mention the return type of a method. What data type is returned by a method is not part of the signature, so as long as you follow the five rules above, the issue of return type can be ignored.

Passing by Value vs. Reference

As mentioned in the first part of our segment on methods, a method can take any number of parameters but can only return a single value. But what if you want, or need, for the method to actually return multiple values? One trick you could do is to declare an array as the return type, but that presents problems of its own. For example all elements of an array have to be the same type and you might need to return different data types. So, what is the solution? The trick is something called passing by reference. However, before we can talk about that, let's talk about something you already know, but are probably not even aware of – passing by value.

If you recall, when I first introduced methods and the passing of values into a method using the parameter list, I pointed out that the value you pass into the method gets copied into the method's parameter variable. (When you fax a sheet of paper to a friend, you still have the original paper in your hand. The fax machine has made a copy of it and your friend is holding that copy. If your friend scribbles notes on his copy, yours is not affected.) If I were to change that value within the method, the original value from the calling routine is not affected. This is called passing by value and is what we have done with all methods until now. Actually, passing data this way is the most common way of getting data into a method. However, there are times when it would be nice to give the method the ability to actually modify the variable passed into it directly and have that change be reflected in the calling routine.

Think of variables in memory as being like a collection of Post Office boxes. Each little cubby hole is a variable into which I can put a single slip of paper that holds the value of the variable and where the number on the box is the name of the variable. When a method is called by value, the compiler takes the slip of paper that holds the value to be passed in out of the cubby and copies it onto another slip of paper. The first slip of paper goes back into the original cubby hole, and the second slip goes into a new cubby hole that the method owns. As the method works, it might scribble all over its slip of paper but the original one is not modified.

Passing by reference is a little trickier. Instead of a fax machine, imagine a passport. You give your passport to the customs official, who then stamps it and hands it back to you. The passport you hold is the same one you gave to the official, not a copy of it, but it has been changed by the addition of the new stamp. In this case, the paper from our cubby hole is not copied, but rather the original value is changed to a new value.

Another example, more true to computer memory, goes back to our cubby hole and its door. In this case you have a paper you want signed or stamped for you – not copied, but the original one modified, sitting in a cubby hole. Instead of making a copy of it and placing it into a new cubby hole with a new name, I just put a second number onto the door of the original cubby hole. The method is given this box number to use as its own variable. Since two variables now hold the same address, as one modifies the paper inside, the other will also see the changes.

Because passing by reference is not the default behavior of a method, the compiler needs to be explicitly told that we want the address of the variable passed along and not the value of the variable. The keyword to make this happen is "ref" (for "reference"). The compiler is so insistent that it be told about this, that you have to use the ref keyword on both sides. You have to use the ref keyword not only in the methods declaration list, but also during the call to the method.

To demonstrate passing by reference we are going to make a version of our Adder method from before (but without the overload). This time the method will not return the result of the addition, but rather will put the result into a variable passed to it by reference and that was originally declared within the calling method. After the method is finished, the result will "magically" appear within the variable inside our Main method. Let's code!

Once again, start a new console project, this time calling it "CH12b". When ready we will create a new class again called "MyMath", and inside it a new version of the Adder method. Notice that the method has a void return type, and is also declared to be a static class. This is so we do not have to instantiate the class before being able to use the method. Finally, notice the keyword "ref" inside the method's parameter list. With all that said, here is the class and method:

```
class MyMath
{
    static public void Adder(int num1, int num2, ref
int theAnswer)
    {
        theAnswer = num1 + num2;
    }
} // end of class MyMath
```

Not much to it, eh? That's all right; sometimes the most powerful things can come in the smallest packages! Notice how within the body of the Adder method we are assigning the result into the variable theAnswer, which was passed in by reference (notice the keyword ref) from the Main method. If this were to be passed in by value (in other words without the keyword ref), then making a change to what would now be a local variable would have no affect outside of this method.

One more important element of the Adder method: notice that the keyword static is at the beginning of the declaration. If you recall, from our explanation of the static vs. non-static methods, by making this routine a static I do not have to make an instance of the MyMath class. I can call this method directly. Of course, we could have written this as a non-static method and instantiated MyMath in order to access the Adder method, but this way just saved us a bunch of typing!

Now that we have our method, let's write the calling routine into Main. For simplicity's sake, I'm not going to ask the user for the values to be added, but will assign them myself (If you want to modify it and have the program prompt you for the values, go ahead!).

```
static void Main(string[] args)
{
    int val1 = 5, val2 = 6, result = 0;

    Console.WriteLine("Before: val1: {0}, val2: {1},
result: {2}",
        val1, val2, result);

    MyMath.Adder(val1, val2, ref result);

    Console.WriteLine("After: val1: {0}, val2: {1},
result: {2}",
        val1, val2, result);

    Console.ReadLine();
} // end of Main
```

Two things I would like to point out. First, notice how I had to initialize the variable result to 0. If you leave that step out, the compiler will complain that you are trying to use an uninitialized variable, which is not allowed. The easiest solution is to just assign a dummy value to it. For now, we just assign a zero to it and make the compiler happy! Second, notice how I have the `WriteLine` both before and after the call to our Adder method. This is simply to show the three local variables and how they are changed as a result of what the Adder method does. Run your program and verify that it works.

Pretty cool, right? Even though this is a pretty simple example it still shows some very complex and powerful behavior:

- We can pass variables by value (`val1` and `val2`) and by reference (`result`) at the same time.
- The names of the variables passed by reference in the calling method (`result`) and in the Adder method (`theAnswer`) are different, even though they both point to the same spot in memory. This is like having two address numbers on the outside of a PO Box.

There is one more item that I should point out. When I declared the Adder method, I made sure to put the variable passed by reference as the last item on the parameter list. If you are using .Net 3.5 or later, this is no longer an issue. You can put the reference parameter anywhere in the list. However, for earlier version of .Net, there was a requirement that all parameters passed by value had to be listed before any passed by reference. Though it is no longer enforced, it is good practice to keep to this rule.

The Out Keyword

Think of passing in by value as a one-way street – information flows from the calling routine into the called method but nothing is able to come back. When you want changes to come back as well, you use the `ref` keyword to pass by reference. This will allow changes made in the called method to be reflected back in the calling routine. In fact, a variable passed by reference can also carry data into the method. For example, that 0 we had initially assigned to the "`result`" variable in the Main method. We did not have a choice in the matter. The compiler gave us an error noting that we were trying to use an uninitialized variable, so we had to give it a value for the error to go away. Effectively, we passed a value, the 0, into the Adder method even though we did not really want or need that 0 to be passed along.

In cases such as this, there is a specialized form of the `ref` keyword that works almost the same way. That keyword is "`out`" and it solves the problem of having to initialize a variable in the calling routine. After all, we know the called method will place a value into this variable, so why does it have to also be set in the calling method?

To test this, modify your CH12b project by changing the keyword "ref" to the keyword "out" in both the Main method and in the Adder method parameter list. That's it! Run your program and verify that it still works as expected. So far it does not seem to do anything different than the keyword "ref" does... True, but we are not finished changing our program yet! To see the difference, remove the "= 0" from after the declaration of the "`result`" variable in Main. Compile the program (F6). Oops, we still have the uninitialized error (Figure 82)!

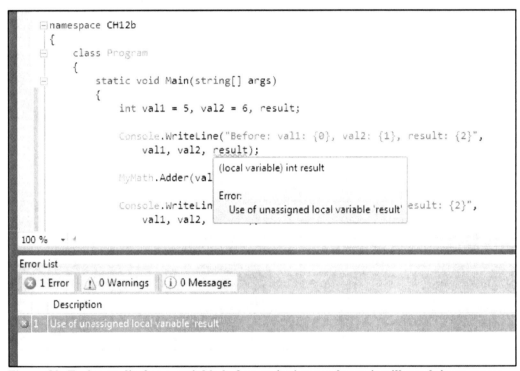

Figure 82: Trying to display a variable before assigning a value to it will result in an error

Hum, we are still getting this error, but why? It is telling us that we are trying to print out a variable which has no value yet – that cannot be done, hence the error. If you let your mouse hover over the highlighted word, the error shows up there as well. Delete or comment out that first `WriteLine` and try again!

This is actually a pretty subtle difference and an argument could be made that instead of using the `out` keyword, just always use `ref` and remember to initialize your variables. While technically that is true, there really is a purpose for the use of `out`. Not only does it prevent data from coming into a method where you only expect data to flow out, but it also gives somebody reading your code a good visual reminder that the flow of data here is one way only.

Parameter Array

All of the methods discussed so far, have had a specific number of parameters defined. When calling those methods, we provided the exact same number of parameters as were specified in the method declaration. Sure, using overloading we can create multiple copies of a method with different numbers of parameters to them, but still it would be a finite set. Yet we have been using a method from the beginning of this book which would appear to violate this very critical rule. Have you noticed that when we have called the `WriteLine` or `Write` methods, we have passed it differing amounts of parameters without any regard to the count? That's a pretty neat trick – bet we could come up with ways of using those ourselves as well.

In fact, let me propose a very common situation where having a non-predetermined number of parameters would be very useful. We have written a few different versions of a method called Adder, whose job it was to add two numbers and return the result. Ok, adding two numbers up is quite nice but what if we have three, four, or even a dozen or more to add like in these overloads below?

```
static public void Adder(int num1, int num2)
static public void Adder(int num1, int num2, int num3)
static public void Adder(int num1, int num2, int num3, int num4)
static public void Adder(int num1, int num2, int num3, int num4, int num5)
```

It turns out that C# has a method by which you can define one special parameter which can take any number of values. Perfect for the kind of addition routine we were just talking about. As you might have guessed from the heading of this section, this is called a Parameter Array.

Let's think of a new super Adder function. While we can write a single routine to handle as many values as needed, we will have to overload the function to handle additional data types. For our example we are going to stick to just ints. Though we could modify our last project, I think it would be better to start fresh. Please create a new project called "CH12c". Keeping with tradition, please create a new class called "MyMath" after the Program class and copy the following method into it:

```
class MyMath
{
    static public int Adder(params int[] theNums)
    {
        int theAnswer = 0;

        foreach (int num in theNums)
        {
            theAnswer += num;
        }

        return theAnswer;
    }
} // end of class MyMath
```

Notice the new keyword "params" before our parameter array declaration. It is this keyword that tells the compiler that what we are expecting is not a user defined array, but rather an array of parameters. The size of which is to be determined by the number of parameters on the line calling this method. After the params keyword we have to specify the data type of the incoming parameters and after the data type we need to put in the open and close square brackets to indicate that this is an array. Finally, we need to provide a name for the parameter.

Once we have the array in hand, we can use it in a number of ways. In this routine, I used a foreach loop to cycle through all the elements of the parameter array, but I could have just as easily used a for loop, with the length parameter of the array as the end point. If you want to try this using a for loop, change the loop to look like this:

```
for(int ct = 0; ct < theNums.Length; ct++)
{
    theAnswer += theNums[ct];
}
```

While the result is the same, this one takes a bit more to type. In the end, which method you prefer is entirely up to you.

Now that we have this great little routine, let's put it to the test! Use the following code within your Main routine:

```
Console.WriteLine("The answer is: {0}",
    MyMath.Adder(5, 6, 9, 4));

Console.ReadLine();
```

In this example, I currently have four values to be added up but I could have put in any number of integer values. Try it, change the values and the amount of the values to the Adder method and verify that it works.

As mentioned before, the data types of all these elements must match, so if I wanted to have a way to add up a series of `doubles`, I would have to overload the Adder method using `double` as a data type.

While this is a very flexible solution, it does have a few very important limitations:

1. You can only have one parameter array for each method. Of course, your method can still have any number of other parameters, passed in either by value or reference, but only one parameter array.
2. The parameter array has to be the very last element of your parameter list.
3. While you can have many elements passed into the array, they all have to be of the same data type.

As long as you keep these rules in mind, using a Parameter Array is quite easy but very powerful!

Points to Ponder

- Overloading is a way of creating multiple methods all with the same name. As long as the method's signatures do not match, they will be treated as different methods.
- The signature of a method is determined by the permission level of the method and the number and type of incoming parameters
- When calling an overloaded method, you just use the common name and, based on the signature, the compiler will know which one to execute
- IntelliSense will show you all of the overloaded signatures when you enter the name of the method and show you which parameter set each one expects
- By default, all parameters passed into a method are passed by "value", meaning they received a copy of the value
- Since they are copies, any changes made within the method will not be reflected in the calling routine
- Passing in a parameter by reference, as opposed to by value, means the value received is not a copy but the actual object itself. If your method changes the value, it will also be changed in the calling routine.
- To call by reference, you put the keyword `ref` in front of the parameters in both the definition of the method and where you call it
- The `out` keyword also passes by reference but it does not require the variable to be initialized before being passed into the method
- Parameter arrays allow for an unspecified amount of parameters to be passed into a routine
- Within your method, the parameter array is going to be an array of the values passed in – hence the name "Parameter Array"
- To declare a parameter array, you must use the keyword `params` before the parameter's name

Challenge

1. Create a method that takes two parameters. The first is a single character containing either '+' or '*'. The second parameter is a parameter array that either adds all the values up or multiplies them together, depending on the character in the first parameter. Return the result from the method or, if the first character is unknown, return 0.

2. Change your method to not have a return value but rather take another parameter in, this one by reference, and set the result into that variable

Review Quiz

1.) What does a return statement do inside a method with a void data type?
   O a. Returns execution to the caller
   O b. Returns the code to the top of the function
   O c. This is not allowed

2.) These signatures are?
   O a. Same
   O b. Different

```
public int abc(int i) {}
public void abc(int i) {}
```

3.) These signatures are?
   O a. Same
   O b. Different

```
public void abc(int i) {}
public void abc() {}
```

4.) These signatures are?
   O a. Same
   O b. Different

```
public int abc(int i) {}
public void abc(int s) {}
```

5.) These signatures are?
   O a. Same
   O b. Different

```
public static void abc(int i) {}
public void abc(int i) {}
```

6.) These signatures are?
   O a. Same
   O b. Different

```
public int abc(out int i) {}
public int abc(int i) {}
```

7.) These signatures are?
   O a. Same
   O b. Different

```
public int abc(out int i) {}
public int abc(ref int i) {}
```

8.) In the figure to the right how many unique signatures are present?

O a. 1
O b. 3
O c. 5
O d. 6
O e. 7
O f. 8
O g. 9

```
public void abc(int i) {}
public void abc(int i, string s) {}
public void abc(string s, int i) {}
public void abc(int i, int t) {}
public void abc(int i) {}
public void abc(int i, int t, string s) {}
public void abc(int i, int t) {}
public void abc(string s, int i, int t) {}
public void abc(int i) {}
public void abc(int i, string s) {}
```

9.) What is a more efficient way to do the following overload?

```
public void abc(int i) {}
public void abc(int i, int j) {}
public void abc(int i, int j, int j) {}
public void abc(int i, int j, int j, int k) {}
```

O a. public void abc(int i) {}
O b. public void abc(params int[] i) {}
O c. public void abc(int i, int i, int i, int i) {}

10.) Assuming you have an array of integers called mySeries, what are two ways you could call the AddAll function?

```
public static int AddAll(params int[] nums)
    {
        int ttl = new int();
        foreach(int i in nums)    {ttl = ttl + i;}
        return ttl;
```

☐ a. AddAll(5, 6, 7)
☐ b. AddAll(mySeries)
☐ c. MySeries(AddAll)
☐ d. AddAll({1, 2, 3, 4, 5})

11.) In what three ways can parameters be passed?
   ☐ a. Typecast
   ☐ b. value
   ☐ c. reference (ref)
   ☐ d. transgression
   ☐ e. out

12.) What type of parameter passing is default and requires no extra keyword?
   O a. Typecast
   O b. value
   O c. reference (ref)
   O d. transgression
   O e. out

Notes

Chapter 13 – Intermission

We have covered a lot of very tough material since our last break, so I think it is time for another one!

Formatted output

From the beginning of this book, we have displayed a lot of numbers but always in their "natural" state – in other words, we just had C# print out the value without any formatting to it. For example, if we had a variable hold 4112.83 and we knew this value represented a dollar amount, wouldn't it be nice if we could have it print out like $4,112.83? Sure, putting the dollar sign in front is pretty easy – just type it in within the quotes before your variable placeholder. However, trying to break it down into its parts so the commas could go into the right places would be challenging. How about trying to show a very large decimal value where we only want three places after the decimal point? For that matter, how about printing a hexadecimal value? As it turns out, all of these are easily achievable using the built-in formatting abilities of C#.

The trick is quite simple. Within the placeholders that we supply to `Write` or `WriteLine`, we just have to append a colon followed by a "format specifier". This specifier is a single control character, sometimes followed by an additional digit for precision. For example, assuming I have a `double` variable called "val1" and it contains the value of 1234.5678, this is how I could display it as a dollar value:

```
Console.WriteLine("The price is: {0:C}", val1);
```

Notice how we have the placeholder followed by a colon and then the format specifier for currency, which is the letter "C". This will give, as an output, the string "$1,234.57". C# will automatically resize the decimal portion to two digits, automatically roundup the value, add a dollar sign and even put a comma into the correct place. However, one valid question you might ask is, "What if I live in another country where we do not use the $ sign for our currency or commas to separate our thousands?"

Ah, C# is smart and doesn't automatically assume an American audience. Actually, it uses the Currency format specification from the "Regional and Language Options" page of your Control Panel. So, if you are in the UK and your Regional settings are setup for the UK, when you run this line, you will get the pound sterling symbol instead of the dollar sign!

(By the way, note that I have only provided you with a code fragment, specifically a single `WriteLine`. This far into things, I am assuming that you can put this single line of code into a program and test it out without my having to show you the entire program's code block! So, please feel free to try all of these little fragments and see the results for yourselves!)

Normally, we use only two decimal places for currency, though there are exceptions (gasoline prices come to mind). In that case, the "C" format specifier takes an optional precision value, which specifies how many digits of precision you want. For our gasoline example, which normally has three digit precision, we would write our line like this:

```
Console.WriteLine("The price is: {0:C3}", val1);
```

This will result in an output of "$1,234.568". Pretty neat, right? So what other format specifiers are there? Here is a list of the most popular ones (all the samples assume 1234 or 1234.5678 as input)[23]:

Specifier	Name	Description
C	Currency	Uses the Operating System's currency format information to format the output. Can take an optional precision value to specify number of digits after the decimal point. Sample: $1,234.57
D	Decimal	Only for integer values. Precision is optional, but without simply displays the value as it comes in. Pads the value with leading zeroes to make the output length equal to precision value. Sample: 01234 (with precision of 5)

---

[23] For the full official list of all the format specifiers, please see http://msdn.microsoft.com/en-us/library/dwhawy9k.aspx.

E or e	Scientific (exponential)	Converts the value to the scientific notation. Precision value specifies number of places after the decimal point, default is 6. The case of the letter "e" in the output is determined by the case of the specifier. Sample: 1.234568E+003
F	Fixed point	Similar to the Currency specifier, but without the leading currency indicator. Precision specifies number of places after the decimal point. Sample: 1,234.57
P	Percent	Multiplies the value by 100 and puts a percent sign after it. Precision specifies number of places after the decimal point, default is 2. Sample: 123,456.78%
X or x	Hexadecimal	Only for integer values. Converts the value to hexadecimal. The case of the letters A-F in the result will depend on the case of the specifier. Sample: 4D2

Date Formatting

Dates are another item that everybody wants formatted differently. (Don't even get me started on m/d/y vs. d/m/y!) C# will always provide you with the current date using the object System.DateTime.Now but the default format will be based on your Operating Systems's regional settings. Even if that format suits your style, you may only want or need a certain piece of it, such as the day of the week, or just the time.

Once again, the solution is a set of Format Specifiers. For each of the examples below, assume that the current date is December 25th, 2009 at 1:23:45 PM.

Specifier	Name	Result
d	Short date	12/25/2009
D	Long date	December 25, 2009
t	Short time	1:23 PM
T	Long time	1:23:45 PM
f	Full date & time (short)	December 25, 2009 1:23 PM
F	Full date & time (long)	December 25, 2009 1:23:45 PM
g	Default date & time (short)	12/25/2009 1:23 PM (depends on OS Region settings)
G	Default date & time (long)	12/25/2009 1:23:45 PM (depends on OS Region settings)
M	Month & day	December 25
Y	Year & Month	December, 2009

Since a date is a composite value, in other words made up of multiple parts, you cannot just assign it as if it were a single value, such as an integer. For example, this will not work:

```
DateTime dt = "12/25/2009 1:23:45 PM";
```

So then, how can you assign a specific date value to a variable? The trick is to use the `Parse` function of the `DateTime` class, similar to way we parse out an integer from a console input. Using our sample date from above, this is the correct syntax:

```
DateTime dt = DateTime.Parse("12/25/2009 1:23:45
PM");
```

In this example, I have provided all the elements that a `DateTime` variable can hold, which includes the date (month, day and year), as well as a time (hour, minute, second and the AM/PM designator). Because a date can be a flexible construct, meaning I might have a date but not the time, you can simply enter whatever parts you wish and the `Parse` command will figure it out.

Command Line Parameters

We have already covered both regular arrays and parameter arrays (using the keyword `params`), so we can finally cover something I promised to cover way back in the first chapter. If you recall our very first program, we went through it line by line, but when we got to the declaration for Main I skipped over the meaning of its parameters.

```
static void Main(string[] args)
```

By now, you have probably figured out that we are looking at an array of strings called "args", but what is it for? After all, the Main method is called by the compiler in order to start executing our program. So, where could the args parameter come from?

If you have ever spent any time working with command line utilities, you are probably aware of command line switches. If not, don't worry. Command switches are a very simple concept – think of it as a way to send information into the program before it even executes. Normally, to execute a command line program, you would type its name at the command prompt and press enter. As soon as you press enter, the program launches and does its thing. But what if you wanted to alter what the program does? Command switches allow you to make the program behave in a different way, or to provide it information (parameters) that it might need to function.

Even the built-in Windows commands support these command switches, such as the ever popular "dir" command. Dir, which stands for directory, simply shows you all the files and folders (known as directories among the command line aficionados) that are located in the directory you are currently in. So, what command switches does dir support?

Take a look at Figure 83 below – it shows the "dir" command when run by itself, as well as with a switch (/w), which changes how the output looks.

Figure 83: The "dir" command with and without a command switch

So, how do you normally use a command line switch or parameter? If running a program at a command prompt, you simply type the name of the program followed by a space and then enter any command switches or parameters. When you press enter, the program is executed and all of the switches and parameters entered after the program name are provided to the program to evaluate or use as needed. Traditionally, a command line switch is made up two or more characters where the first character is a forward slash. The following characters specify which switch you wish to activate. A command line parameter has no such designator it is just a bit of data. Figure 84 is an example of the "dir" command with both a parameter (*1.txt) and a switch (/w). The parameter restricts the listing to text file(s) which have a 1 as the last character of their name, while the switch tells dir to display this in wide format.

```
C:\z>dir *1.txt /w
 Volume in drive C has no label.
 Volume Serial Number is 083A-2D98

 Directory of C:\z

file1.txt    note1.txt
                 2 File(s)               12 bytes
                 0 Dir(s)  87,714,983,936 bytes free

C:\z>
```

Figure 84: The "dir" command with both a parameter and a switch

One standard among nearly every command line utility is a help function which usually describes what the program does and what switches, if any, it supports. Under Windows the standard way to get this help listing to show up is to type the name of the command followed by "/?". The forward slash before the question mark signifies that this is a command switch and not a parameter.

Go ahead and try it! Open up a command prompt window. The easiest way is to click on the Start button, type in "cmd" and click Ok. When the Command Prompt window comes up, type in "dir /?" (without the quotes of course) and press enter. You should get a screen similar to Figure 85, but the exact output will depend on the version of Windows that you are using.

Figure 85: Typing a forward slash and then a question mark "/?"

The array of switches and parameters available with dir allow you to customize the output it gives you in all sorts of ways. How does this relate to our console applications?

All of the programs we have been writing so far have been Console Applications, which have to provide any command line parameters entered by the user to the code for processing. This is done through the "args" array, which at run time will contain these optional parameters. Any switches or parameters you pass into the args array can be used and processed in Main. That's great, but what if we run our program through the Visual Studio environment? Ah, that has been thought of! There is a way that you can provide command line parameters to your programs when running it through the Visual Studio debugger environment but it is a bit hidden.

Each project has a set of options that can be applied to it on a case by case basis using the Properties page. We have already visited the properties page when we covered variable overflow and underflow. There we found a switch by which we could make our project check on this condition automatically. As you recall, one of the ways to bring this page up is from the Project menu by selecting "<project name> Properties". Once you have the Properties page open, from the left hand side click on the "Debug" tab (Figure 86).

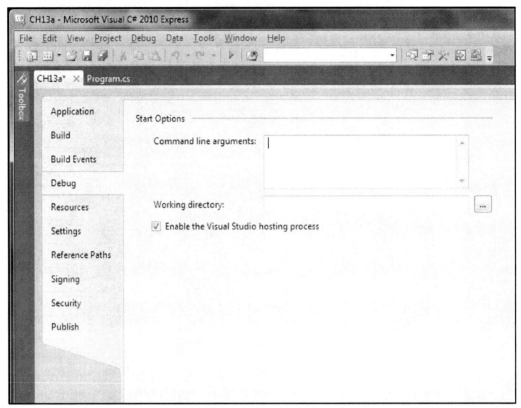

Figure 86: You can specify command line arguments by accessing the Debug page of the Project Properties

There are not too many options on this page but we are only interested in one – and it is easy to find! See that large box labeled as "Command line arguments"? Anything you enter into this box will be available within your project by accessing the `args` variable of the Main method. We can try this with a very simple project that will just step through all the elements it finds in `args`, check for a specific switch, and display everything else for us on the screen. Please start a "CH13a" project and use the following code in your Main method:

```
foreach (string item in args)
{
    if (item == "/hello")
        Console.WriteLine("Hello user!");
    else
        Console.WriteLine("{0}", item);
}

Console.ReadLine();
```

Thanks to the `foreach` loop, this is a very short and simple program. If you have already put something into the Command Line Arguments text box on the project Properties page, please remove it. We should run the program first without any entries in there, to simulate the program executing without giving it any command line arguments. Go ahead and run it!

The results are a bit underwhelming, since nothing shows up – as expected! After all, we did not provide any parameters so there is nothing in the array. Therefore, the `foreach` loop had nothing to process. So, if nothing shows up without any data being provided, why did I get you to run this? Mostly to demonstrate a difference between C# and some of the other C based languages. Under C, for example, if we had run this exact same program there would actually have been one entry in the `args` array – the name of the program itself. With C# only the actual parameters are provided to your application, something that could be confusing to anyone with a background in other programming languages, such as C.

Now that we have seen what happens with no parameters, I think it is time to try it with something actually provided. Open up your project's Properties page and enter something into the Command Line Arguments box. You can use anything you would like but for my test I entered "item1 item2". Run your program and you should get an output like Figure 87.

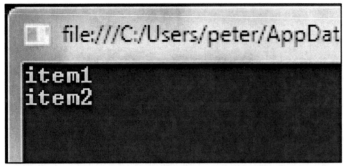

Figure 87: Running the project from Visual Studio, we can see both parameters that were passed in

Just as we expected, two entries are displayed. If we were running our program outside of the Visual Studio environment, we would simply have entered these values (item1 and item2) after the name of our program (Figure 88).

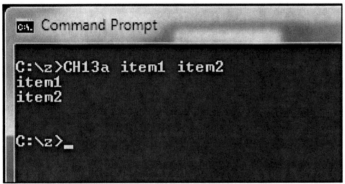

Figure 88: Calling on your CH13a program from the command line shows both parameters that were specified

Now, in the `foreach` loop, we are also examining our parameters against a very specific entry, the /hello flag. If we find this entry we are going to display a special message instead of the parameter value. Go back into your project's properties page and add this switch somewhere into the Command Line Arguments box (Figure 89), then run your program.

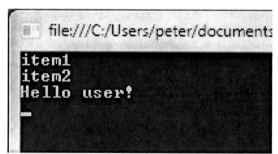

Figure 89: Add the /hello switch into your command line arguments box

When the `if` statement sees that switch, it prints out our friendly hello message (Figure 90). This is a very simple example of how you can process incoming parameters and switches.

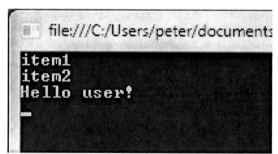

Figure 90: The switch causes the hello message to be printed

Try different types of input to see how it shows up within the args parameter array.

The important concept to pick up from this example is that we can get information into our programs via the command line and that spaces are used to separate the individual entries.

Forbidden Knowledge

At some point during my high school years, I read something that has always stuck with me. While I cannot recall where I read it, or even the exact quotation, the gist of it was that knowledge by itself is neither good nor evil. It is up to us to use our knowledge for either good or bad. Why do I bring this up in a book about C#? Because, there is a subject that I am almost hesitant to bring up but for the sake of completeness I really have to. Since the earliest days of programming, there has been one consistent rule among all programming languages and all developers – goto is bad and should never be used. As with most such statements, there is some truth to it but, of course, in life things are never as easy as that.

So, what is goto? Do you remember a game called Monopoly? In that game you move sequentially around the board by the number thrown on your dice. Except when you land on a space called "Go directly to Jail", then instead of moving sequentially around the board, you just jump to the space labeled as Jail. The sequential flow of your path has been altered by this "Go directly to Jail" space.

In the very simplest of terms, goto is a command used to alter the flow of execution. By that definition, it is not all that different from other statements such as if, switch or even looping commands such as for and while. The difference is how goto works as compared to any of these other examples. With an if statement, for example, we can see that the program flow might change depending on the condition but it is done in a logical and predictable method. On the other hand, a goto statement is pretty much what it sounds like – a command to jump to another point in the code without any conditions or checks.

The reason this is so universally considered a bad idea is that it leads to something called "spaghetti code" (think of a plate of tangled spaghetti), which is programmer speak for "something hard to follow and understand". The funny thing is, in the very early days of programming, before languages such as C and Pascal, goto was a critical programming element and was used to create loops, logic conditions and other such things. In fact, if you go back to the beginning of this book and take a look at Figure 1 you can see a simple Basic program that used a goto.

So, one final warning. I will show you an example of the goto statement, but whenever you consider using it, I ask you to reconsider and find an alternative.

By the way, most companies have a process called a Code Review, where before any code can be accepted into a project it has to be reviewed by a team of developers. This group makes sure that the code makes sense, does not contain any obvious errors and can be understood by others. Nearly all of these companies have a policy that any code which uses a goto will immediately fail code review and needs to be rewritten. You've been warned!

There are actually two parts to the goto statement, one of which is the goto command itself followed by the name of a label where you wish execution to jump to. The other part, of course, is the label to which the goto statement will refer to. The best way to explain this is with a bit of code:

```
int ct = 0;

loopStart:
    if (ct == 5)
        goto loopEnd;

    Console.WriteLine("Ct equals {0}", ct++);
    goto loopStart;

loopEnd:
    Console.ReadLine();
```

This is the hard way to write an iterative loop. We start by declaring a counter and setting its initial value. To function, the loop needs two labels to indicate landing points for actions and two goto statements for the actions. The "loopStart:" is the label that we can jump to using a goto later on in the code – it has no other purpose and causes no output, change in variables or any other observable affect when executed.

To avoid the creation of an infinite loop, we need to specify a condition under which the loop is exited. We do that with an if statement and another goto command for a jump when our exit condition is met. Next, a simple message is displayed along with the value of the ct variable and at the same time its value is increased by one.

Until that condition is met, we continue to execute the WriteLine and goto loop start statements. When the condition is met, we are sent to the loopEnd landing point.

Granted, this is just an example to show you how a goto statement works. It also shows how, whenever you feel the urge to use it, there is always a better way to accomplish your task. Just take a look at how long this code is as compared to the equivalent if it had used either a for or a while loop.

Have I mentioned that you should never, ever use a `goto` statement? I'm not kidding!

Points to Ponder

- You can format the output of variable on the `Write` and `WriteLine` commands. For example, you can display a number, such as 12, as a dollar value so it looks like this: $12.00.
- To format an output variable, you use a colon after the output placeholder value followed by a command character and optional parameters. For example, to format a numeric value as a dollar value you would use ":C".
- When writing a command line application, your Main method has an incoming parameter array for any command line switches that are provided to it by the user
- You can provide command line parameters to a program, even if you are running within the Visual Studio environment, by modifying your project's properties page
- C# has a `goto` keyword, but it is evil and should never be used under any circumstances!!

Review Quiz

1) You have an integer variable called `bal` which contains the value of 4200. How could you generate the following output? (Choose 2 answers.)

> Your balance is $4,200.00

☐ a. `Console.Write("Your balance is {0}", bal);`
☐ b. `Console.Write("Your balance is {0:C2}", bal);`
☐ c. `Console.Write("Your balance is {0,2}", bal);`
☐ d. `Console.Write("Your balance is {0,C}", bal);`
☐ e. `Console.Write("Your balance is {0:C}", bal);`

2) You need to assign a specific date to the variable `dt`. Which is the correct way to accomplish this?

O a. `DateTime dt = "10/31/2009";`
O b. `DateTime dt = (DateTime) "10/31/2009";`
O c. `DateTime dt = DateTime.Parse("10/31/2009");`

3) The following parameters are provided to your program:

> entry1 entry2 entry3

In your program, you are only interested in the first parameter (entry1). Which line of code will print that parameter out?

O a. `Console.WriteLine(args[0]);`
O b. `Console.WriteLine(args[1]);`
O c. `Console.WriteLine(args[2]);`
O d. `Console.WriteLine(args[3]);`

4) Using a `goto` is an efficient way to change the flow of execution in your program?

O a. True
O b. False

Notes

Chapter 14 – Classes

When we discussed Classes earlier, we only touched upon the proverbial tip of the iceberg, but it was enough to introduce the concept. Now we need to take a look at some of the more advanced properties of classes.

Classes are the primary means by which we create objects – they allow you to create structures that range from the very simple to the highly complex. Some of the elements by which you can give power to your classes have to do with how internal data and methods are accessed, how data is initially entered into a class when it is being instantiated, and how they can inherit, or how they can allow others to inherit abilities from them. Oh, foreshadowing! Actually, the concept of inheritance will be introduced in our next volume – we have plenty of other stuff to cover here!

Constructor

At my house I have a universal remote control that is linked to my TV set, cable box, and DVD player. By themselves none of these three devices are really useful, but when combined I can watch my movies or TV shows. Knowing this, when I programmed the universal remote's on button, I set it up so by pressing one button all three devices are turned on. For the one action that I take (pressing the on button), three different events occur on my behalf (the TV, cable box and DVD player are all turned on). This is similar to what the constructor of a class does, where by the simple action of instantiating a new class any number of additional steps can occur.

Simply defined, a constructor is a special method which can be used to set the internal data fields of a class, prepare other data structures, or to open external connections. It is automatically executed when an object is instantiated. As usual, the best way to truly explain this is with a simple example. In fact, we are going to use this same example for the rest of this chapter, expanding upon it with each new subject. Please start a "CH14a" project.

When ready, find the end of the Program class and create a new class called Person. Initially, it will be a very simple class with just a pair of fields:

```
class Person
{
    public string name;
    public byte age;
}
```

Simple it may be, but this is a complete class and will do just fine for our purposes – but before we can use it, we need some code in our Main method to actually put this class to use. For that, please use the following code:

```
static void Main(string[] args)
{
    Person thePerson = new Person();

    thePerson.name = "Joe";
    thePerson.age = 21;

    Console.WriteLine("Name: {0}, Age: {1}",
thePerson.name, thePerson.age);

    Console.ReadLine();
}
```

Nothing special in here so far, and even before running this program you should be able to make a good guess as to the output. However, let's examine one part of this code a bit more carefully. Take a look at that pair of open and close parentheses at the end of the instantiation line (that is the line with the keyword new on it). Looks sort of a like a call to a method, doesn't it? In fact, that is exactly what it is!

All classes have something called a constructor which is just a special method that is called when an object is instantiated. Now, we did not write any methods within our class yet, so what is being called? If you do not provide a constructor for your class, C# actually creates one for you, though it doesn't show in your code or do anything obvious.

However, a default constructor does do something. It initializes all instance fields to their default values. For numeric data types the default value is a 0, for Booleans it is false and for a string it is a null string. This is why it looks like we are calling a method, because we actually are!

Instead of taking the default constructor, I think we need to write one of our own.[24] However, this is not just any method but a very special one and as such there are some rules to follow:

1) The name of the constructor method has to be the same as the name of the class
2) A class can have only one constructor though it can be overloaded as many times as you want to
3) It cannot have a return type but it should not be marked `void`. C# knows that a constructor always has a return type of `void` so giving it any return type, even `void`, will generate an error!

Modify your Person class to look like this:

```
class Person
{
    public string name;
    public byte age;

    public Person(string aName, byte theAge)
    {
        name = aName;
        age = theAge;
    }
}
```

A nice, simple constructor for a simple class! We carefully followed each of the three rules, accepted two incoming values and then assigned those values into the two fields of the class. But by doing this, we broke something in our Main method, specifically the line where we instantiate the object (Figure 91). (If you are not seeing the yellow popup with the error message, just let your mouse hover over the part of the code underlined in red.)

---

[24] So, what happens to the default constructor if you also write one yourself? Ah, great question! Be patient and all will be revealed!

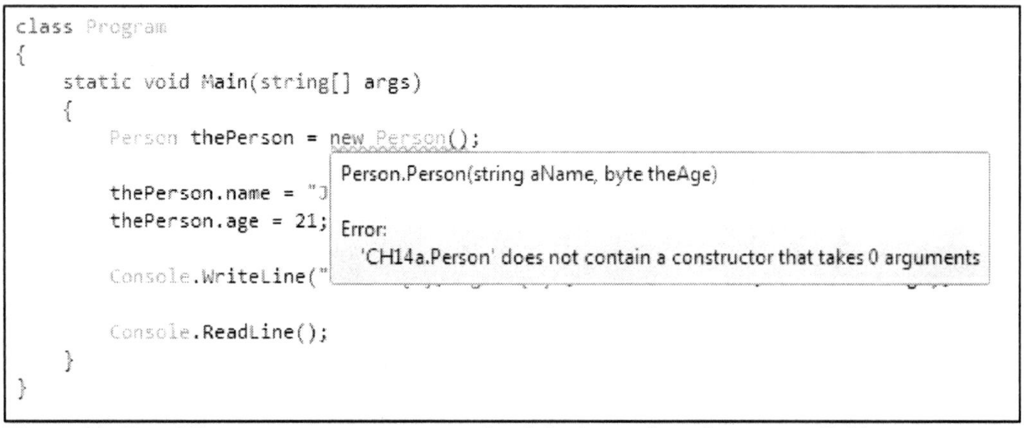

```
class Program
{
    static void Main(string[] args)
    {
        Person thePerson = new Person();

        thePerson.name = "J
        thePerson.age = 21;

        Console.WriteLine("

        Console.ReadLine();
    }
}
```

Person.Person(string aName, byte theAge)

Error:
'CH14a.Person' does not contain a constructor that takes 0 arguments

Figure 91: By adding our own constructor, the default one is no longer available

Hmmm, that is an interesting message. It is not saying that the compiler cannot find the constructor, rather it cannot find one which takes no arguments – which is what an empty open/close parentheses set means. If you remember, one of the constructor rules is that, like any other method, it can be overloaded. So far, the only constructor we have takes two parameters but the instantiation line is trying to call one without any parameters. Since that version of the constructor does not exist, we get an error! To fix this, let's modify the code in our Main method like this:

```
static void Main(string[] args)
{
    Person thePerson = new Person("Joe", 21);

    Console.WriteLine("Name: {0}, Age: {1}",
thePerson.name, thePerson.age);

    Console.ReadLine();
}
```

This time, when we create an instance of the class, we can provide the initial values to our two data fields all on one line, allowing us to remove the two lines which provided the initial values before.

For the purpose of our demonstration, the best solution was to move the assignment of the name and age values into the instantiation, but we could have fixed the error another way. We could have written another constructor (remember a constructor can be overloaded) which takes no parameters, and which would have had no lines of code to execute. That would have given the instantiation line a valid method to run, allowing our Main routine to remain untouched.

```
class Person
{
    public string name;
    public byte age;

    public Person()
    {
        // Empty constructor
    }

    public Person(string aName, byte theAge)
    {
        name = aName;
        age = theAge;
    }
}
```

Now, if you are asking yourself why we had to provide a blank constructor – after all, before making our own constructor all of this worked fine, thanks to the C# compiler providing a blank constructor on its own – then pat yourself on the back for asking a great question! The reason is simple: C# does provide a blank constructor, but only when we do not have one (or more) of our own defined. As soon as we created our own constructor, the one automatically generated is no longer being provided. If we still have a need for an empty constructor, then it is up to us to provide it.

What else can you do inside a constructor? Well, pretty much anything you can do in a method you can do in a constructor, although generally a constructor is used to prepare the object that was just instantiated. Since the constructor is called automatically, once during the setup of the object, it is best for one-time tasks instead of repeating processes.

That last sentence has a very important concept in it that you should not miss. Notice I said that the constructor is called automatically. Does that mean that I cannot call a constructor manually? Correct! This is a special method that is only called during the instantiation of the object, and is not available for general usage. In fact, IntelliSense knows this and will not provide the constructor in the list of methods available to your object (Figure 92). The only things available are the publicly accessible fields (age and name), and the 4 standard methods that all objects share.

```
class Program
{
    static void Main(string[] args)
    {
        Person thePerson = new Person("Joe", 21);

        Console.WriteLine("Name: {0}, Age: {1}",

        thePerson.
                    ┌─────────────────────┐
                    │ ◈ age               │
        Console.Re  │ ◈ Equals            │
    }               │ ◈ GetHashCode       │
}                   │ ◈ GetType           │
                    │ ◈ name              │
class Person        │ ◈ ToString          │
{                   └─────────────────────┘
    public string name;
    public byte age;
```

Figure 92: IntelliSense shows all you class members, but does not show the constructor

Static Constructor

In our discussion of constructors in the preceding section, it was mentioned that the constructor is executed whenever a new instance of a class is created. This kind of a constructor is more precisely know as an Instance Constructor, or Class Constructor. However, your class definition can also contain static methods, which are available without having to create an instance of the object – meaning an instance constructor will not be executed. Som what can you do if you need to prepare something (such as variables) which your static methods will need?

The solution is a Static Constructor. The purpose for these is the same as for an instance constructor; the difference is when they are executed. While an instance constructor will be executed each time a new object is instantiated from a class, the static constructor will be executed only once. More specifically, it will be executed just before you call any static method of a class, for the first time. Let me rephrase that. The very first time you call any static method of a class, the static constructor, if one exists, will be executed. If you then call on a `static` method again, the same or another one, the static constructor will not be executed again.

Defining a static constructor is very similar to that of an instance constructor, the only difference being the keyword `static` in front of the method. So, if our Person class were to get a static constructor, it would look like this:

```
class Person
{
    public string name;
    public byte age;

    public Person()
    {
        // Instance constructor
    }

    static Person()
    {
        // Static constructor
    }

    // Rest of code here
}
```

There are a few additional rules that you must know when defining a static constructor:

1. You can only have one static constructor in a class
2. A static constructor cannot have any parameters
3. Static constructors cannot be overloaded

All of these rules basically refer to the same issue. Since a `static` constructor is called automatically by the compiler before executing a `static` method, there is no way for you to provide it any parameters. Because of this, there is no way for it to be overloaded and therefore you can only ever have one!

Constructors and Structs

Besides a class, you can also create and use constructors within a `struct` (If you need, see Chapter 9 for a refresher on `structs`). The same rules apply: the constructor has to be named the same as the `struct`, it can be overloaded, and it is primarily used to allow for the `struct` data fields to be populated during the instantiation of an instance of the `struct`. While in the chapter where we introduced the `struct`, we simply declared a variable of the data type of the new `struct`, as we would for any other data type. However you can use the same instantiation method as with a class using the keyword new. For example, if we have a `struct` called Square and it has a constructor to set its two data fields, we can create it like this:

```
Square mySquare = new Square(5, 6);
```

Even though it looks just like the instantiation of an instance of a class, it is actually used for a `struct` with a constructor.

There are two major differences between constructors for a class and those for a `struct`:

1. A `struct` cannot have a parameter-less constructor. This is because a `struct` is considered a data type, which is automatically initialized to a default value on creation (0 for numeric types, empty string for string types, and false for bool).
2. Even if you create a constructor of your own, the system provided blank constructor remains!

To demonstrate both of these points, take a look at this code block:

```
struct Square
{
    public int height, width;

    // The following constructor is wrong, and will
    // generate an error since parameter-less
    // constructors are not allowed!

/*  public Square()
 *  {
 *      height = 10;
```

```
*          width = 10;
*     }
*/

    public Square(int h, int w)
    {
        height = h;
        width = w;
    }
}

static void Main(string[] args)
{
    Square mySquare = new Square(5, 6);
    Console.WriteLine("Height: {0}, Width: {1}",
        mySquare.height, mySquare.width);

    // This will work, since a struct does not lose
    // its default constructor even if we have
created
    // one of our own!
    Square anotherSquare = new Square();
    Console.WriteLine("Height: {0}, Width: {1}",
        anotherSquare.height, anotherSquare.width);

    Console.ReadLine();
}
```

The struct Square has a constructor defined which takes two integers and then sets its member values to those two integers. There is also a parameter-less constructor, but since that is not allowed I had to comment it out. In the Main code block, we declare a new object called mySquare from the struct and use its constructor to set the member fields to 5 and 6 respectively. So far, pretty normal and looking very much the same as it would for a class.

However, the next example is most definitely not like that of a class! Notice how when we create the object anotherSquare, we do not provide any values for the constructor. If this were a class based object then for this to work we would have had to create a constructor that takes no parameters, but that is not allowed for a struct! Yet the code works! This is because a struct, unlike a class, does not lose its default constructor even if you write a constructor of your own!

Back in Chapter 9, when we declared a `struct` variable in our code, we did not use the keyword new. We simply declared the variable as we do with any other data type. In other words we did this:

```
Square yetAnotherSquare;
```

We know this is legal (since we used it all through Chapter 9), and it does actually still call upon the default constructor that is provided with each `struct`. The reason this works is because declaring a `struct` variable without the keyword new is considered a shortcut. When the compiler processes this line, it actually converts the line for itself to look like this:

```
Square yetAnotherSquare = new Square();
```

While both methods are legal, and used quite commonly, I personally prefer the full version with the new keyword. Yes, it is a bit more typing but it makes for code that is easier to read and understand at a later date, and reminds me that there is an implicit constructor being called on my behalf.

I Don't mean That, I mean This!

Let's take a look at our Person class's constructor code again:

```
class Person
{
    public string name;
    public byte age;

    public Person(string aName, byte theAge)
    {
        name = aName;
        age = theAge;
    }
}
```

Notice how the names of incoming variables to the constructor (aName and theAge) are not the same as the fields of the class (name and age). This is not by accident. After all, if we had named the parameters of the constructor the same as the class fields, how would we (or for that matter the compiler) know to which one we were referring? In other words, what if we had written the constructor method like this:

```
public Person(string name, byte age)
{
    name = name;
    age = age;
}
```

In fact, please go ahead and modify our project's constructor method to look like this. Yep, that is pretty confusing. Are we assigning values that came into the method to the class fields, or the other way around? Sure, any human reading this code would immediately assume that we want to assign the incoming values to the fields of the class, but assumptions can be wrong. More importantly, the compiler never makes assumptions and, in fact, it would be quite confused by this code (Figure 93).

```
class Person
{
    public string name;
    public byte age;

    public Person(string Name, byte age)
    {
        name = Name;
        age = age;
    }                (parameter) byte age
}
                     Warning:
                        Assignment made to same variable; did you mean to assign something else?
```

Figure 93: Using the same identifiers of name and age for your parameters and class members gives you a warning

So, besides using better (i.e. different) variable names, how else could we tell the compiler what we really meant? The keyword this is here to help! Basically, the keyword this always refers to the current instance of the object and will clear up the confusion to the compiler. To test this, please put the keyword this followed by a period before the names of the class's fields, like this:

```
public Person(string name, byte age)
{
    this.name = name;
    this.age = age;
}
```

That took care of our errors! Once we make an instance of the class, we can refer to its elements by using the instance name followed by a period and then the name of the field we wish to access. The `this` keyword does the same thing but works internally to the class regardless of what name you might have instantiated it to externally. While, for our example here, the better solution is to use clearer names for our class fields and the constructor parameters, there are times when you might not have that choice and need to make it clear to the compiler to which variable you are referring.

Finalizer

In nature, there is always a balance between things – male vs. female, birth vs. death, day vs. night. It turns out, that even programming languages have to follow nature. So, if a constructor is used to help create an object then there needs to be something to help destroy it.

Imagine yourself on a beautiful warm day, walking around with a nice fountain drink in a paper cup with a lid and a straw. The cup, lid and straw are necessary for you to enjoy your drink while walking around. The moment you take your last sip and your cup is empty, what do you do with it? Since it is no longer needed, you look for a proper place to discard it – after all, once the cup is empty it is no longer of use to you. What if you never threw any of your paper cups away but picked up a new drink every afternoon? Eventually, you would have more cups and straws then you could carry and it would render you unable to function. Obtaining a necessary object in memory but failing to let them go when no longer needed is called a memory leak.

It is common for objects in programming to run by creating connections to other objects. These connections take up computer memory. Earlier on, I mentioned that C# has a garbage collector, which automatically cleans up variables and their memory when they go out of scope. That is also true for instantiated classes but there are some things that the garbage collector is not able to do. Let us take a look at an example. If the constructor that you create makes a connection to an external database, what happens to this connection when the object goes out of scope? Most likely, it would stay open, using up memory in the process. This could lead to a severe memory leak which might crash your program. In such cases, you can write a finalizer routine within which you could close this database connection.

This leads to the question of exactly when does a finalizer get executed? Once your object goes out of scope, the garage collector will clean up any variables that your object used. Since the purpose of a finalizer is to clean up things which the garbage collector cannot, such as open connections which are stored within your class, it needs be executed just before the garage collector runs.

While not as commonly used as the constructor, a class can also have a finalizer method, which is called automatically when the object falls out of scope and is removed. (A finalizer can also be called a destructor, which to me always sounds like some kind of a comic book bad guy, so we'll just stick with finalizer.) Just as C# provides a blank constructor if you do not manually create one, it also creates a default finalizer. Unless you have a need or a custom finalizer, it is not required to write one.

So, how do you write a finalizer? Just as our constructor has the same name as that of the class, so does the finalizer but with one addition. You need to put a tilde (~) before the name, which marks it as the finalizer method. Using our Person class from before, here is what the finalizer method would look like:

```
~Person()
{
    <some code>
}
```

That's it! There are no parameters, no return type and no security modifier. This is a very simple declaration to be used only in the unique situation where something needs to be done which is outside of the scope of the garbage collector. Since this is used only to clean up after the class, it cannot take any parameters nor can you overload it. (By definition, overloads are used to allow for different types of incoming parameters, which a finalizer cannot have.) Unless you have a very explicit reason for needing a finalizer, do not create one – in fact, we are going to leave this out of our project as well.

Properties

In my High School science class, the teacher showed that a glass of water will eventually reach the same temperature as the air that surrounds it. For example, if we put some ice cold water on a counter in a room with an ambient temperature of 72F, in a few hours the water will also become 72F. Now put the same glass into a 38F refrigerator, once again, after a few hours the temperature of the water will become that of its surroundings. However, there are limits. If we now put this glass of water into a freezer, which is at -25F, the water in the glass will never reach that temperature. It will go down to 32F and not go any lower. The same holds true at the upper end – the temperature of our water will never become higher than 212F[25]. The water will not "throw an error" if you try to go outside of this range, it will simply stay at one of these limit values. Using Properties, we can also enforce limits on the values which can be assigned to the data fields of objects.

Until now, we have always referred to the internal data values of a class as fields and have been able to access them directly. However, in most cases the ability to externally modify an object's data fields is probably not a good idea. What if we have to impose limits on a particular field and if we exceed those limits our code would either crash or the results would simply not make any sense? By allowing direct external access to these fields, such as we have been doing all along, we cannot guarantee that a process would honor our limit requirements.

So, what is the solution? What if, instead of allowing direct access to these fields, we mark them `private` and restrict access to class methods within which we can impose our limits? That solves the problem of outside processes directly messing with our fields. However, it leaves the problem of how to set or read values.

What if we wrote a method to do the following?
- Take the incoming value(s)
- Verify them as acceptable
- If the values are acceptable, set the fields
- Write another method that returned the field values to the calling process

---

[25] Ok, I know that water past 212F will become steam and that the steam can be of a temperature higher that 212F, but for our example we are sticking with water and not steam. (Same for water becoming ice at below 32F.)

Even better, we could give our method the same name as the field! That would hide from the calling process the fact that it is not accessing the field directly. Rather, the called field is accessed by a method that has control over the process. This turns our fields into properties.

Actually, this is a very common scenario and, in order to accomplish it, a set of keywords (`get` and `set`) exist to make your life easier. Let's take our Person class and enforce some rules on the age field – any value below 1 or above 125 will not be valid. If they are outside of these bounds, we will set the age to the nearest limit. To make this happen, we need to make two changes to our Person class. First, please change the permission level of our two fields from `public` to `private`. Now that we can no longer access these fields directly (Figure 94), we need to provide an alternative way to accomplish the same thing.

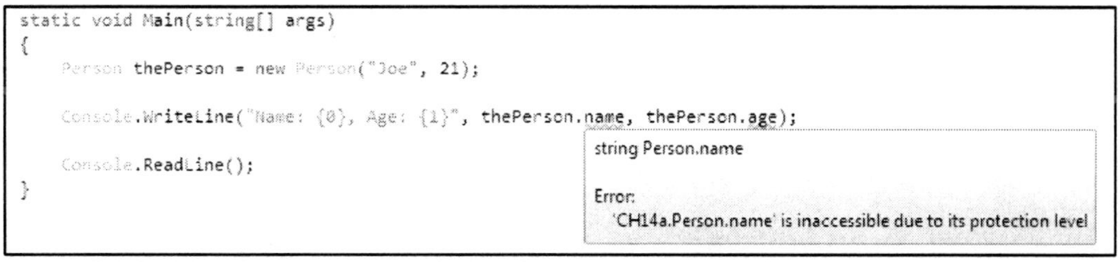

```
static void Main(string[] args)
{
    Person thePerson = new Person("Joe", 21);

    Console.WriteLine("Name: {0}, Age: {1}", thePerson.name, thePerson.age);

    Console.ReadLine();
}
```

string Person.name

Error:
'CH14a.Person.name' is inaccessible due to its protection level

Figure 94: Making fields `private` in another class, makes their values inaccessible to your calling method

For that, please add the following two methods into our Person class, just after the constructor (We can actually put it anywhere, there is no requirement that it be after the constructor):

```
public string Name
{
    get { return name; }
    set { name = value; }
}

public byte Age
{
    get { return age; }
    set
    {
        if (value < 1)
            age = 1;
        else if (value > 125)
            age = 125;
        else
            age = value;
    }
}
```

In order to allow external access, we wrote two methods named the same as the variables, but we used an upper case letter since we cannot use the same name twice in the same scope. (Remember C# is case sensitive, so by changing the case they are considered two different names.) The two methods are set to `public`, since we have to be able to access them from the outside in order to set or read the field values.

Hmmm, there is something very strange about these methods – notice how they do not have a parameter list, even though they will accept a single incoming value. (Actually, they look almost like field definitions!) How is that possible? Because within the method we use the keywords `get` and `set`, the compiler knows that these methods has very special functions with regard to data fields, namely to either assign them an incoming value or return the current value. Which of these two tasks it does, depends on how an external process calls upon this method (more on that in just a bit).

When the request is to read the value of the field, the `get` block is executed. Within this block, you must have a return statement which then sends a value out. The value that is returned is totally up to you. Normally, you would just return the field's value but you could have code in there to do something special and return something totally different. (For example, if the name is equal to "Joe" return not the name but the string "he is a great guy!")

The only other ability these methods have is to write a new value into one of the data fields, which is done using the `set` code block. The keyword `value` holds the received value, which you can either assign to the field immediately or run any kind of a check or process on before using it. In our example code above, we check to see if the value is outside of the range of 1 to 125 and if it is, we just set the field to the nearest limit. Otherwise, we use the value directly.

So, how does the compiler know if you want to `set` or `get` the value of the field? This depends on how you use this property – if you try to read from it then the `get` block is executed, but if you write to it then `set` is used. Right now the code in our Main method is trying to illegally access the two fields, so we have to rewrite it in order use the objects properties instead. Change your Main to this:

```
static void Main(string[] args)
{
    Person thePerson = new Person("Joe", 21);

    Console.WriteLine("Name: {0}, Age: {1}",
thePerson.Name, thePerson.Age);

    thePerson.Name = "Jenny";
    thePerson.Age = 18;

    Console.WriteLine("Name: {0}, Age: {1}",
thePerson.Name, thePerson.Age);

    Console.ReadLine();
}
```

Within the code of Main, we are using the constructor to set the initial values, which we then extract for display by accessing the property. This causes the property method to get executed and because we are reading the value, the `get` side of the method is used.

On the next two lines, we then replace the initial values ("Joe" and 21) with new data ("Jenny" and 18). Again, the property method is executed but now we are assigning a value to the property the `set` side is used.

Besides the protection that this offers to the data fields of our class, we also see another powerful feature at work here. Notice that for both pulling the value out as well as for setting it, we use the exact same syntax: `thePerson.<field name>`.

Points to Ponder

- A constructor is a special method within a class, which is automatically executed when an instance of the class is instantiated
- A constructor method is always named the same as the class, but has no return type and needs to be marked as public
- Structs can also have a constructor method
- The keyword `this` always refers the current instance of the class
- A finalizer is an optional method for a class which is automatically called and executed when the class goes out of scope and is removed from memory
- Normally, you do not have to worry about creating a finalizer, since the compiler takes care of it. But if you have a special process which needs to clean up some memory or close a connection to a file, the compiler cannot do that for you. You have to take care of it by using a finalizer method.
- Finalizer can also be called a destructor
- Fields are variables within a class
- Properties are special methods written to allow access to privately marked fields of a class
- The code within the property method of class can be used to do data validation before assigning the value(s) to the field(s)
- The `get` and `set` keywords for a property allow you to receive or send values out when the property is accessed
- You do not have to use both a `get` and a `set`. A property with only a `get` is considered a read-only property, while one with just a `set` is a write-only property.

Challenge

1) Create a class for a very simple note taking application. The class should have the following fields: Name (string), Day (byte), Year (ushort) and

Note (string). In Main, create an instance of the class and populate the fields. Display the results to the screen.

2) Add constructors to the note class so that the user can either specify all of the fields or none at all. If none of the fields are provided, assign a default value where Name defaults to "unknown", Day to the current day of the week (1-7), Year to current year, and Note to blank.

3) Change the fields to private and turn them into properties by creating the methods to allow access to them. Put in verifications so the day value has to be between 1 and 7 and year has to be above 1975. If the values are outside of these ranges, set them to the defaults as described above.

Review Quiz

1) When are constructors called?
   O a. When the application starts
   O b. When the object is created
   O c. After the object is garbage collected
   O d. Before the object is garbage collected

2) If you do not have a constructor...
   O a. The object is considered static
   O b. The application throws an exception
   O c. The runtime provides a default constructor
   O d. Then methods cannot be overloaded

3) You use Visual Studio .Net to create a Windows-based application that will track candy sales. The application's main object is named Candy. The Candy class is created by the following definition:

```
public class Candy { }
```

You have to write code that sets properties for the Candy class. This code must be executed as soon as an instance of the Candy class is created. You need to create a procedure in which you can place your code. Which code segment should you use?

   O a. `public bool { }`
   O b. `public void Candy() { }`
   O c. `public Candy() { }`
   O d. `Candy() { }`

4) When does the default constructor exist?
   O a. If the class has no other constructors declared
   O b. If the class has constructors declared which do not conflict with the default signature
   O c. If the class has a declared constructor with an empty parameter list

5) What is true about constructors? (Choose 6 answers)
- ☐ a. They can be overloaded
- ☐ b. At least one constructor always exists
- ☐ c. One constructor can call another constructor
- ☐ d. They can use private access modifiers
- ☐ e. Can use initializers to keep from duplicating code
- ☐ f. Can preserve the default constructor no matter how many constructors the developer writes
- ☐ g. Are called by the `new` keyword
- ☐ h. Can be static

6) What is the constructor call in the following code:

```
Patrol p = new Patrol(55);
```

- O a. p
- O b. `new`
- O c. (55)
- O d. Patrol

7) What are some restrictions that static constructors must adhere to that instance constructors do not? (Choose 2 answers)
- ☐ a. Cannot be overloaded
- ☐ b. Cannot have a default
- ☐ c. Cannot be named after its class
- ☐ d. Cannot use the `this` keyword
- ☐ e. Cannot be used to initialize member values

8) When does a destructor get called?
- O a. When the application starts
- O b. When the object is created
- O c. After the object is garbage collected
- O d. Before the object is garbage collected

9) What is true about a destructor? (Choose 2 answers)
- ☐ a. Must start with a #
- ☐ b. Must start with a ~
- ☐ c. Can have more than one parameter
- ☐ d. Must have no parameters
- ☐ e. Can have a return type

10) What is called first when an object is getting destroyed?
   O a. Destructor
   O b. Memory is de-allocated
   O c. Constructor

11) What is called last when an object is getting destroyed?
   O a. Destructor
   O b. Memory is de-allocated
   O c. Constructor

12) Which two of the following type of methods cannot have any parameters?
   ☐ a. Class constructor
   ☐ b. Destructor
   ☐ c. Static constructor
   ☐ d. Overloaded method
   ☐ e. Any private method

13) An overloaded function results in…
   O a. No constructor calls
   O b. One constructor call
   O c. Many constructor calls

14) You develop an application that includes a class named Pilot. You must create an instance of Pilot. You want to write the most efficient code possible. Which code segment should you use?
   O a. `Pilot Colin = new Object();`
   O b. `Pilot Colin = new Pilot();`
   O c. `Object Colin = new Pilot;`
   O d. `Pilot Colin = new Object;`

Notes

Chapter 15 – Error Checking

No matter how carefully you write your program, errors will occur. Coding and syntax errors, such as missing semicolons or curly braces, misspelled keywords, etc., will all be caught by the compiler, so they shouldn't ever make it into the final code. These are quite easy to deal with.

Some errors are logical errors and could be due to an oversight of the programmer (variables too small for expected values, typing a * instead of a +, and so on), while others might be due to users entering invalid values. These can be quite difficult to catch, since they will only show up while your program is running, and can result in anything from unexpected values to full blown system crashes. In either case, your code has to be robust enough to deal with these errors in a controlled way instead of just allowing it to crash.

A Nice Game of "Catch"

Recently I purchased a new desk from Ikea and after getting it home started to assemble it. As soon as I started to put the parts together, I noticed that a bag of the dowels used to hold the parts together were missing! Luckily, on the instruction sheet there was an 800 number provided, which I called to request the missing parts. This is not all together different from what can (and does) happen in code. As the program runs, it can come across a line of code which cannot be executed due to some unexpected error. Instead of just letting the program crash, we can provide it with some alternate code to run when such an unexpected error occurs.

C# provides a structure called `try` within which you can put the code that might generate an error. While finding the error is great, it does not help much if you do not have a way to respond to it. So, each `try` block has to be followed by one or more `catch` blocks. It is within the `catch` block(s) that you can respond to the error and can either correct it silently, tell the user what happened and gracefully shut down, or, depending on the error, ask the user to correct it.

Notice I said "one or more" `catch` blocks – that is not an error on my part. Since there are different types of error conditions (for example, division by zero vs. data overload), you can provide different responses based on the error. For each specific error that you want to deal with, you need to provide a different catch block with code appropriate for the error in question. We will deal with handling different errors and multiple catch blocks, but before we can deal with the error we have to first find one!

Using our Ikea desk example from above, the assembly of the desk was in the try block, and the phone number to call is in the catch block. Most of the time you do not expect to call upon the action in the catch block, but it is there in case it's needed.

The way to try to find the error is to enclose the code you suspect in what is called a try block. Yes, this does mean that you have to anticipate in advance where an error might occur, instead of just responding to general errors from across your entire application. This actually makes a lot of sense once you think about it. Within a single application, there are likely to be different areas where you might expect an error. However, the ways to respond to the error(s) that might occur in each area is likely to be different. Common areas where you can expect an error are places where the user has to provide a value (for example, you expect a numeric input but the user types in a string), mathematical operations (division by zero, overloading result variables, etc.), trying to open external connections (files, database connections, etc.), and so on.

In fact, before we try to deal with an error, let's create a situation where an error can easily occur. Once we have that, we can make our code robust by trapping the error and dealing with it in a nice way. To do so, we are going to start a new project, "CH15a". Once ready, enter the following "bad" code into you Main method.

```
byte myNum = 0;

Console.Write("Please enter a number: ");
myNum = byte.Parse(Console.ReadLine());

Console.WriteLine("\nYou entered: {0}", myNum);

Console.ReadLine();
```

This is a simple program; in fact, it is not so different from a number of others we have already written. Yet within the five lines of code that make up this program, I can easily see at least two very common errors. To be more precise, the source of both of the errors I am thinking of is a single line of code. Can you figure out which line I am talking about, and the errors likely to occur?

On the third line of code, the user is asked to enter a number, the result of which is then parsed into a byte variable. Even without knowing the data type into which the result is to be placed, one potential error comes to mind. What if the user's input is not numeric, but is a string? Should the input be numeric, there is still the possibility of the number being larger than the size of the data type. In that case, the attempt to parse would throw an overflow error. One little line, yet so much potential for error! I think we need to keep our eye on this line...

As for the rest of the program, I think we are ok with all of the other lines. The rest of the program consists of steps which, due to their nature, are not likely to generate an error. All they do is create a variable, display text to the screen, or wait for an input before terminating the program. While we could try to put error monitoring around these lines as well, there really isn't much to gain since an error here is unlikely.

Actually, before we try and deal with the errors, I think we should see what happens, if the errors are not properly handled. Go ahead and run the program. When the prompt comes up, enter in a value above the limit that our byte sized variable can handle[26] (Figure 95).

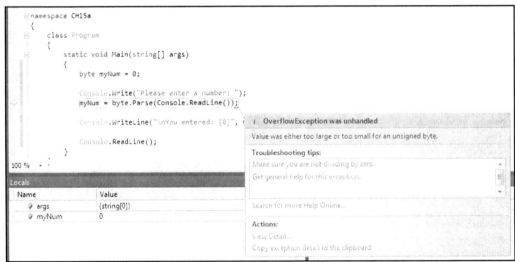

Figure 95: If the user enters a number greater than the 255 capacity of a byte, then you get an OverflowException

---

[26] You do remember that the limit of a byte variable is between 0 and 255, right?

Since we are running our program within the confines of the Visual Studio debugger, instead of a blue-screen crash that a user would experience, we get a debugger session with the error displayed and the line on which it occurred highlighted. Just as we anticipated, the value overloaded our little `byte` variable and generated an error of type "OverflowException" (as noted in the title bar of the error details dialog). Keep that error name in your mind; we will be dealing with it by name in just a little bit. Stop the program and re-run it. This time don't even enter a number, but type in a non-numeric input (your name, for example). What error does that generate (Figure 96)?

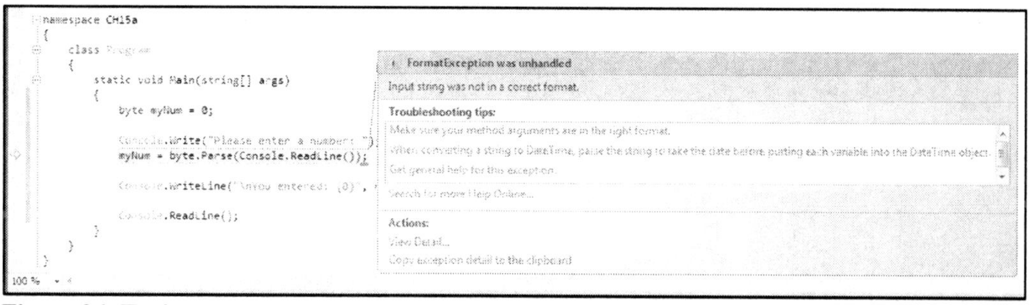

Figure 96: Trying to parse non-numeric data into a `byte` throws a FormatException error

This time the name of the error is "FormatException", which is the compiler's way of saying we gave it something incorrect for the data type into which it is trying to parse. These two tests give us some very useful bits of information. First, we learned that the compiler will show us exactly where the error occurs. Second, it tells us exactly what kind of an error occurred. Both bits of information are valuable but for different reasons. By knowing on which line the error is occurring, we know which line we have to wrap error checking around. Knowing the exact error allows us to craft specific error handling code for each error.

The first thing to work on is the code to catch the error. This is done by using the keyword `try` before the block of code which exhibits the error. We wrap that block of code in curly braces. Modifying our five lines of code gives us this:

```
byte myNum = 0;

Console.Write("Please enter a number: ");

try
{
```

```
        myNum = byte.Parse(Console.ReadLine());
    }

    Console.WriteLine("\nYou entered: {0}", myNum);

    Console.ReadLine();
```

We are not done yet, so don't try to run this code!

Any error occurring on the line or lines of code within the try block is now up to us to deal with. How we do that is by adding another block called the catch block, which must immediately follow the try block. For now, all we want to do within the catch block is display an error message to the user:

```
byte myNum = 0;

Console.Write("Please enter a number: ");

try
{
    myNum = byte.Parse(Console.ReadLine());
}
catch
{
    Console.WriteLine("Uh oh, we found an error!");
}

Console.WriteLine("\nYou entered: {0}", myNum);

Console.ReadLine();
```

With all this new code in place, we should see how our program behaves under three different cases: correct input, non-numeric input and non-valid numeric input (aka above 255). No surprise for correct input. After all, the error catching code will only run if there is an error so things work just as they did before. However, in the cases where we have invalid input, we get our expected error message as well as something odd. We get our error message, as we wanted, but we also get a funny output line which tells us that you entered 0, which we didn't, so what gives (Figure 97)?

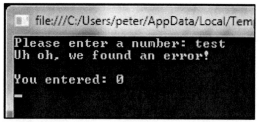

Figure 97: An error in the `try` means the variable never got assigned and it displays the value as zero

Actually, our program is doing exactly what we told it to do. Pesky computer, so very literal! Regardless of the error condition, the last two lines we run are the output line where we display the entered value and the `ReadLine` to pause the program. The `myNum` variable gets initialized to 0 during its creation. When an error occurs, there is no assignment of a new value to it so when the display line comes around, it shows that 0. Hmmm, if we get an error in which a non-valid input was entered, do we still want the dummy initial value to be displayed? Probably not. So we need a way to keep that `WriteLine` from executing when an error occurs.

There are actually two solutions to this. The first is to modify the `catch` block so that it stops the program before the output line is executed. For this solution, put a `return` into the `catch` block (as well as another `ReadLine` so we can see the error message):

```
byte myNum = 0;

Console.Write("Please enter a number: ");

try
{
    myNum = byte.Parse(Console.ReadLine());
}
catch
{
    Console.WriteLine("Uh oh, we found an error!");

    Console.ReadLine();
    return;
}

Console.WriteLine("\nYou entered: {0}", myNum);
```

```
Console.ReadLine();
```

The second solution is a bit more elegant but not as obvious. Instead of leaving that display line at the end of the program just past the try/catch block, move it inside the try block. Since we do not expect this line to ever generate an error, why move it inside the try block? Simple! The way the try block works is that as soon as any line in there generates an error, the execution of that block of code stops immediately. The program flow then moves into the catch block. As long as the output line is after the parse line, it will only execute if the parse works without an error. Not only is this more elegant but also requires fewer lines of code!

```
byte myNum = 0;

Console.Write("Please enter a number: ");

try
{
    myNum = byte.Parse(Console.ReadLine());

    Console.WriteLine("\nYou entered: {0}", myNum);
}
catch
{
    Console.WriteLine("Uh oh, we found an error!");
}

Console.ReadLine();
```

Go ahead and try both of these solutions. It might be helpful to run the program using the debugger, enter an invalid bit of data and follow the flow of the program.

Catching Specific Errors

We know that our last example generates an error for each of two very different situations – non-numeric input and a numeric input larger than the range of a byte. Right now our program responds to both errors with the same message –

wouldn't it be nice to tell the user why they are getting an error? For that we would have to know which kind of an error occurred and display an appropriate message.

As it turns out, the `catch` block can take an optional parameter that tells it to which error to respond. For example, we know that our program can generate at least two types of errors, OverflowException and FormatException. (Remember those from earlier on?). If we provide one of these error types after the keyword `catch`, then that catch block will respond only to that specific error. Notice I said it will respond ONLY to that specific error – so what about other errors? For each `try` block you can, and usually do, have multiple `catch` blocks. Each one deals with only one specific type of an error.

What if you have an error you did not expect and therefore did not provide a specific `catch` block for it? You can, and really should, always provide a generic `catch` block which will catch any errors for which you have not provided a specific catch block.

Now, this is important and it is very commonly done incorrectly. When an error occurs within a `try` block, the compiler goes through each `catch` block in order until it finds one that matches the error that occurred. When it does, the program flow jumps into that `catch` block and executes all of the lines it finds there. When it finishes, it ignores all of the other catch blocks and program flow jumps to the line following the last `catch` block.

In other words, no matter how many catch blocks you have written, only one will ever get executed per error. Because of this, you must put your specific error catches first and put the generic one last. If not, the generic block will catch the error, regardless of what it is, and the specific one will never be executed.

With our program we anticipate two specific errors and to be on the safe side we will also provide a generic one for everything else. This means we have to write three `catch` blocks, each with a different error cause and message. Putting this into code, our program now expands to look like this:

```
byte myNum = 0;

Console.Write("Please enter a number: ");

try
{
```

```
        myNum = byte.Parse(Console.ReadLine());

        Console.WriteLine("\nYou entered: {0}", myNum);
    }
    catch (OverflowException)
    {
        Console.WriteLine("Error: Invalid number! 0-255
only!");
    }
    catch (FormatException)
    {
        Console.WriteLine("Error: Please enter numbers
only!");
    }
    catch (Exception)
    {
        Console.WriteLine("Uh oh, an unknown error was
found!");
    }

    Console.ReadLine();
```

Modify your project with the new code and run it. Generate each kind of error and verify that the correct message is displayed. Hmmm, getting the OverflowException and FormatException messages is easy, but how do we get the generic error message to show up? Ah, that's just it – that message is for an error that we did not anticipate. In fact, OverflowException and FormatException are only two errors that could possibly come up for a `byte.parse` command. However, it is good practice to always have a very generic `catch` clause for any errors that could come up but for which you did not write code to handle.

Additional Information in a Catch Block

Besides the type of exception that you want the catch block to handle, there is one more optional element you can provide to the `catch` keyword. After the exception type that is being handled, you can provide a variable name, traditionally "e" or "ex", which will get populated with the details of the exception. The most common information provided within this variable would be a description of the error that occurred, which you can provide to the user. Modify your Overflow `catch` block to look like this:

```
catch (OverflowException ex)
{
    Console.WriteLine("Error: Invalid number! 0-255
only!");
    Console.WriteLine(ex.Message);
}
```

Run your program, enter an invalid number and examine the output. Notice the message displayed – "Value was either too large or too small for an unsigned byte". While this is a really nice error message, it might be too confusing to a user since it provides information they do not need to know. Do you really want them asking what an unsigned `byte` is? While displaying this message for either of our known and expected error conditions might be too much, it probably would be very useful in the generic `catch` block. Since the whole purpose of the generic block is to catch any errors which you did not anticipate, having all the information in that case is probably a good idea.

So, what other information can you get from this error variable? Besides messages, you can also display a link to a help file where the user could get additional information (which you can define yourself), the name of the source application where the error occurred, the name of the method where the error occurred, and something called the stack trace. We have not talked about a stack trace yet since it is rather complex, but in short, it can provide tons of information about the state of your program at the time of the error.

Finally

Besides the `try` and `catch` blocks, there is one more block that you can use as part of the error handling structure. As I'm sure you have guessed by now, this block uses the keyword `finally` and is executed as the very last thing in an error block, regardless of whether you had an error or not. That last part is important – the finally block is executed whether or not an error was caught! The best way to understand this is to see it in action. After your last `catch` block, type in the following lines:

```
finally
{
    Console.WriteLine("Executing the finally
block");
}
```

Please run your program a few times, using both correct input and input which you know will generate an error. Notice how each time the output from the finally block is displayed. What could the purpose of this be?

Imagine a program that is supposed to get some input from the user, open a connection to a database, write the input to a table, close the connection, and tell the user if the process was successful or not. After successfully getting the input from the user, you open a connection to your database without any problems. The next step is to write your data out to the table, but due to some other process the table is locked and you are unable to write the data.

Luckily, you had this block of code in a try/catch block so instead of crashing, you get an error which tells the user that something went wrong and the data was not written. Your program is now done, so it ends. Great, but what happened to the open database connection?

Had the table not been locked, you would have written out your data, closed your connection, and given your user a nice happy message. However, the error short circuited your program. The closing of the database connection never occurred and now your database has an open connection left hanging – yep, that is a "Very Bad Thing". No matter how your app ends, that connection should be closed. By putting the code to shut down the database connection into a finally block, you guarantee that it is executed regardless of any error(s) that may or may not occur.

If you remember the finalizer block from our previous chapter on classes, the finally block sort of has the same purpose. It is a way to make sure you can clean up regardless of what happens. While it may not be needed very often, it is nice to know it is there should you need it.

Throw Me an Error

All errors, until now, came from only one source, the compiler, and were caused by an invalid entry, data overflow, bad math, and so on. However, there is another way that an error can be generated and that is by our code throwing an error directly. This seems sort of counterintuitive. After all we want to avoid errors not generate them, yet this can be a useful tool.

Using our code from before, let's come up with an additional error condition which is by our doing and not by the compiler. Our `byte` data type has a valid data range of 0 to 255, and we know that if we enter any value outside of this range we will get an OverflowException error. Great, but what if we had a more specific range limitation for some reason? For example, what if we could not accept a 0 as a valid value? If the user enters a 0 into our program it will happily take it, since that will not cause a parse error or an over Overflow error. But we can change that…

We already have a nice error message if the user enters an invalid number. It would be nice to be able to use that same error if a 0 is entered. We are going to put a check into the `try` block so if the user enters a 0 it will cause, or more correctly `throw`, an OverflowException error. Of course, we also need to modify the error message in the current OverflowException `catch` block to show that 0 is not within the range of acceptable values.

Here is what the entire program should be, with the new `throw` inside the `try` block:

```
byte myNum = 0;

Console.Write("Please enter a number: ");

try
{
    myNum = byte.Parse(Console.ReadLine());

    if (myNum == 0)
        throw new OverflowException("Zeros not
allowed");

    Console.WriteLine("\nYou entered: {0}", myNum);
}
catch (OverflowException ex)
{
    Console.WriteLine("Error: Invalid number! 1-255
only!");
    Console.WriteLine(ex.Message);
}
catch (FormatException)
{
    Console.WriteLine("Error: Please enter numbers
only!");
}
catch (Exception)
{
    Console.WriteLine("Uh oh, an unknow error was
found!");
}
finally
{
    Console.WriteLine("Executing the finally
block");
}

Console.ReadLine();
```

As you can see, the throw command is pretty simple, though there are some unexpected things to notice in there. First, you have to tell the compiler that you are generating a new error, hence the keyword new and second, you have open and close parentheses after the name of the exception being thrown. Optionally, you can put a message inside the parentheses, which will be provided to the `catch` block within the message parameter.

Points to Ponder

- Errors can occur in your program due to invalid data from a user
- To prevent an error from crashing your program, you need to write code to identify and deal with the error
- The `try` keyword defines a block of code within which you expect an error
- For each `try` block, you must have at least one `catch` block
- A `catch` block can be used to catch only a specific error or every error
- Since only one `catch` block will ever be executed, you have to place your most specific `catch` blocks before the generic one
- Within a `catch` block, you receive detailed information on the error that was caught if you provide a variable to store this information
- A `finally` block will always be executed regardless of whether an error was generated or not
- A `finally` block is optional
- You can generate your own errors using the keyword `throw`

Challenge

1) Ask the user for two integers. Divide the first number by the second and display the original numbers as well as the answer to the user. Use try/catch blocks to make sure the user only enters numbers for the two entries and to make sure you do not get a "division by 0" error. Display appropriate messages for each error.
2) Write a program to display a menu of 4 items. For items 1-3, just display a message for which item was selected and for item 4, exit the program. If the user enters anything else (non-numeric input, number larger than 4), redisplay the menu and prompt for another input. To keep things clean, use `Console.Clear()` before displaying the menu. (Hint: use a while loop and try/catch blocks.)

Review Quiz

1) Which two types of statements always raise exceptions (choose two)?
   - ☐ a. try
   - ☐ b. catch
   - ☐ c. throw
   - ☐ d. checked with overflow
   - ☐ e. Checked without overflow
   - ☐ f. finally

2) Which two types of statements will run after an exception is thrown in a try block? (choose two)
   - ☐ a. try
   - ☐ b. catch
   - ☐ c. throw
   - ☐ d. perry
   - ☐ e. checked
   - ☐ f. finally

3) What is the last error handing statement to always run?
   - O a. try
   - O b. catch
   - O c. throw
   - O d. perry
   - O e. checked
   - O f. finally

4) What is the difference between raising an exception with a `try` vs. a `throw`?
   - O a. `try` = system defined exception. `throw` = user defined exception.
   - O b. `throw` = system defined exception. `try` = user defined exception.

5) When organizing the catch blocks what is a good rule to adhere by?
   - O a. Place the catch blocks from most general to most specific.
   - O b. Place the catch blocks from most specific to most general.

6) The identifier of a catch block is... (choose 3)
   ☐ a. Optional
   ☐ b. Required
   ☐ c. Contain exception info
   ☐ d. Is read-only
   ☐ e. Is read-Write

7) You are taking over somebody else's C# application. The original author included the following debugging code: Which output is produced by this code?

```
try
{
    Console.WriteLine("Inside Try");
    throw(new IOException());
}
catch (IOException e)
{
    Console.WriteLine("IOException Caught");
}
catch (Exception e)
{
    Console.WriteLine("Exception Caught");
}
finally
{
    Console.WriteLine("Inside Finally");
}
Console.WriteLine("After End Try");
```

O a. Inside Try, Exception Caught, Inside Finally, After End Try
O b. Inside Try, IOException Caught, Inside Finally
O c. Inside Try, Exception Caught, IOException Caught, Inside Finally, After End Try
O d. Inside Try, IOException Caught, Inside Finally, After End Try

8) You need to write additional code that will handle all mathematical exceptions with a minimum amount of code. Which code segment should you use?

O a.
```
try { // Existing code goes here. }
catch (DivideByZeroException e)  { // Insert
error-handling code. }
catch (OverflowException e)  { // Insert error-
handling code. }
catch (NotFiniteNumberException e)  { // Insert
error-handling code. }
```

O b.
```
try { // Existing code goes here. }
catch (ArithmeticException e) { // Insert error-
handling code. }
```

O c.
```
try { // Existing code goes here. }
catch (DivideByZeroException e)  { // Insert
error-handling code. }
catch (OverflowException e)  { // Insert error-
handling code. }
```

9) You have a catch block that keeps catching a general exception. You need to debug and find which line number is throwing the error. Which property of the Exception class shows the line number?

O a. Source

O b. Message

O c. StackTrace

O d. InnerException

10) You need to write code that will call on the `ArithmeticException` class if the integer called floor is equal to 13. What code segment should you use?

O a.
```
if (floor == 13)
{ return Marshal(ArithmeticException) }
```

O b.
```
if (floor = 13)
{ return Marshal(ArithmeticException) }
```

O c.
```
if (floor == 13)
{ ThrowException(ArithmeticException) }
```

O d.
```
if (floor == 13)
{ throw new ArithmeticException("13 not allowed")
}
```

Notes

A Final Word

With that, we come to the end of the first book in our journey through C# programming. No longer a complete stranger to programming, C#, the compiler and all of the other cool stuff we have learned, you are now ready to move on to more advanced subjects. However, the material presented here is the basis upon which the rest of the language is built, so having a really good understanding here is quite important.

In the next two volumes, Intermediate, and Advanced C# Programming, I will cover the rest of the material which makes up the entire C# and .Net programming universe. Among the many wonderful topics still in our future are things such as Lists (think of arrays but without the limitations that arrays have), Generics, reading and writing of files, networking, events and delegates and many, many more!

See you soon!

Appendix A – C# Keywords

Compared to many other languages, C# has a relatively small set of keywords; in fact there are only 77 of them in the list below. Keywords can be easily identified in Visual Studio by the blue color that IntelliSense automatically colors them. Since these are all reserved, they cannot be used as names for variables, objects, classes, etc.

abstract	float	return
as	for	sbyte
base	foreach	sealed
bool	goto	short
break	if	sizeof
byte	implicit	stackalloc
case	in	static
catch	int	string
char	interface	struct
checked	internal	switch
class	is	this
const	lock	throw
continue	long	true
decimal	namespace	try
default	new	typeof
delegate	null	uint
do	object	ulong
double	operator	unchecked
else	out	unsafe
enum	override	ushort
event	params	using
explicit	private	virtual
extern	protected	void
false	public	volatile
finally	readonly	while
fixed	ref	

Appendix B – Quiz Answers

Chapter 1

1) a, c, d

All classes are stored in .cs files and a single .cs file can store multiple classes. However, it is considered good practice to put each class into a .cs file of its own.

2) b

All C# programs start in the `Main` method. Remember that C# is case sensitive so Main has to start with an uppercase letter!

3) b

Classes are grouped together into a namespace.

4) d

The compiler is used to convert source code into an executable file.

5) a

Always remember to open up the solution file (.sln extension) and not the C# file (.cs extension)

Chapter 2

1) a

The `WriteLine` method is used to write things out to the console and then move to the next line. The `Write` method is also used to write things to the console, but it does not then move to the next line.

2) b, d

Both `Write` and `WriteLine` are used to display things onto the console window.

3) a

When using a placeholder with a `Write` or a `WriteLine` method call, you start at 0, not at 1!

4) b

Both `Write` and `WriteLine` are methods of the Console class.

5) d

The size of a variable (how much memory it takes up and how much data it can hold), is determined by the Data Type of the variable.

6) c

All variables have to be given an identifier when declared and are then referred to by using this identifier.

7) b

The keyword `ushort` is shorthand for System.UInt16. See the Data Types table in Chapter 2 for the both the official Type name and the more common shorthand alias names.

Chapter 3

1) a

An `if` statement without a curly brace enclosed block, will only run the next statement

2) b

You can chain multiple `if` statements together using the `if else` syntax.

3) d

While an `if else` statement is useful for two or three nested `if` conditions, for anything more complex a `switch` statement will usually work better.

Chapter 4

1) b

Memory is measured in Bytes. Even though a single byte can be broken down into smaller components (nibble or bit), we consider a Byte as the smallest amount of memory.

2) a, c, e

Each of these answers is equivalent in that when executed, the value of the Amt variable will be increased by one. Option B is wrong since C# does not use the dollar sign symbol and D is wrong due to the order of the elements.

3) b, c, e

Using more than one * or / in a row is not a valid C# operator, so answer A is incorrect. Answer D is incorrect due to the order of the various elements, and F is incorrect since programming languages do not use the () notation to mean multiplication – a notation common among mathematicians.

4) c

The notation for the modulo operator is the percent symbol, and the shorthand for all these operators is to use the operator symbol first, which is then immediately followed by an equals sign.

5) d

The reason option D is correct is due to the Order of Precedence, which states that the multiplication takes place before the addition. This means the problem is interpreted as 1 * 10, which is 10, to which you add 5, or 10 + 5.

Chapter 5

1) a

The initialization is the first section of the `for` loop statement, and is used to set the initial value of the loop counter.

2) d

This loop will run 10 times (from 1 to 10). The 1 is set by the initialization and it will stop at 10 because of the `i <= 10` condition.

3) b

The `break` keyword causes the loop to abort and jump to the next line of code after the loop block.

4) b

With a `do` loop the condition is at the bottom, guaranteeing you at least one pass through the loop body.

Chapter 6

1) b
The // symbol comments out only one line. Even though you can also use the /* */ notation from Answer D to comment out just a single line, it is normally used only when commenting out multiple lines.

2) b
To get your program execution to halt, you have to insert a breakpoint.

3) a
You can change the values of variables in the watch window.

4) a, c, d
This can be tricky, so look over the code carefully! Notice the ! symbol at the beginning? That turns the logic around, so the line will only be printed when n is not 5 or is less than 7. 7 gets printed because the n > 7 section is `false`, which becomes `true` due to the !.

5) b
F6 will build your code, but not execute it.

Chapter 7

1) d
Initializing an array occurs when you set the size and dimensions of the array using the `new` keyword.

2) b
To declare an array you use a pair of square braces after the data type name followed by the identifier you want to use. The reason answer D is not correct, is that D is initializing an array that has been declared. While this is quite common, the question was asking only about declaring the array, not initializing it!

3) a
Since arrays start at 0, the first element is always 0 regardless of the size.

4) c

Since arrays start at 0, the last element is always 1 less than the total number of elements that it has.

5) Length = 8, GetLength(0) = 4, Rank = 2

Remember for a multi-dimensional array, the Length property returns the total number of elements across all dimensions. GetLength returns the number of elements in a given dimension, and Rank returns the number of dimensions.

6) c

Because arrays are 0 based, the number of elements is always 1 greater than the index of the last element.

7) a, c

You can use either a `for` or a `foreach` loop to iterate through an array. You can also use other loops, such as `while` or `do while`, but those were not offered as options.

8) a, b, d, e

Answers C and D are opposites of each other, so if one is true the other cannot be. Since we know that an array size is set during its initialization, answer D is correct and therefore C cannot be. Answers E and F are also mutually exclusive. Because arrays are 0 based, the first element is always 0.

Chapter 8

1) b

Since the quotes symbol is used to mark the beginning and end of a string, you cannot use it within a string, unless you escape it using a backslash.

2) b, c

The two ways to tell the compiler to display a backslash without treating it as an escape sequence, is to use two backslashes or to put an @ symbol before the string.

3) c

Since strings start at 0, just as an array does, the letter 'a' is located at location 8, even though it is the 9th character.

4) a

The Replace function will replace all matching strings with another string. Substring would not work, since it is used to pull characters out of a larger string, and option C is wrong, since you cannot modify a string as if it were an array.

Chapter 9

1) d

When assigning from a larger variable (`int`) to a smaller variable (`byte`), you must cast the larger value to a data type which will fit into the smaller type.

2) a

In this case you are assigning from a smaller data type (`byte`) into a larger data type (`int`). Because an `int` can hold the full value of a `byte`, you do not need to do a cast. While technically you could, making answer C correct, the question specifically asked for the "shortest way", and not using the case is shorter!

3) a

To define an `enum` (or a `struct`), you first specify the data type you are defining, followed by its name and then the members that make it up.

4) a, c

You can either use the . notation to refer to a member of an `enum` (for example Calendar.Feb), or cast a number to the `enum` data type. Remember that, like arrays, the index of `enum`s start at 0.

5) b, d

Answers A and C are both system defined, therefore they cannot also be user defined. User defined data types are `enum` or `struct`s.

6) b

The keyword `ushort` is a short cut to the full name of the data type which is System.UInt16. (Take a look at the table of system data types in Chapter 2.)

Chapter 10

1) a

While it is quite common for a method to have at least one parameter, it is not required. Therefore the answer is 0!

2) c

The keyword `void` is used to tell the compiler that your method will not have a return value.

3) c

Since the return value of the Adder method is being put into a variable of type `int`, and it runs without an error, the method must be returning an `int`. If it were to return a different type, even one which could be safely put into an `int` value without casting, the compiler would flag it as an error or a warning.

4) a

Ah, this is tricky so be careful! Notice how the value of the parameter that is passed into the Greeting method is changed. However, this change is to a local variable (v1 was passed into the Greeting method by value), therefore the value of the variable in the calling method, v1, is not changed.

5) b

The reason this will not compile is because in the declaration of the method you promise to return an `int` value, yet do not do so anywhere in the code. The solution is to put a `return` statement into your method.

Chapter 11

1) c

You use the keyword `using` to import a namespace into your project. Answer A cannot be correct since it is not a valid C# keyword. Answers B and D are valid keywords, but cannot be correct. Namespace is used to declare a new namespace, while System is the name of an already defined namespace.

2) d

You can import in as many namespaces as you need.

3) a

The access modifier `public` allows for full access from any other calling code.

4) b

The access modifier `private` keeps the object restricted to access only within the class.

5) a

A fully qualified call to a method includes the namespace, class and method name, all connected by periods.

6) a

You use the keyword `using` to import a namespace into your code. Once imported, you can call any method from that namespace by its short name. In other words you can leave the namespace component off, but the class part is still required!

7) a, b, c, d

All of these statements are true, except for answer E – a namespace cannot be marked as `private`.

8) b

By default, any member of a class is marked as `private`, but it is still considered good practice to always specify an access modifier, even if you want the default setting.

9) c

Within a single namespace, all classes must have unique names.

Chapter 12

1) a

You can use a `return` statement inside a method marked as `void`, however you cannot actually return a value. All it does is cause the method to end at that point and return to the calling code.

2) a

Both methods have the same parameter count and data types. The only difference is that one returns a value and one does not. Since return type is not considered part of the signature, these have the same signature.

3) b

The two methods have a different number of parameters, therefore the signature is different.

4) a

The return types are different, but that does not count. The parameters are of the same data type, even though the local names are different, therefore the signature is the same

5) b

Both methods have the same return type and parameter list. However one is static and the other is not, which means they are considered to have different signatures.

6) b

The only difference is that the first method passes its parameter by reference while the second passes by value. This makes the signature different.

7) a

Both methods are passing their parameters by reference therefore the signatures are the same

8) d

Of these ten entries, there are six unique signatures. (Lines 1, 2, 3, 4, 6, and 8)

9) b

Whenever you need to pass in multiple parameters, each of the same data type, the most efficient way is to use a parameter array.

10) a, b

A parameter array can take any number of discreet inputs or a single array. Answer D would be correct if not for the curly braces around the values.

11) b, c, e

Values can be passed either by value or by reference. The keywords ref and out both pass by reference.

12) b

Passing by value is the default way to pass values and requires no additional keyword.

Chapter 13

1) b, e

The parameter of :C inside a `Write/WriteLine` placeholder will format your value to a currency style. Both of these answers will display the same value. The difference is that answer B specifies two places after the decimal point, while answer E uses the system default. On a standard US system, two places after the decimal point is default, so the result is the same.

2) c

The `DateTime` data type cannot be assigned directly since it is a composite type, meaning it is made up of multiple parts. You need to use the Parse method of the DateTime object to correctly assign its value.

3) a

As with all arrays, you start counting at 0! The first parameter will be in `args[0]`, not in `args[1]`!

4) b

It is never efficient to use `goto`!

Chapter 14

1) b

The constructor of an object is called when the object is created.

2) c

If you do not write a constructor, the system will provide a default one.

3) c

The constructor of a class must be named the same as the class and a return type is not provided.

4) a

The default constructor is only available if there is no user provide constructor. As soon as you create a constructor, the default one is no longer available.

5) a, b, c, e, g, h

Constructors can be overloaded, there is always at least one available (the default one), and one constructor can call another one. You use an initialize to call another constructor, which saves having to duplicate code. The constructor is called when the object is instantiated, by the keyword new on the instantiation line. Finally, constructors can be static.

6) c

The constructor of a class is called when the () parameter on the instantiation line is encountered by the compiler. The value(s) within the parenthesis are sent to the constructor method as parameters.

7) a, d

Static constructors cannot be overloaded and cannot use the this keyword. A static constructor is executed when you first call a static method of a class, so having an overload makes no sense – there is no instantiation for static methods, therefore there is no way to provide values to a static constructor. As for the this keyword, the purpose of this is to allow you specify which instance of an instantiated class is being referred to, which is not possible with static methods, since there is not instantiated object to access.

8) d

The destructor (or finalizer) method is called before the memory of the object is released and the garbage collector can clean it up.

9) b, d

A destructor method is named the same as its parent class, but is started with the tilde symbol (~). It also must have no parameters, since it is called automatically when releasing an object, therefore there is no way to provide a parameter.

10) a

The first thing called when releasing an object from memory is the destructor.

11) b

The last thing called when releasing an object is the garbage collector so memory gets de-allocated and released back to the system to reuse.

12) b, c

Neither a destructor nor a static constructor can have any parameters, since they are both called in a way which prevents a parameter from being provided.

13) c

You are allowed to overload constructors, meaning you can have many constructors.

14) b

You instantiate a new object by the use of the keyword new, followed by the name of the object being instantiated.

Chapter 15

1) c, d

The keyword throw is used to generate an exception, and an overflow will also generate an error when it is inside a checked block. Try, catch and finally are all incorrect since they are part of the error checking structure, but by themselves do not generate errors.

2) b, f

When an error is generated within a try block, the code inside one of the catch blocks is executed. Code within the finally block is always executed. Try, throw and checked cannot be correct, since they are used to look for an error (try or checked) or generate an error (throw). Finally "perry" cannot be correct, since it is not even a valid C# keyword!

3) f

The final block of code to run within a try/catch structure is always the code within the finally block.

4) a

Try is used to enclose a block of code within which an error may occur, while throw is used to generate a user defined error.

5) b

As soon as code inside a try block generates an error, the compiler starts to look at each of the following catch block(s) until it finds one which catches the found error. Once it has found a matching catch block, it will not look at any of the other catch blocks, so having your most specific blocks first will allow the specific errors to be caught as expected, instead of in a generic error block.

6) a, c, d

The identifier of a catch block is where you specify which error that block responds to, and into which variable to place the exception info. Once this error variable is set with the error data, it becomes read only. If you leave out the identifier, the catch block will catch all errors but the exception data will not be provided to your code – therefore the identifier is optional.

7) d

The error process starts with the code inside the try block, so the Inside Try line will always be printed out. The next command is the throw, which generates an IOException error. The catch block specific to this error prints the line "IOException Caught". Since there is no additional code in there, execution shifts to the finally block, which is always executed, from where the "Inside Finally" line is printed. The final WriteLine will always be executed as soon as we are finished processing the error.

8) b

While both answers A and C would also catch some mathematical errors, only answer B contains a catch block that will catch all math related errors.

9) c

Additional information about the error that was caught is provided to your code inside the identifier specified for the catch block. There is much information provided with this, including the StackTrace, which contains the line number of your error.

10) d

The way to generate an error is to use the throw command. To specify which error type to throw, you also need to use the keyword new followed by the name of the error type.

Index

CPSIA information can be obtained at www.ICGtesting.com
Printed in the USA
LVOW052045080512

280881LV00017B/47/P